THE
SPIRIT OF CLAY

THE
SPIRIT OF CLAY

A CLASSIC GUIDE TO CERAMICS

Robert Piepenburg

Pebble Press Inc.

To my loving wife Gail and to our family
Wendy, Matthew, Shanna, Jessica and Leah.

The Spirit of Clay

Copyright © 1998 by Robert Piepenburg

Pebble Press Inc.
24723 Westmoreland
Farmington Hills, MI 48336-1963

Publisher's Cataloging in Publication Data
Piepenburg, Robert.
    The Spirit of Clay/Robert Piepenburg.—Revised Ed.
    1. Ceramics - Pottery.   2. Creation - Art - Inspiration.
    3. Self-Perception - Self-Awareness.   4. Self-realization in art.

ISBN: 0-9628481-4-X

Library of Congress Catalog Card Number: 98-065059

Cover drawing by Gail Piepenburg
Front cover: *Richard DeVore, "#729," multi-fired stoneware vessel, 14" × 10 3/4".*
Back cover: *Gail Piepenburg, "Triptych," raku fired wall relief, 24" × 35".*
Frontispiece: *Kris Nelson, "Stoneware Coffee Pot," anagama fired, natural ash glaze, 9" × 9" × 5".*

Printed In the United States of America

Contents

When we creatively interact with clay we unearth the realities of the human spirit from the circumstances of life, engage the passions of our heart, and honor the uniqueness of our being in a way that touches all of humanity.

ROBERT PIEPENBURG

A Letter . . .

Dear Student,

This is a book about the self, the creative self, and the making of ceramics.

Beginning experiences in ceramics generally turn out to be more technical in nature, but they don't always remain so. It is inevitable that many technical aspects and skills must first be encountered and understood to make clay objects, and a large part of this text addresses just such things. Fortunately, not many skills are necessary to successfully form clay. In a relatively short amount of time you'll accomplish much of what you technically need to know and be able to make the transitions of putting more of self, more spirit, into your clay work. Because your relationship with clay is ultimately more human than technical, you will more often than not find yourself on a path of self-formation that will be every bit as rewarding as your path of clay-formation.

Such transformations of human expansion are not unprecedented in the arts. It's just that with ceramics and it's primal connections to physical elements such as earth, water and fire, and thousands of years of history (with roots in Eastern traditions) that it becomes more immediate. The spiritual connections between the ceramic arts and human nature are intuitive and essentially inherent. The evolution of your self-actualization with clay may appear not as a series of slow transformations but as quantum leaps. The first clay class I took as a junior in college was for elective credit and a personal example of this natural union. I had no prior interest in clay but needed one more class to fill out my schedule. I half heartedly thought I might enjoy working with and changing clay. Little did I know that when I took the class that clay would end up working on me; changing my life, if not my entire being, in the most dramatic of ways.

I now know that clay can be a fertile growing ground of the spirit. I've seen this same spiritual birthing scenario occur time and time again with students of mine who were new to clay. What I didn't know then, but have come to know now, is that you don't actually find your self with clay . . . you make yourself with clay. We are inherently defined by what we do and what we do with clay identifies who we are.

At times it seems ironic that the oldest of art forms, rich with tradition, is the new art of our age.

Today when living leaves many restless and desirous of experiences that feel true inside it is not surprising that the unspoken humanity of the ceramic experience is so appealing. Aside from any suggestive tone of salvation it is not an experience devoid of natural wholeness, a wholeness which is accepting of our human side and which values dignity and creative freedom. In this sense ceramics is about the spiritual and is not technical. Here the goal is not to make a perfect pot, but to give our most ordinary of lives depth and value. This, dear student, is the challenge of ceramics: to use your imagination creatively. Not just to make objects of continuous beauty but also to cultivate an expressive life. This part of ceramics is not tangible, but a dimension of meaningful living. At the moment, your way into this adventure called ceramics will be more difficult to locate and adjust to than your way beyond it. The other side, the spiritual side, is where the technical struggles of the beginning are no longer relevant and where, for the rest of your life with clay, the creative self emerges as the directing force.

As a teacher and as a human being I have seen many students look to an experience with clay for relief and guidance as they choose to rediscover themselves and to restore the wisdom that comes from knowing and touching the heart of the deeper self. The human spirit hungers for identity and, like love and happiness, it is ultimately revealed in relationship, understanding and compassion. Creative work and inner growth are age-old counterparts. Developing a living, working relationship with clay enhances one's ability to respond humanly. This involvement, this connectedness, more than anything else; more than natural pleasure, more than personal passion, is a movement toward self. If you're new to clay much of this is preconscious, but I hope that with time you will come to view clay work as an essential part of your spiritual diet.

Traditionally, the teaching of ceramics has been a technical process separate and somewhat removed from the creative context and sensibility that nurtures the human spirit. The technical is quite different in scope from the creative. The technical is about solving, fixing, improving until some problem-free ideal of perfection exists. It's also about physical memory, a quest to make a deeper bond between material and skill. Because ceramics begins with a material (clay) and is grounded physically in the recognition of the known (object), it's spiritual dimensions can easily go unnoticed. Yet, it is precisely at this junction where your response to the clay experience can make life meaningful. For midway between the known and the unknown, between knowingness and unconsciousness, lies your imagination.

With respect for the imagination comes respect for human capacities and a context central to humanness: spirituality. It's the spiritual dimension that makes it meaningful. Elusive as it may be the spirit must be cultivated

Richard DeVore, #713, Stoneware with multi-fired low temperature overglazes, 14 1/4" × 13". His subtly sensitive and classic-like forms are eminently sensuous.

with as much soulful caring and crafting as is given raw ceramic materials. The rewards, although humble, can empower human life and give the greatest depth and texture to works of clay.

Ceramics as a secular craft is not complete until it incorporates the creative imagination so sacred to the making of art. The entire history of art is a recurrent enactment of individual displays of imagination. Craftsmanship, or the quality of workmanship, by itself is never enough, and certainly is not art. For your clay work to succeed not only must it be well made, it must also be creatively conceived. When this integration is fully realized the object becomes a telling instrument of feeling and spiritual insight. The alliance between creative imagination and craftsmanship allows the clay object to assume a long and powerful life by existing as a catalytic support for revisioning, exploration and future growth.

In ceramics, technique and spirituality need to be viewed almost as if one. The kind of connection I'm making here is often arguable, hard to access and by certain standards unsecured; but it fuels essential breakthroughs. Just as creativity requires an open attitude, a willingness to see in new ways, your personal work in clay is best served by bridging these two worlds.

Thus, this book focuses not only on the technical aspects of ceramics, but on bringing a sense of spirituality to your life both as a human being and as a ceramist. What is important, as you walk this path of clay, this path without end, is the transformation of your creative capacity and your spiritual wholeness. Again, speaking as a teacher, I know there is no substitute for experience and that some things can only be caught not taught. My wish to you now is that you pursue your clay activities with a joyful and open spirit; that you find the truths that lie within your affections and that you and your clay works live fully within them.

With fondest regards,

Robert Piepenburg

Robert Piepenburg, Festival of Wings and Looking Up, raku fired, 42″ & 45″ tall. In one sense I equate these ceramic sculptures to writing. Each part of the piece, like each word in a sentence, has its own aesthetic content, its own meaning. Yet, when arranged into a compositional whole they convey a greater visual message.

Patrick S. Crabb, Rimmed Plate Series, 3" × 22". Patrick's earthy plate, with its aura of unending energy, began as a slab of clay draped inside a plaster mold. Later, after stiffening, a wheel-thrown rim was added and freely detailed to animate the clay and evoke an inspired feeling of movement. The encrusted textures are the result of extra heavy applications of glaze multi-fired in an electric kiln at cone 04/06.

Gail Piepenburg, Steel and Clay Series, 5" × 14" × 34". The carved, broken, pierced and raku fired clay draws strength from its aesthetic relationship to the etched steel stained with rust and gun bluing.

THE
SPIRIT OF CLAY

Peter Voulkos, Hunya-Hunya, wood-fired stoneware stack piece, 24" × 46" high. Part of why this California artist has been such an influential person in contemporary ceramics is that his clay work is fused with spirit. His ceramics will forever endure because his spirit resides in his creations, rendering them timeless.

1

Clay

What it is . . .

Clay is the earth. It is her material body and, in some bequeathed visions, the dawning material body of human beings.

Clay is a natural and incredibly malleable medium. Its organic innocence is ripe with new beginnings and all are blessed who experience the joys that it embodies.

As a raw material clay is a hydrated alumina-silicate. Its two main minerals, alumina and silica, first began as igneous feldspathic rock which resulted from the cooling of molten magma that now forms over fifty percent of the earth's surface. Igneous rocks, when pulverized after millions of years of erosion, weathering, disintegration and decomposition, become amazingly plastic when mixed with water and it is in this intriguing state that we know it as common clay.

As one of earth's most abundant and available raw materials, clay can easily be shaped by hand when wet. The particles that make up its composition are flat and very thin, so the water helps them stick and slide against each other, thereby allowing for a unique property of mysterious workability we call plasticity. Plastic clays are very flexible and able to withstand a great deal of physical manipulation and stress without collapsing. When clay dries it becomes fairly hard yet retains it's shape. As the water evaporates the flat, hexagonal plate shaped clay particles draw closer together causing some shrinkage in size. Different types of clays shrink at different rates, but on an average about 10%. That is to say, a pot ten inches tall at the time of making may be only nine inches tall after drying.

TYPES OF NATURAL CLAYS

Primary Clays

Clays that remain close to their original source are known as primary clays. These residual clays are generally of coarse grain and light in color as they have not been pulverized or stained by movement.

Secondary Clays

Clays that have eroded to a bed far from their origin are known as secondary clays. These sedimentary clays make up the other half of the two main categories geologists use for classification based upon site of origin. Secondary clays are of a finer particle size due to the crushing, crunching consequences of their continuous journey; a journey which also renders them more plastic. Along the way these clays pick up organic materials and other impurities such as iron, which further affect their color and working properties.

Kaolin Clay

Kaolin or China clay is the purest of the *primary clays* and the most well known. The whitest of high-firing clays, kaolin was first found in China long before deposits were discovered in England, Germany and the United States. It is a highly refractory (non-melting) non-plastic material primarily used in the making of porcelain, the queen of clay bodies. Edgar Plastic Kaolin and #6 Tile Kaolin are the popular favorites of the day and can be found stockpiled in many studios, waiting at the ready, with all the facsimile of a nondescript ammo dump.

Ball Clay

The most plastic *secondary clays* are the ball clays. The most well known deposits are found in Kentucky and Tennessee. These smooth-textured, light colored clays are of the finest particle size and greatly improve the workability of any clay body on the potter's wheel. Due to excessive shrinkage, however, they cannot be used alone and need to be mixed with other less plastic clays.

Fire Clay

As a *secondary clay* that is both plastic and highly refractory (resistant to melting at high temperatures) fire clays can be mixed with water and used solo to form a decent clay body. Experience suggests, however, that a diversity of particle size in any clay body, obtained by the addition of one or more other clays, further enhances its strength and workability. Because they contain little or no iron, fire clays range in color from a light to medium gray.

Stoneware Clay

Stoneware clays contain a mixture of particle sizes that are smaller and finer than those of fire clay. Unlike fire clays, which are abundant and readily available the world over, stoneware clays are scarce and near impossible to obtain. At one time Jordan clay was the favored stoneware clay in ceramics but is now unobtainable. A blended clay called Kentucky Stone is now being marketed as its substitute. Generically, the term stoneware is now used to refer to any clay body that can be high-fired.

Common Clay

Common clays are *secondary clays* that have traveled further from their source than other clays. They vary greatly in particle size and generally contain a considerable amount of organic impurities. These impurities coupled with large quantities of iron greatly affect the clay's color and firing temperature. Their maturing temperature is fairly low, often leaving the work porous. As a surface clay, found almost everywhere in the world, its fired colors can range from buff to a dark terra-cotta red. Sometimes characterized as a natural earthenware, these clays are frequently used to alter the color or to lower the firing temperature of clay bodies.

Bentonite

This *secondary clay* is extremely plastic. In fact, it is so "sticky" that it is often referred to as a plasticizer and need only be added to clay bodies in amounts of 2% or less to significantly improve their working qualities. The results are immediate and there is no need to wait for the beneficial effects of bacterial growth achieved through aging to keep the clay from being short and unworkable. Bentonite, like ball clay, also adds to the dry strength of clay in the greenware state. Both of these fine-grained clays contain some iron impurities but bentonite is far more plastic than ball clay.

FILLERS

A filler is a course material added to a clay body. Each filler possesses unique properties for improving the working or firing characteristics of the clay. In general they reduce shrinkage, prevent warping, add strength and enhance refractory qualities. Their particle size is measured by screening; fine (60 mesh), medium (35 mesh) and course (20 mesh). Added in varying percentages, the range for use in throwing bodies can vary from 0 to 15% and go as high as 50% for those used in handbuilding. I like to think of fillers as performing the same function as that of bones in our bodies: to improve posture. I also view fillers as secret prerequisites for successful firings . . . especially if the work is thick or large. Every ingredient has its part to play and if you intend to work big, add lots of filler to your clay body. Also, dry and fire the work very slowly.

Grog

Grog is a refractory clay that has been fired and crushed to a certain mesh size. Having been preshrunk as a result of being fired to a high temperature I often refer to it as sanforized clay. As the most commonly used filler it is an excellent choice, especially in the coarser mesh sizes, for adding texture and porosity and ultimately for building much thicker clay walls. Molochite, a white grog made from vitrified china clay, is used when the white color of a porcelain clay body is to be maintained.

Sand

Sand is second to grog in popularity as an ingredient for reducing warping and cracking. For throwing it is often structurally preferred to grog. Not only is it less expensive but clay sticks to sand in a way that it doesn't to grog, thereby allowing for a much thinner and stiffer clay wall. At high temperatures, however, the white silica sands may soften, contributing to cracking and a roughness in surface texture. To avoid the quartz inversion of silica I use a Lake Michigan beach sand obtained from a local foundry supplier.

Kyanite

Kyanite is a heavy duty refractory. As a black alumina-silica ore with a shiny silver appearance, I have come to call this additive magic dust. This stuff is simply amazing. Not only does it aid in strengthening the clay but it expands during firing, providing unbelievable resistance to thermal shock and cracking. To everyone's satisfaction this is true not only at high temperatures but at the lower temperatures of raku where sudden changes in temperature and cracking are all too intimately related. Mullite, formed by the calcination of kyanite at extremely high temperatures, can also be used in clay bodies for its refractory qualities. Kyanite and mullite have a unique physical characteristic. When crushed the small particles are needle or rod like in shape. These rods overlap to form a strong interlaced structure whereas sand and grog simply bump up against each other. As a result the interlocking helps to prevent clay body failure.

Sawdust

Screened sawdust can be used as a filler to open-up the clay by providing greater porosity and weight reduction. Unlike kyanite, which adds to the overall weight of the body, sawdust burns out leaving a sponge-like wall full of air pockets. Sawdust bodies can be used on the wheel but more often than not are used for handbuilding. It's interesting to note that the introduction of this organic material into the clay body has the effect of immediately aging the clay; rendering it plastic almost overnight. Other non organic ingredients such as pearlite, zonolite or vermiculite can be used in clay recipes, up to 50%, for texture and weight control.

Reinforcers

Synthetic materials, generally of a thread-like nature, added to clay to help hold it together are called reinforcers. The most common, nylon fiber, comes pre-chopped in half inch lengths and can be mixed or wedged into

A fairly wet mixture of 50% clay and 50% pearlite being worked by Ben Pearlman into a plaster support mold for drying. Although this textured body has limited plasticity it does minimize shrinkage. Fired to high temperatures it becomes extremely strong and light-weight for its thickness.

clay to create thin walled slabs that do not crack or warp during drying. Basically the nylon filaments perform the same function as that of steel reinforcement rods or mesh in poured concrete: to prevent a slab or structure from cracking and breaking apart. Fiberglass, although not as popular, can also be used for this purpose, only it becomes a part of the clay when it melts and does not burn away like the fine nylon strands. Frequently, fiber-reinforced slabs have to be cut or trimmed with scissors.

PREPARED AND MIXED CLAYS

The quality of the clay you work with is *extremely* important. If it's a substandard clay body it will affect your work and sense of self in an alienating way. If, on the other hand, it is a good clay body, one that feels right and performs beyond expectations, it will nudge your work forward while quietly nourishing the inner self. Clay can reveal what is inherently meaningful, yet often hidden. In ceramics, physical work need not be at odds with inner values.

As I have mentioned, ceramics can become a mere technical experience of physical memory and performance or, in a more relevant and influentially powerful form, it can become a primary source for one's deepest growth and maturing. Working with clay is both a singular and a universal place where creative work and the human spirit converge. Universal in the same way that the sun or the moon, regardless of one's location, are known, and singular in that it is always a place of private intimacy.

If ceramics is recognized as a genuine link between universal physical experience and that which lives deep inside us, then it can also be recognized that the condition of the clay we work with has as much to do with either disturbing or cultivating such a relationship. In this sense, there is a direct correspondence between outer and inner material. In other words, the clay you work with has an effect not only on the direction your forms take but on the direction you and your imagination take. Tend to its preparation well. Know it as earth, as mud, but also know it as a material beyond interpretation.

As I see it, there are two ways to obtain a good clay body. One is to mix it yourself from the best raw materials you can acquire. The other is to purchase commercially prepared bodies that are becoming increasingly more sophisticated and desirable. In the choice of the latter you want to chose a supplier of proven consistency and quality. Fortunately, there are many available.

Good suppliers of premixed clays (such as the Standard Ceramic Supply Company, Seattle Pottery Supply or the Laguna Clay Company) usually offer a wide range of bodies that fire to different temperatures and colors. Some recipes are formulated for throwing, others specifically for handbuilding, and many for both. There are also clays designed for certain firing procedures such as *oxidation, reduction, raku* or *salt* firings.

One of the most difficult decisions for a practicing ceramist to make when first setting up a studio is whether to purchase already prepared clay, or thousands of dollars worth of mixing equipment, either in the form of a mechanical clay mixer, a pug mill or both. Many choose the former approach. Initially it is less expensive and continues to remain so unless several tons of clay a year are consumed. Also a great deal of studio floor space is required for mixing machines and the storing of raw materials that may not be available. Ideally, clay mixing should be done in a separate room that is well ventilated, as a great deal of clay dust can be generated during mixing. In addition to concerns for personal safety, the decision to mix or not to mix is also one of convenience. Time saved can be a freeing priority if it allows greater participation in other areas of personal quest.

Mechanical Mixers

Many mechanical clay mixers are former dough mixers or modeled after commercial dough mixers. These are large, heavy duty machines with revolving blades capable of mixing 200 pounds of bulk clay at once.

As a general procedure, the clay ingredients are first dry mixed in the

This mechanical mixer, once used to mix dough for coffee cakes, does an exceptional job at mixing a 250 pound batch of clay in less than three minutes.

hopper prior to the addition of water. But, just as in baking where the dry powders are added to the liquid to prevent lumps, clay can be added to the water and then blended for several minutes. After this initial mixing the dumping bucket should be opened and the clay examined. What you will be checking is its moisture content. If too moist and soft, add more powder and continue mixing. Repeat this simple adjusting process until the clay's consistency is satisfactory and exactly right for your needs. It is extremely important here to point out the successful advantage of not adding all of the dry ingredients to the water at once. Let me explain why, as the hidden simplification of this sensible approach is not without an earthly reason. Which is to say, a more workable clay body can be constructed if the dry ingredients are added in small but proportional amounts to the hot water at various intervals for some prolonged mixing while still in a "soupy" consistency. Make sense? If not, mix one batch without going through an extended period of saturated wetness and compare the differences. Also, if you want a "super" plastic clay body don't forget to first mix a small amount of bentonite in with the water *before* adding the other clays.

The squeeze test, when given, is a good indicator for telling when a batch of clay is ready for unloading. Remove a small sample of the clay and place it in the palm of your hand. Gently squeeze it between the fingers and release. The open fingers should be fairly clean having removed themselves from the clay without sticking, indicating that the mix is capable of holding its shape without adhering to everything it makes contact with.

To take the mixing of clay one step further, the creation of a good batch closely parallels the mixing of concrete where particle size and thoroughness of particle distribution are of mutual importance. For a clay body to have strength and resist cracking (due to excessive shrinkage) its ingredients should be thoroughly mixed for as long a time as is practical. Prolonged mixing of materials in the dry state can cause the fillers and heavier particles to settle to the bottom of some mixers. Long mixing times in the wet state allow the raw materials to become well distributed and more tightly packed. Good packing reduces shrinkage, and a clay body made up of a diverse mixture of particle sizes naturally packs better. Concrete, which is a blend of powders, sand and gravel, has a strong, workable density that is directly related to particle size variation. Conversely, clay batches made up of ingredients of the same or similar particle dimensions possess very little dry strength and remain very porous and weak when fired.

Pug Mills

Pug mills have a long horizontal auger like blade. Ingredients are added to a small hopper, compressed, mixed and extruded from a barrel-like opening.

The pugging units in most studios are used for recycling damp clay scraps. Sometimes, as when reprocessing scraps, the clay needs to be re-pugged an additional time or two. For superior clay, pug mills are frequently used to further remix pre-made clay bodies (clay made in mechanical mixers) to improve their working qualities. If equipped with a vacuum pump for de-airing the clay, the need for wedging can be eliminated by the pugging process.

Reprocessing Clay

Clay scraps, wet or dry, are best recycled by drying them out prior to breaking them up into small chunks and covering them, in a bucket, with water. Left to settle a day or two, the scraps slake down to form a thick slurry that can be poured onto plaster bats to stiffen, or loaded into a clay mixer in place of water to create a new and usable mix when blended with enough dry ingredients. Clay that has been reprocessed in this way is always preferred to a new mixture of powdered clay and water. The bacterial growth that takes place, over time, with old moist clay will greatly improve the workable qualities of any new batch of clay it is mixed with.

AGING CLAY

Mixed clay that has been allowed to age becomes more plastic. As an organic material clay improves over time as colloidal bacteria sets in and breaks down the clay platelets into even smaller particles. Aging over night helps, one week is better; two weeks even more so. Longer is better. Months, even years of storage make for a more workable and cooperative clay body. Some try to hasten this ripening process by adding Darvon, vinegar, beer or yogurt. Aged clay, once experienced, fosters appreciation and becomes exuberantly connected to the successful making of clay objects. Potters who realize the exceptional capabilities of such clay embrace it with a passion, always seeing to it that a musty smelling batch is forever incubating as they work; that even an extra bucket's worth of the oldest, truly premium stuff, is set aside for those special parts such as handles. Tending to the aging of your clay is fundamental if not inseparable to satisfactions that can be long lasting and deeply inspiring.

Steven Hill using a rolling pin to flatten twisted coils of well-aged clay into teapot handles.

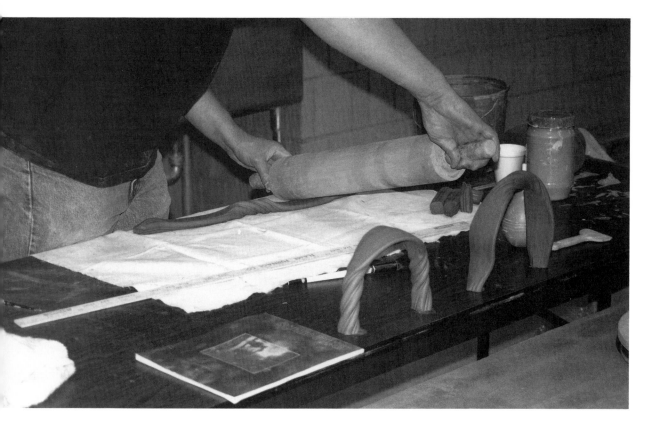

WEDGING

Wedging is a process of kneading premixed clay by hand prior to use. Its primary function is to remove any existing pockets of air and to homogenize the clay. When it comes to success on the potters wheel, well wedged clay is a necessity.

The other function of wedging, one that many potters feel to be of equal importance, is the unspoken dialogue that is initiated between the potter and the clay. Time spent wedging is a time of intimate contact that establishes a mood for thinking and for working. It also serves to initiate and direct future courses of action. For example, if the clay is soft it might be saying, "I'm not feeling very strong just now . . . perhaps it's better if I become something low and flat like a plate." Or, if it is stiff, the message it might be communicating is that it is willing to become a thin, tall form, such as a bottle, without collapsing. As you wedge your clay, listen.

Clay is best wedged on a canvas covered board or on a wedging table with a plaster slab for a top. It's wise to cover a plaster wedging surface with canvas to keep tiny chips of plaster from being picked up by the clay. Bits of plaster in a clay wall will eventually expand and cause the surface clay to flake and break away. Since wedging is generally done from a standing position, where the whole body is part of the motion, the surface used should be securely anchored and located just below waist level. The height of this surface is important and should be individually determined, whenever possible. An inch or two up or down will exercise and develop different muscles, or in some instances, fatigue.

The two common methods of wedging are *spiral wedging* and *ram's head*, also known as *bulldog wedging*. Both techniques remove air from the clay while simultaneously working to provide a smooth and even consistency throughout. If the clay appears too soft for use at this time, its consistency can easily be stiffened by the addition of powdered clay, or it can simply be wedged for a longer period of time on a moisture absorbing surface. It's also worth noting that clay ages better if it is first wedged prior to storage.

Spiral Wedging

Technically, spiral wedging originates from a twisting of the wrists and is often credited with lining up the clay particles in a circular formation consistent with the turning of the potters wheel. I'm not certain as to how much truth there is to this concept but I do know that spiral wedging is preferred by throwers.

To start the sprial wedging process, quickly roll your piece of clay into the shape of a cone. If you are right handed, place the cone in front of you with the base facing to the left and the point to the right.

With the left palm covering the base, place your right hand on the side of the cone and with the combined weight of your hand, arm and shoulder, simultaneously push down and to the right with the heel of the palm in a clockwise rotation. The left hand does very little as it follows through in its support of this pivoting motion.

Prior to repeating this maneuver, the fingers of the right hand should partially lift the clay and turn it, on end, towards the stomach. This slight clockwise twisting of the clay keeps its mass together while repositioning it for continued wedging.

Repeat this sequence several times over, trying to establish and maintain a natural rhythm as you work. Stop when it feels right and finish up by carefully rolling the newly created folds of clay back over on themselves and back again into the shape of a cone. The wedged cone of clay is now ready for centering on the potters wheel.

Clay being wedged for throwing using the spiral technique.

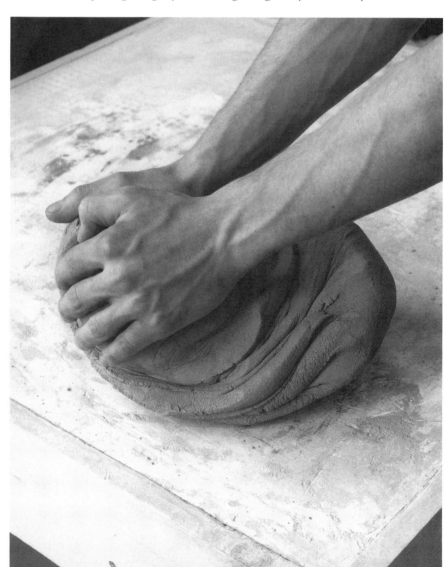

Ram's Head Wedging

While not as popular as the spiral technique, the ram's head technique is much easier and faster to learn. It simply involves the placement of your hands on a ball of clay followed by a downward, slightly sideways pressure from the heel of both palms after which the far side is lifted, rotated forward and again pressed downward and sideways. After many such repeated actions the end result is an animal-like facial form with overlapping folds of skin. If the amount of clay being wedged is relatively small these folds can resemble the head of a bull dog; if a larger amount of clay is handled in the same manner spiral folds are generated on each side of the hands that resemble the curved horns of a ram, hence the descriptive name ram's head wedging. This symmetrical form, although de-aired and tightly compacted, is not in a shape that can be easily centered on the wheel. Before it can be used for throwing it needs to be carefully rolled into the form of a cylinder or slapped between the hands and into the shape of a ball. In doing so, the risk of trapping additional pockets of air is increased, not a serious concern but one that adds complexity and demands consideration.

With the ram's head technique clay is wedged with an equal force from both hands.

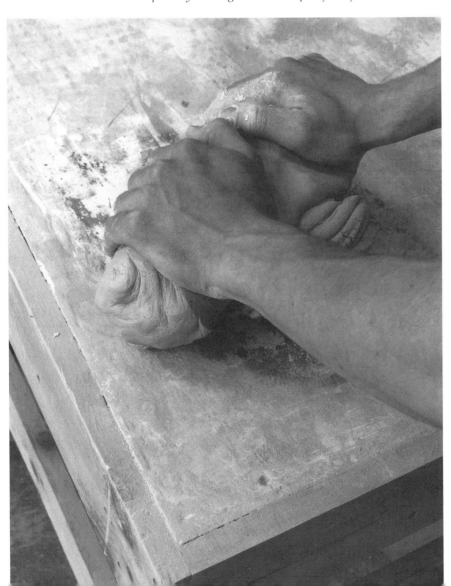

PERSONAL CLAY TOOLS

One of our most important personal clay-working tools is our own mind. Clay is naturally responsive to our touch—to our fingers. It is also receptive to impressions—to the imprints of other materials both natural and man-made. Still, its shape and surface become precious when it celebrates the creative imagination of our very own being and finds itself united with all that we are. When that energy which ultimately shapes our clay also embraces our personality, passions, visions . . . all of our life experiences, then that clay is shaped and charged with the greatest of all tools . . . the spirit of our own life.

Standard Tools

"Tool". What is a tool? It can be a hand operated instrument. It can be something used to perform an operation. It can be a necessary aid for doing one's work. Broadly interpreted, a ceramic tool is a device for shaping our clay. The standard tools of the trade, the ones used most often in the ceramic profession, are the:

SPONGE: the small, fine-grained sponge is essential for throwing and handbuilding. It is used for transferring water, smoothing clay surfaces and an infinite number of other spontaneous applications. The natural ones (sometimes called elephant ears because of their shapes) are the ones most favored, but the newer synthetic "Sugarloaf" potters' sponges and the traditional round cellulose makeup sponges are fine—just don't leave home without one of them.

NEEDLE TOOL: a long, strong needle attached to an even longer wooden or metal handle. It's used for all sorts of cutting and joining operations. Sometimes called a pin tool, it is frequently used as an instrument for drawing and signing but in such instances the conventional lead pencil often works better.

FETTLING KNIFE: a narrow, long bladed knife. The blade is relatively stiff, with a minimum amount of flexibility, and has no true substitute. It is the faithful workhorse of hand builders when it comes to modeling and cutting.

RIB: a thin, flat form made from either wood, metal or rubber. They come in many shapes and sizes but the kidney shape is commonplace and seems to prevail as a traditional favorite. They are used primarily for shaping and smoothing. The wooden ribs are used almost exclusively for throwing, while the metal and rubber ribs—which are flexible—are used for both throwing and handbuilding. The stainless steel ribs, often referred to as scrapers or steels, make an excellent scraping tool for leveling rough clay surfaces and are equally as proficient at shaping thrown contours. Of the three, the metal rib is the champion; a serious shaper of clay. The spiffy rubber ribs are sensibly called finishing ribs in honor of the astoundingly smooth finishes they can impart on the clay surface. They come in different colors, coded to match different degrees of flexibility. The blue ones, which are fairly soft and flexible, work well on soft clay.

WOOD MODELING TOOL: a long wooden knife-like tool for working clay in a variety of ways. They come in 6, 8 and 10 inch lengths and in many, many different shapes. One end is usually blade-like and is extremely useful for trimming newborn pots that are still wet and in an upright position on the potter's wheel. The other end is often contoured to resemble the tip of a finger. In practice, it's often used as an extension of the finger.

LOOP TOOL: a looped ribbon of steel attached to a wooden handle. It's used primarily for trimming leather-hard pottery while inverted on the pottery wheel. The flat ribbon loop tool should not be confused with the thin wire loop tools used for clay modeling and sculpting. With use, the flat steel will lose its edge and need sharpening.

CUTTING WIRE: a 20 inch length of fine wire or nylon line attached, at each end, to short lengths of wooden dowels. It is used for separating thrown pots from wheel heads and for cutting through clay.

CHAMMY: a thin piece of pliable leather. Made from tanned sheep's skin, a 6 inch length of this silky soft hide can effortlessly clean-up and refine an otherwise ruffled clay edge; leaving it elegantly smooth and polished looking. A chammy does the same thing to the rim of a thrown pot that sandpaper does to the surface of a piece of fine woodworking.

Found Tools

As important and as useful as the standard and commercially manufactured tools are, they aren't nearly as exciting to acquire or as pleasurable to use as those that are found. There is something personally meaningful about intuitively being drawn to an object that either your experience or super consciousness immediately connects with and recognizes as a useful companion to your clay work. Such tools are the ones that help reawaken feeling and bring personality to the work. In time they begin to dominate the tool box as the value of their special contributions grows. Curious things begin to occur from ready-to-use found objects; new approaches to working evolve and loyalties to certain individual tools develop. Before you realize what's happening some tools become dependable favorites; capable of initiating momentary anxiety at their mere misplacement.

A list of found clay tools would be endless, just as the sources for them are. Go to the kitchen; rattle some pots and pans, open all the drawers, look for intriguing objects that can leave an enrichment mark, a design or a decorative texture on the clay when pressed to it. What about those eating utensils, that butter paddle, those cookie cutters? On second thought, for-

get about the cookie cutters, the cheese cutter or better yet, what would that spool of heavy twine look like freely rolled into the clay and then pulled away? Hardware stores! I love hardware stores, especially the older ones where items are still found in bins and not in plastic packages—it's as if they were partially stocked for the ceramist: nuts, nails, pipe fittings and an immense supply of intoxicating stuff. Try looking in your grandparents garage or garage sales in general. My favorite source is the lumber mill yard. I'm especially fond of working with scrap pieces of wood and wood moldings. The rough-sawn ends of some scraps have an authority about them that is evocatively flattering when pressed into the clay like rubber stamps.

TYPES OF CLAY BODIES

A clay body is a mixture of two or more clays or clay and some non-clay materials. Usually one clay is dominant, often chosen for a specific set of characteristics such as firing temperature, workability, strength and color. Other clays are added in smaller amounts to provide a variation in clay particle size and to function as modifiers. As a modifier each clay type is unique, with a potential to provide some sort of desirable adjustment such as a change in color, plasticity, or in a formula's maturing temperature. Non-clay additives such as flint (silica) increases density and material hardness by raising the firing temperature. Feldspars, on the other hand, lower the firing temperature while simultaneously strengthening the clay and rendering it waterproof. The non-clay *fillers*, as you remember, help reduce shrinkage and warpage.

Porcelain

Porcelain is not only a clay body but a mystical dimension for experiencing an ordinary material of extraordinary beauty and poetic depth. In its most refined form it is pristine white. As a delicately thin surface it is exquisitely translucent.

The formula composition for porcelain is split fairly evenly between clay and non-clay materials. In fact, the all-American base formula for porcelain is 25% kaolin, 25% ball clay, 25% feldspar and 25% flint. This formula, like that of any other clay body, can be altered or customized in an infinite number of ways. For example, the white porcelain grog, molochite, could be added for improved stability. The ratio of kaolin clay to ball clay could be varied, as could the percentages of feldspar and flint. Substitutions can also be made. Soda feldspar can be substituted for potash feldspar, No. 6 tile clay for EPK china clay, or Tennessee ball clay for Kentucky ball clay. Case in point, translucency is greatly improved by simply increasing the amount of potash or custer feldspar. The possibilities are endless and the results are often dramatically noticeable.

The richness of porcelain's translucency is also enhanced by firing at high temperatures. To fuse the materials into a vitrified glass-like state, a true porcelain clay needs to be fired to cone 10 (2345°F) or higher. Lower maturing porcelains can be formulated by increasing the amounts and kinds of flux. For example, the amount of feldspar already in the clay body can be increased, or nepheline syenite, whiting and even Gerstley borate can be added as a body flux.

As a workable clay body porcelain has a few shortcomings that can prove challenging. Its limited clay content reduces plasticity and the length of time that it remains moist and usable. It can be workable for the longest of times, then suddenly become stiff and dry. Fortunately, porcelain is highly moisture absorbent and can be readily softened. As a dense, high firing clay, further compromises have to be made in shape and size to avoid warping and slumping. Still, ceramists have always learned to cultivate solutions to such chronic annoyances and to artfully seek out adjustments that both benefit and embrace their work.

John Albert Murphy, Patience, porcelain vessel that was thrown and press molded, 6" × 9" × 3". The surface pattern was masked, sprayed with colored mason stain slips and fired to cone 6 inside an electric kiln.

Stoneware

As the most popular of all types of clay bodies, stoneware is a mid to high temperature firing body. It is strong and dependable when used for culinary or functional ware. Many find its rugged, natural surface character appealing, with or without a glaze.

Stoneware bodies are highly refractory (melting or fusing at temperatures higher than 2300°F) and, on the average, contain at least 80% clay. The main ingredient, fire clay, accounts for the bodies ability to withstand a wide range of mishandling and firing temperatures. These clays mature anywhere between cone 6 and cone 10 (2194°F and 2345°F) and maintain a strong, stone-like surface appearance.

Relative to the type of kiln atmosphere they are fired in, stoneware clays can range in color from a light unspeckled buff to a deep speckled brown. The speckling is the result of unseen iron impurities in the clay itself. Electrically fired kilns do not reveal these metallic specks, so potters often add granular oxides such as illmenite or manganese to improve the fired surface appearance of the ware. Others, who are unsatisfied with the overall pale color of electrically fired (oxidation) clay, add colored clays such as Redart clay or Barnard clay to the body during mixing. The true, rich character of stoneware clay, however, is best revealed after being fired in a gas kiln. These kilns provide a reducing atmosphere that is deficient of oxygen. During combustion, this shortage of oxygen (reduction) chemically alters the color of the clay by taking oxygen away from the metallic oxides. The result can be a warm toast brown or orangish clay with occasional outbreaks of dark iron specks.

Earthenware

Natural low temperature clay bodies that mature around cone 04 (1922°F) are often referred to as earthenware. Structurally, these soft, nonvitrified, relatively porous clay bodies lack strength and durability. Earthenware vessels are not waterproof unless glazed. Their low density, although not always a functional advantage, makes these clays a good choice for large nonfunctional or sculptural shapes. The openness of the clay reduces shrinkage and allows for the creation of forms that are massive yet light in weight. Often common iron-bearing surface clays account for a large part of the bodies makeup, and tend to fire to a reddish brown. Yet, depending on the source of the clay, any color, even white, is possible.

Low-Fire

The term low fire has come to be associated with white and light colored clay bodies that become highly vitrified—glassy hard—around the cone 05 (1888°F) range. When fired a little higher, they are sometimes referred to as medium, low-fire or soft stoneware. Most formulas contain enough non-clay ingredients, such as feldspar and talc, to provide the necessary strength and density to make these clays tough and appealing. Although waterproof, and not in need of glazing, their lightness of color makes the bright low-temperature glazes look exceptionally brilliant over their surfaces.

Ron Nagle, S.D.#1 - Eleventh Hour, handbuilt, multi-fired glaze and china paints, 3 1/2" × 4 3/4" × 3 1/4". Ever since the late 1960s, shortly after he started using the cup image as his major frame of reference, Nagle has been a master of small, intimate low-fire ceramic forms. His imaginative use of surface texture and exquisite glaze colors aid in rendering his objects all that more precious and jewel-like.

John Harris, Cricket Pot, raku fired clay with copper-iron halo brushwork over terra sigillata, wrapped with raffia ties, 5" × 4".

Raku

A raku clay body is one that has a high thermal shock tolerance: an ability to withstand a sudden or dramatic change in temperature without cracking or breaking. To obtain this type of endurance the clay needs to be very *open* or porous. Most raku bodies achieve this *openness* with the addition of 20% to 30% filler in the form of kyanite, sand or grog. The remainder of the composition is often all clay. Practically any kind of clay can be utilized, although the common choice is fire clay. Raku clay bodies are fired near cone 07 (1783°F), but adapt to lower temperatures for pit or smoke firing.

Lorraine Capparell with her Three Ages Of Women ceramic sculpture installed at the Palo Alto Cultural Center. The two 6 foot supporting columns form the gate with the Maiden on the left and the Matron on the right. The remaining five Crone columns forming the temple are 8 feet tall.

Developing A Clay Body

Many potters buy their clay premixed. Those that own an electric mixer or pug mill purchase the ingredients separately and custom blend them with water. These materials are obtained in the powdered form, usually in 50 and 100 pound bags, and are used in the clay formula in amounts that are appropriate to the specific fabricating and firing needs of the individual.

Learning to formulate your own recipe for a clay body will take some time. Knowledge and understanding of how and what the various ingredients contribute come from experience. You'll have to experiment and test, eventually coming to know the subtle differences between materials: which are plastic and nonplastic, which are fluxes, which affect shrinkage, and even how to manage the water content to your liking. The chart on the next page should be of some help.

Material	Low-fire	High-fire	Wheelwork	Handbuilding
A.P. Green Fireclay (28 mesh)	30%	75%	60%	75%
Hawthorn Bonding (30 mesh)	30%	50%	50%	50%
Goldart (200 mesh)	50%	75%	75%	75%
Redart (200 mesh)	40%	20%	20%	40%
Kentucky Ball Clay	25%	30%	30%	25%
Tennessee Ball Clay	25%	30%	30%	25%
EPK Kaolin	25%	50%	25%	25%
No. 6 Tile Clay	30%	40%	30%	30%
Georgia Kaolin	25%	40%	30%	25%
English Kaolin-Grolleg	25%	40%	40%	30%
Feldspar	30%	30%	30%	20%
Bone Ash	30%	30%	20%	20%
Flint (200 mesh)	25%	25%	25%	25%
Talc	50%	20%	15%	20%
Nepheline Syenite	30%	30%	30%	20%
Spodumene	20%	25%	25%	20%
Silica Sand (40 mesh)	10%	10%	10%	15%
Beach Sand (35 mesh)	10%	10%	10%	20%
Kyanite (35 mesh)	20%	20%	15%	35%
Kyanite (48 mesh)	20%	20%	25%	15%
Mullite (35 mesh)	20%	20%	15%	30%
Molochite (20 mesh)	5%	5%	0%	20%
Fine Grog (48 mesh)	15%	15%	15%	15%
Medium Grog (30 mesh)	10%	10%	10%	30%
Coarse Grog (20 mesh)	0%	0%	0%	25%
Screened Sawdust	15%	15%	10%	25%
Nylon Fiber (1/2″ chopped)	0%	0%	0%	5%
Wollastonite	4%	4%	4%	6%
Boroflux	5%	0%	0%	2%
Bentonite	3%	3%	3%	3%

**Clay Body Materials:
Maximum Formula
Allotment**

The world's largest student pottery sale is held annually in Michigan on the first weekend in December by the students at the Royal Oak campus of Oakland Community College. The college offers a two year associate's degree in ceramics and when instructor Charles Blossor first organized the show twenty one years ago total sales were less than $2,000. For the last five years sales have been over $300,000. This year 25,000 pieces were sold and sales toped out at $350,233.

MOTHER EARTH

Before you go off and begin your work with clay I have something to relate to you . . . your works in clay are ultimately gifts from your mother: the great Mother of nature we call earth. We are all her children. Mother Earth has given us life and nourishment in ceaseless infinitude. Her creative capacities and deeds are powerful forces that we are unable to fathom, yet alone match. As potters we can learn from her, work in collaboration with her, become one with her but we cannot live and experience meaning without her.

The clay experience before you, like the landscape, is very broad. Its horizon extends beyond our vision. Yet in our new-born awareness, within a community of other respectful beings, we should do our utmost to always care for her welfare. With creative consciousness, we should honor her in every piece of clay touched and with every pot formed so that each becomes a collaborative voice for our own life and that of our sacred earth Mother.

What you do with clay is very primal and will be naturally related to your connectedness to the earth. Out of this spiritual relationship simple, yet beautiful, ceramic forms will evolve that have been previously formed in your unconsciousness. As it is part of our nature to honor and advance certain virtues of our mother.

As a living organism, the earth is symbolically associated with motherhood and growth. As you journey with clay, stay alert, be receptive and be open. The Earth allows the clay to transmit her wisdom—her secrets. So touch, look and embrace all; miss nothing. I encourage you to take the journey seriously, to make it sacred and not just physical. Let these words be an affectionate reminder to not undertake it without a heart-felt sense of enjoyment or without letting your receiving be filled with acknowledgment and gratitude.

Adrian Arleo's House II is based upon a fertility/pregnancy image that, with minimal detail, creates a sense of intimacy as it explores a nurturing relationship. The 50" tall sculpture is supported on a 1/2" diameter armature welded to a 1/4" steel plate that is 12" square.

The Australian Aboriginal

From the very first inhabitants of the planet, tribes and peoples of various lands shared many common environmental concerns, spiritual beliefs and meaningful values regarding the earth. The cultural practices of the Australian aboriginal for the past 40,000 years reflected an overlapping network of sacred, social, ceremonial and artistic traditions that are directly related to the earth and a natural order to the cosmos.

To varying degrees, aboriginal identity is centered on a spiritual concept referred to as *Dreaming* or the *Dreamtime*. These terms are permeated with supernatural elements and beings. They chronicle the ancestors of creation and mandate a harmonious relationship with the universe. Dreaming engages the Earth, her natural forces and life forms, and exists as the bonding link of equilibrium between man and nature. A *walkabout,* normally a trip for gathering food and water, becomes a special opportunity to connect with Dreamtime. The aboriginal is inseparable from the land, and any trip that provides the traveler a spiritual opportunity to reflect on the geography of creation becomes a Dream Journey, or a pathway of sacred renewal.

Art is important in aboriginal life and history. The ceremonial ground paintings and rock engravings are sacred expressions of Dreaming and a powerful means for staying connected with the past and honoring the earth. They painted images of spiritual power on the earth's surface and on their bodies with colored clays. They danced their ritual dances of ancestral life and personal Dreamings on prepared surface areas of clay to become part of the land.

To the aboriginal the land does not belong to people, or any one person. People belong to the land. With this state of mind they are able to live in deep harmony with their environment and peacefully flourish as a people. Their values are spiritual, not material, and their earth has sacred dimensions.

Clay has sacred dimensions because of its expressive potential. As you work with clay, be aware that some things become irrevocably sacred when they continuously summon-up feelings related to the spiritual nature of life. Clay is objective and subjective. Objectively it possesses utilitarian value. Subjectively it possesses an evolutionary history of our environment and human beliefs. The value-laden power of clay is that it can manifest the spiritual nature of our being: giving physical form to our personal insights.

It's no secret that one of the frightening dangers we face today is a loss of our spiritual identity. During these highly technological times, amidst many forms of ignorance, prejudice and inhumaneness, we are reminded through clay work of our interconnectedness with the Earth and of those things in life that are alive with value.

The American Indian

Early Native Americans, like the Aborigines, did not separate themselves from the land. In their wisdom, the Earth was sacred and full of spiritual meaning. To receive her natural gifts one needed to give of oneself. This spiritual practice of reciprocity is still in practice today. Because the land was sacred and manifested spiritual gifts and powers it was treated with reverence and complemented with tribute and offerings. Certain parts of the landscape became spiritually symbolic and were designated as holy places. These centers of spiritual awakening were so significant that tribal traditions allowed them to be approached only for visionary or purification experiences.

The native people of the Southwest, perhaps more so than any other group of American Indians, have a special and enduring connection to the land. To the Southwestern Indians the land was their primordial source and the spiritual link to the past: to their ancestors. Through this interrelated identity with the earth, pottery evolved from a utilitarian object to a spiritual artifact.

The traditions of pottery making in the Southwest go back 2,000 years, replacing 6,000 years of basketry as the prominent interfacing art form between daily living and spiritual equilibrium. While their clay works have been tremendous achievements in human terms, many people today fail to see, yet alone understand, the underlying subtlety of their connections to spiritual experiences or how the creations of spiritually inspired art objects parallels ones connection to the earth.

At times it is easy to overlook life's elusive meanings and abstract connections, especially if one is unaccustomed to, or is unsuccessful at, relating to the world out of a sense of wholeness. Through any number of developments, technology and modern forms of communication for example, false feelings of being a connected part of the universe can emerge that appeal to the senses, albeit with displaced impulses of objectivity and openness, but that still remain far removed from Indian consciousness or vision.

The American Indian was not lost in a circle of confusion, insecurity or incompleteness, but lived in relationships with the whole of nature and within a sense of oneness with the great universe. If they struggled with anything, I imagine it would have centered on how to best maintain their union with the Earth herself.

What is most remarkable, especially in comparison to the idealized activities of mankind today, is that the American Indian and the Australian Aboriginal were phenomenally successful as caretakers of our Earth. The story of our own history, as short as it is, engulfs us with less marvelous images and lived truths as it tells, in freighting detail, of how the Earth has been spiritually abused, ecologically endangered and made to suffer in its present state of environmental vulnerability.

Julian and Maria Martinez of the San Ildefonso Pueblo decorating and burnishing pottery on the patio of the Palace of the Governors in Santa Fe, New Mexico in 1912.

However brief or extensive your involvement with clay becomes, know that you are making a living connection with the Earth and that because of such live moments you will never again be the same. You will have gained some enlightenment. Your touches will be impressionable and, if full of honest passion, you will come to a self-realization that clay, and your bond with it, is in accord with nature and embraces life. The context of this participation with clay should inspire a greater caring for the Earth and all who live through her. So, be on your spirit-hearted watch . . . be prepared for a new uniting.

A Revealed Presence

At the moment this whole concept of Mother Earth may reverberate within you spiritual excitement or sheer unrelatedness. The affinities of an insupportable presence between making pottery and awakening to your inseparableness with the earth is far more confusing than some of life's other metaphysical mysteries. The focus here, however, is on a balanced approach for receiving both the clay and the Earth in a context of wholeness. This implies, of course, that as one's work with clay proceeds changes in perception occur that affect conventional, mater-of-fact thinking.

As I've mentioned, to reach new awarenesses of self and a more balanced equilibrium between Earth and what one does with the earth, the relationship needs to be approached from the spirit-oriented side as well as the physical side. Technical information for working with clay appears in following chapters. Shifts in consciousness, however, are more difficult to frame with reason. They are touched upon throughout the book, and definitely need to be realized. The mechanics for understanding the spirit-substance of clay work are organic. They are embodied in the living and the love of doing. Perhaps the most vital work of the spirit embodied in clay is to simply awaken or strengthen the spiritual values within our own being and to bring us to a life-sense understanding that will allow us to live on the Earth in equable wholeness.

In many ways the voice of nature has been lost to us. Through pottery the Earth is given a voice, and as you take up the clay that voice is yours. Speaking together the messages are shared. Together both are served with dignity. Working together the potter's life is transformed and finds new meaning. With the transformation comes not only an understanding of the spirit of divine oneness between human life and the Earth but also a more intimate feeling toward the functioning of its bond. Within the context of this revelation there is new hope for the ecological crisis that tears apart the fabric of our environment.

*Charles Simonds, People Who Live In A Circle. They Excavate Their Past and Re-build It Into Their Present. Their Dwelling Functions As A Personal and Cosmo-logical Clock, Seasonal, Harmonic, Obsessive. Clay with sticks and stones, 8 3/8"
× 26 1/4" × 26 1/8".*

The Ecological Connection

Our existence is inseparable from that of the earth's. Our destinies are so interdependent that only with and through each other can we both survive.

In the future our lives, our economies and our social-political systems will evolve around ecological concerns in ways that many of us cannot even begin to imagine today. This would become especially true in the case of unprecedented accidental or antagonistic global ecodisasters. My grand-father never heard of acid rain, the ozone layer, nuclear expectoration or global warming. On this present day they are frightening worldwide hap-penings capable of threatening the quality of our existence and altering the hopes of our future. What environmental damages will our children and grandchildren know as a reality that we have not yet heard of? Which re-source extraction industries (timber, construction, mining, ranching, etc.)

will exploit the beauty and ecosystems of their environment? What commercial, political and human issues will threaten their natural world? Will the Earth of their time, along with her water, air and other support systems, be able to provide the nourishment we have known in our time? Will it be an important part of their own identity?

These evolutionary issues speak of urgency. They speak of a separateness; of an imbalance with the natural laws of relationships, communion and community. They also remind us of our commanding role in the functioning of things and the mutual phenomenon of the Earth's presence in our survival. The dynamics of such integrated cycles are intimate and sacred. Within this mystery Native wisdom and "primal" activities, such as working with clay and the spirit of clay, generate a deeper relationship with nature while promoting the emergence of a greater ecological understanding. Humanistically, working in clay provides spiritual significance and an enlightenment that bears little resemblance to the ruinous void consumerism has left on much of the human psyche and landscape. A void that was a consequence of self expression through abundant acquisition instead of interactive giving and a thought form that things had to be consumed to be enjoyed; that anything primordial, natural or untouched was less than desirable. What is so scary about such a non-spiritual, exploitative attitude is that today, for the first time in the history of the world, technologies exist that can over power our environment in devastating ways.

A world view of ecology is essential to the future well being of the earth and our presence as ceramists is related to our identity with the natural world. Working with clay gives us an opportunity to stay in touch with our Earth and to recognize the web of life that sustains us. Throughout history, indigenous peoples have understood the spiritual meanings of the land. As potters, working in these times, we have an inroad to this spiritual heritage and the opportunity to inherit the heart of humanity through our interactive behavior with clay. As we become more intimate with clay our sense of responsibility to the Earth expands. Personal feelings of affection and protection arise that heighten our ecological perceptions and leave us to ponder, ever so more deeply, our role as human beings, as ceramic artists and as Earthkeepers. In the presence of our pondering it is not difficult to feel that the Earth, our great Mother, is communicating to us through our genetic connections.

THE SPIRIT OF CLAY

Teach your children
what we have taught our children,
that the earth is our mother.
Whatever befalls the earth,
befalls the sons and daughters of the earth.
If men spit upon the ground,
they spit upon themselves.

This we know.
The earth does not belong to us;
we belong to the earth.
This we know.
All things are connected
like the blood which unites one family.

All things are connected.
Whatever befalls the earth
befalls the sons and daughters of the earth.
We did not weave the web of life;
We are merely a strand in it.
Whatever we do to the web,
we do to ourselves.

CHIEF SEATTLE*

*Chief Seattle (originally "Seathl") was the chief of 6 local tribes in Washington State when he delivered his now famous speech in 1854 on living in harmony with the earth and with each other. These few lines are part of a popular version of the speech written by Ted Perry. They are from *How can one sell the air? : Chief Seattle's Vision*, edited by Eli Gifford and R. Michael Cook. Copyright © 1992 by The Book Publishing Company. Reprinted by permission of the publisher.

CLAY BODY FORMULAS

Porcelain

Jasper Porcelain Cone 9
38% EPK Kaolin
25% Potash Feldspar
20% Tennessee Ball Clay
15% Flint
 2% Bentonite

White Knight Cone 9
28% Tennessee Ball Clay
25% EPK Kaolin
25% Custer Feldspar
20% Flint
 2% Bentonite

Hood Porcelain Cone 10
25% Grolleg
25% No. 6 Tile Clay
25% Kentucky Ball Clay
10% Custer Feldspar
10% Flint
 5% Pyrophillite

Russian White Cone 10
40% Grolleg
20% Custer Feldspar
20% Flint
15% No. 6 Tile Clay
 3% Bentonite
 2% Wollastonite

Stoneware

**Chatterley Multi-purpose
Body** Cone 6
45% Goldart Clay
23% A.P. Green Mill Clay
11% Kentucky Ball Clay
 7% Kona F4 Feldspar
 6% Virginia Kyanite (48 mesh)
 5% Mullite (35 mesh)
 3% G-Grog (20 mesh)

**Northern Kentucky
University
All-Purpose White Clay**
50# Hawthorn Bonding Clay
25# Kentucky Ball Clay
25# EPK Kaolin Clay
23# Custer Feldspar
20# Flint
5–15# Sand/Grog

Voulkos's Stack Body Cone 10
50# A.P. Green Fireclay
50# Cedar Heights Goldart Clay
50# Kentucky Ball Clay
50# Grog (48/60 mesh)
20# Custer Feldspar

Four Seasons Body Cone 10
100# Hawthorn Bonding Clay
 30# Tennessee Ball Clay
 30# Kentucky Ball Clay
 15# Custer Feldspar
 15# Grog (30/48 mesh)

Earthenware

Hollister Terra-cotta Cone 04
100# Redart Clay
 50# Kentucky Ball Clay
 50# Fireclay
 20# Talc
 50# Fine Grog
 65 grams Barrium Carb.

Yung Red Earthenware Cone 02
80# Redart Clay
 8# Lincoln Fireclay
 6# Kentucky Ball Clay
 6# Talc
    130 grams Red Iron Oxide

Low-Fire

Funk's WhiteBody Cone 04-06
50% Kentucky Ball Clay
50% Talc
 2% Bentonite

Atlanta White Body Cone 02-06
35% Kentucky Ball Clay
30% EPK Kaolin
20% Talc
10% Flint
 5% Goldart Clay

Arleo Sculpture Body Cone 04
36% Greenstripe Fireclay
27% Kentucky Ball Clay
10% Talc
 9% EPK Kaolin
 9% Flint
 9% Wollastonite
15% Medium Grog
10% Fine Grog
    35 grams 1/2" Nylon
    Fiber/100 lbs.

Raku

Piepenburg Handbuilding Body
100# Hawthorn Bonding Clay
 50# Goldart Clay
 50# Virginia Kyanite (35 mesh)

Piepenburg Throwing Body
100# Hawthorn Bonding Clay
 50# No. 5 Tennessee Ball Clay
 30# Virginia Kyanite (48 mesh)

Ana England's Handbuilding Body
50# Fire Clay
25# Kentucky Ball Clay
25# Foundry Hill Creme Clay
15# Talc
 8# Spodumene
10# Sand
10# Grog

Bryan McGrath Throwing Body
50# Hawthorn Bonding Clay
20# Kentucky Ball Clay
20# Grog
10# Spodumene

Participants in a workshop with Paulus Berensohn arranging clay stones on the floor (in a self-directed yet playful manner) to form an instinctively arrived at pattern which celebrates the creative spirit while speaking to the earth. Just prior to this communion experience each person was asked to create a family of 9 stones that progressively varied in size.

2

Play

One of the most instinctive and useful in-roads for coming to clay is through a simple, yet elemental, phenomenon known as "play".

Play, in any form, is intuitive creativity in action. Inherent in our being is a vast plurality of feelings, images and intuitive responses that originate from the deepest levels of our inner knowledge. Through the freedom of play we are able to penetrate these levels and tap into the guiding force of our own knowledge . . . our own creative self.

As an activity, play is a flexible way of doing something, but it is also a frame of mind and as such becomes an evolutionary source for all that is original. Play is also spiritual in a highly personal context that is both sacred and divine in its relationship to ourselves and our work. In one sense it is the spiritual wisdom of our subconscious—of our very being.

By now you're probably asking, what does play have to do with acquiring techniques for shaping my clay work? The answer, although unassumingly so, is everything. Play is the "mommy" of technique. By continuously playing and experimenting with our tools and materials we learn the necessary techniques for working with clay. As our knowledge expands, clay no longer exists as a material but becomes a medium—a medium for our new found talents, a medium of expression for our senses. With time, you too will understand that the compositional spirit of clay is play.

Verne Funk, Cool, 14″ × 21″ × 7″. With an artistically playfully attitude the ceramist is freer, in both vision and technical inventiveness, to liberate the extraordinary from the ordinary and create intensely exciting clay pieces.

Play As Liberation

Play is a creative way to make use of fabrication techniques. It encourages us to seek other sources for ceramic form beyond the traditional vessel vocabulary. As creative work, with a spectacular spectrum of freedoms, it draws on our personal passions and intuitive feelings, leading us to new insights. Such breakthroughs are to be treasured in that they ultimately provide the new sources, the life giving origins, for our clay work.

Play is the shepherd of metamorphosis that allows ceramics to be more than a process of craft. Through play ceramics becomes a process of passion. Through play we become intrinsically motivated to create with clay out of the pure, simple joy of doing rather than for any extrinsic compensation.

The disciplines of Zen Buddhism, which center around the attainment of enlightenment through self-knowledge, have long suggested that we look within ourselves for the knowledge and peace needed to live in spiritual equilibrium. Through the universal language of play our capacities, as people seeking to be creative with clay, are seeded with personal insights and fertilized with an excitement of freedom. Through play we are able to take hold of our reality and find our creative voice. The Zen concept of the universal self suggests that by letting go, by doing without thinking, we merge with the doing and find our freedom. Through such transformations a person's entire life becomes a creative mosaic and every expression a creative act. Because playing is a form of unhindered doing it is relatively free of attachment and rises beyond any psychological need for control.

This group of students was asked to playfully create a clay piece based upon an interest they each had in common.

Due to individual personality traits its not easy to assess just how far we are able to realize our creative powers through play. For some, resistance may arise out of personal fears or a need for intellectual grounding. For others, more trusting in nature and less anxious about taking risks, play experiences may prove to be more rewarding.

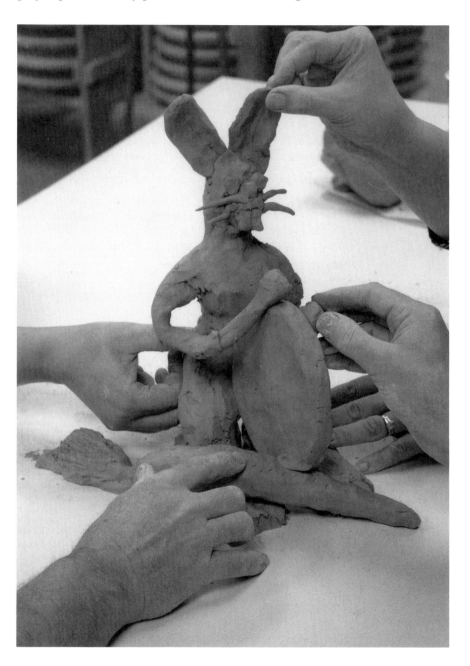

Initially, creative play experiences are less anxious when familiar images are dealt with. Once the known is approached in a playful manner many fears and obstacles are transformed and, minute-by-minute, the play activity itself releases natural desires to be creative in ways that, although maybe not new to the world, are freeing to the participant.

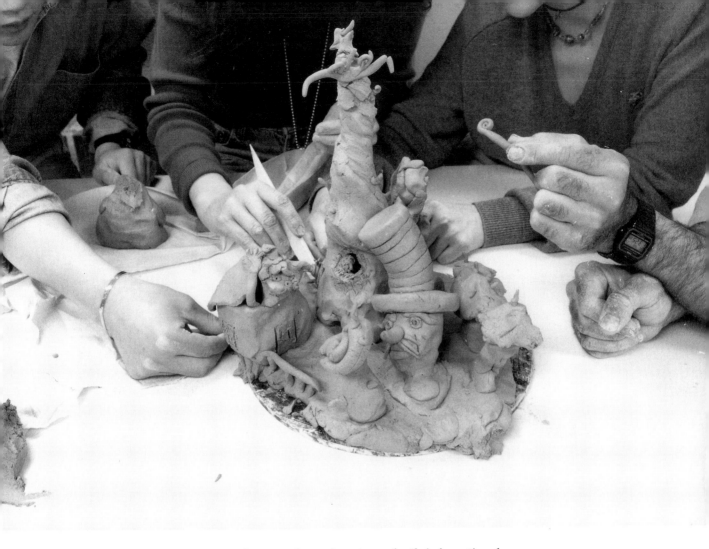

A group of students using Dr. Seuss stories as the gateway for their formative play activities with clay. While serious learning is seldom associated with pleasure, our play develops our creativity, and our enjoyment of it works to mold us artistically.

Playing, like technique, is something we use when creating but it is not what we create with: it is not our creative force. If we were to let either play or technique direct our work we would be surrendering our personal vision and any hope for self-realization along with it. What your future clay work can be already exists within you. It will be an extension of who you are. You may not yet know that part of you or may not exactly know just which part will give birth to your clay next, but in one shape or another it is you who will be its living source and it will be you who will body forth its form. Likewise, you may not know today what you will be choosing for dinner on your upcoming birthday but you will choose something. What playing and technical training have in common is that each help to materialize the clay object by dismantling the obstacles of psychic obstruction. When it comes to freeing up the creative spirit, play provides some of the therapeutic tools, the screw divers, the pliers and the wrenches, for loosening the fasteners of repressedness. Once some of these personal blocks are removed the creative process becomes a powerful resource for experiencing personal wholeness.

CREATIVE CLAY ACTIVITIES

Collaborative Playing

When two or more people come together in play they are united. By sharing the fellowship of the experience information is revealed and exchanged. When the activity ends everyone has gained from the relationship.

If the verb for the noun "play" is playing, the verb for the noun "clay" should be claying. When we play we make new discoveries and often find ourselves in places where we are given new views to our true identity. Out of the surprises and excitement of play travel we re-create new ways in which to structure our lives and artistic processes. Creative doing requires creative thinking. To aid you in imaginative structuring and to add fresh inspirational substance to your efforts the following exercises and guidelines are presented for use as a springboard:

Seeing Through the Nose

Select a classmate, a family member or a close friend and, each with a small amount of clay, assume a relaxed sitting position facing one another. Keep as close together as is comfortably possible and, along with your partner, quietly begin to model each others noses. Using only your fingers and the clay held in your hand, sculpt it to a scale that is life-size or slightly larger. Make a conscious effort to continually look at one another and to carefully transfer the information gained to the clay. Work in silence so that the personal rhythms of shared energy and the intimate dimensions of the experience can more easily be felt and better understood. When it is clear that each of you has finished, set the pieces down and take a few moments to share the feelings the two of you experienced while working together.

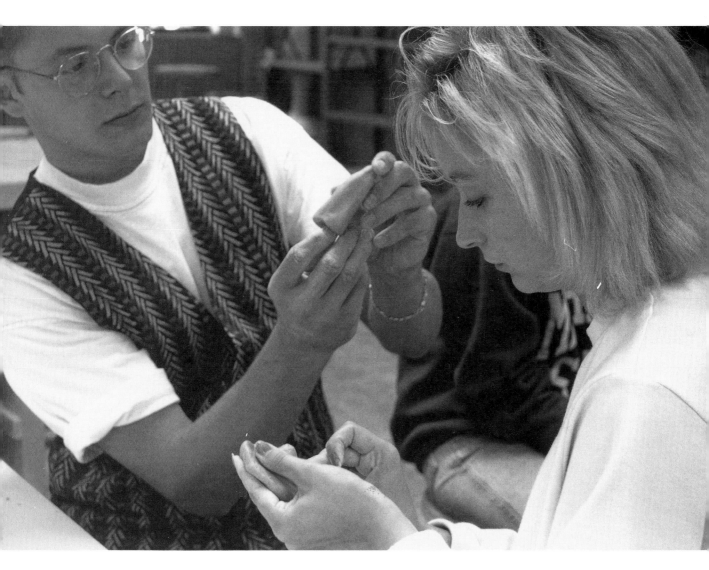

Louis Aiello and Jennifer Merritt sculpting each other's nose in clay.

An exciting aspect of playing in this manner is that no initial expectations concerning a grandiose artistic end product exist. The inhibiting pressures of common adult psychological forces, such as preconceptions, critical judgments and ego controls, don't have the time to surface when the activity is seemingly informal or playfully structured. Extremely valuable things develop that can sweep across whole new horizons when clay is playfully engaged. The resulting nose, for example, could end up possessing great artistic merit: looking quite handsome glaze fired and hanging on the wall as a facial feature fragment loaded with aesthetic and human symbolism. Even if this were not to be the case the experience of the doing itself can be rich with artistic feelings and creative pleasures. In addition to these developments, you are involved, comprehensively, in the dynamics of seeing and in letting your touching parallel your seeing. This exercise could even be one's introductory clay experience. One's first clay piece. If the exercise succeeds in mediating your creative identity with the clay it will also add faith to the process of working with clay.

As a follow up to the nose making exercise, take a ball of clay, big enough to fill your hand, and slowly work it into a flat (1/2" thick) slab. Form your slab by gently pushing the clay onto a table top with short repeated movements of the fingers, knuckles, palm, or any other part of the hand. Stay relaxed as you work. Do not hurry, but take the time to feel the clay, to know your own body rhythm with it, to see the emergence of a textural pattern. If you have not worked with clay before this is good way to become acquainted. In this case you might want to proceed with the eyes closed, thereby allowing your sense of touch to take over and become your guide.

Transforming the physical texture of a clay slab with the intuitive elements of play.

Working a sculpted nose into a textured surface. Transformations made within a context of play perception rather than physical memory arise as creative leaps.

Be aware of your breathing. Remember this is a play experience, so breath from your abdomen and release any tensions. Remain focused on the unfolding surface texture. If you're not happy with what's evolving, experiment with a different textural hand imprint. Continue to work until it feels finished. After some personal reflection, take the nose you've just made and place it on your slab. Repeating the same hand motions and texture marks, work it onto the slab so that the two pieces are visually integrated. Use a clay cut-off wire to separate the slab from the table. If you think it might look good as a wall piece take your fettling knife and bore a hole, from the back side, part way into the nose so that it can eventually hang from a nail placed into the wall.

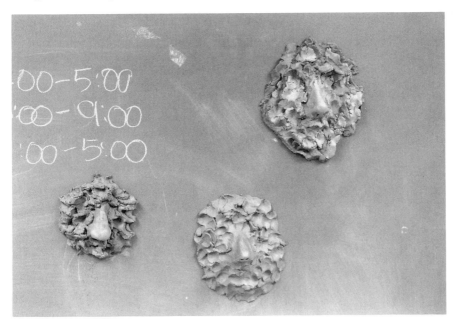

Nose/texture slabs temporarily pressed onto a chalk board for viewing.

As an alternative experience to this exercise hold a ball of clay the size of an orange in your palm and, with the thumb from your other hand, quickly press it into a crude bowl shape. Keep the walls thick so that enough clay is left to form a nose on one side of the rim. Do not hesitate to extend the nose beyond the height of the rim. When the nose is completed, thin out the remaining wall thickness by pressing the clay between your finger tips. Tilt the form slightly so that a new bottom is made from a portion of the wall directly opposite the nose. This will expose the original bottom which can now be pressed, from the inside, out into the shape of a chin. Just above this extended chin use your finger nail, or any straight edge tool, to mark in a mouth.

Nose pots pinched by students from small balls of clay. The trust and excitement one develops in their own process, their own knowingness, through play is immediate and real. At times play may be abstract but it is not passive. At its best, play is learning — a direct means for experiencing and knowing ourselves.

Nose pot that was pinched and smoke fired with sawdust.

After you have completed your nose pot (or chin pot, if that's what it looks like) put it in a place where it can easily be seen as it dries. For the next couple of days, look at it and take time to reflect on what you learned from the exercise. Did you discover anything new about yourself? Did you, if only briefly, make contact with your own creative process? Were there any surprises that popped up? Were you inspired? Did you gain new ideas for future clay projects? What was your response to the clay and how did the clay respond to your handling? Did you enjoy the experience?

With regards to personal growth you may want to consider asking such questions, not only about each new clay piece you make but of each significant event in your life. Life's integrated joys and deeper meanings aren't always obvious. In our quest, often the right questions become more important than the answers and every creative encounter generates new questions.

Nose pot that was glazed and fired to cone 10.

Improvisational Development:
A Communal Play Experience

Together, with a group of 3 to 6 people and 25 pounds of clay, find a relatively quiet, out-of-the-way, area. Sitting in a small circle and without talking, take part in building a single clay piece for the next 15 minutes. The shape of the clay piece will be spontaneous; a mystery evolving out of the freedom of the moment. It will represent play in its purest form, improvisation. Improvisation, as a form of continuos creation in motion, is living wholly in the moment and being in the present, "in the here and the now."

If being an improviser feels a little scary, the event can be structured around a theme for useful direction. Possible theme titles might include: "A Treasure Island", "Under the Sea", "City of the Future", "Living in a Treehouse", "Fantasy Landscape" or "Dreamscape".

When a small group of people cooperatively work together in this manner, the work takes on a social dimension that can introduce, among other things, patience, humor, changes of heart and new friendships. When it is playful, creative and spontaneous it also embodies personal elements of risk, surrender, courage and trust. The overall self-emerging dynamics of such shared activity is consummate in that it encapsulates the personal substance of the creative process while integrating it with the social fabric of human interaction.

Bridges

Working with a companion create a clay bridge . . . create two clay bridges. Create something that might want to use the bridge. In living, we build many kinds of bridges: this page you're reading is one of mine.

Chairs

Working independently, yet among other people doing the same work, create 3 small chairs from clay that are no taller than 3 inches. After fifteen minutes, bring all of the chairs together for a group exhibition, discussion and critique. The results can be unpredictably simple, very amazing and very, very reflective.

Students wholly engaged in the dynamics of working together amidst the social rhythms and elements of play activity as they create a tree-house. In the same way that special qualities of childhood shape the adult, the interchanges that form the tree-house also form the self.

Narrative Shape Shifting

Using your fingers, the top surface of a table and a knife, make 8 clay shapes that are fairly identical. Their longest dimension need not exceed 3 inches. Repeatedly use these clay pieces, in combination, to give physical form to the meaning of the following words: "Support", "Enclose", "Union", "Order". Limit yourself to 3 minutes per concept and compare your end results with the results of those working along with you prior to going on to the next word.

Family

On separate occasions, get together with the youngest and oldest members of your family to playfully share in the making of a clay object of their choosing. Save it, glaze-fire it, and return it to them in the form of a wrapped present.

Dwelling Place

Using your imagination (in a manner that might even cause Freud to raise an eyebrow) work solo or with partner and freely create a scaled-down residence that a specific type of person, spirit or animal might find suitable to live in. If you were a native of a subtropical savannah or, better yet, a wind spirit . . . what kind of habitat would you design? Would it be a summer house and have many openings? Would it have charm? Would it be the world class home quarters of clay play? Imagine being a mollusk (snail), an insect (wasp), a reptile (turtle), a bird (cliff swallow) or a mammal (beaver) . . . what kind of abode might you want to settle in for a long stay or just hang-out in for the day?

Garden Plot

At the very beginning of each new semester I often ask students to spend a few moments with a classmate interviewing one another so they can formally introduce the other person to the entire class along with some personal background. During the introductions it was revealed that one of the class members had just published a book of poetry. When I asked him for the title of his favorite poem, hoping to get a natural, in-born lead for an improvised group exercise, he said it was "Tears of Joy and Pain". I started to ask students what their most joyful or joy-filled memory of childhood was. The very first answer given was "working in my grandmother's garden". The garden theme immediately shimmered with promise. Still, I continued to seek everyone's reply. Two people talked of time spent at cottages, two of hiking in the mountains and another two of swimming. Of them, I calmly asked that they pair-up and, non-verbally, do a 15 minute clay piece of their, commonly shared, childhood memory. The remaining students were asked to work, also in pairs, on garden plots.

Playing in clay, through the memories of those joyful times that energized us as children, enriches our lives in the present. The garden plots al-

A garden plot, with dog, evolves as two students work/play together. Like gardens, the creative spirit grows and thrives when properly cared for.

lowed the students a chance to make discoveries as adults through their personality as a child. Childhood, as an evolutionary time of life when identities are realized, is an inspiring time of playful possibilities and intuitive outpourings. Memories, by provoking the release of these past realities, are a reunion with our former selves. They gather together a lifetime of separate experiences and rearrange them into a single, simultaneous flash of consciousness. The memories from our childhood cultivate today's private gardens of self: giving that self a richer soil to grow in. If you were involved in this epoch project would you include a scarecrow in your garden plot?

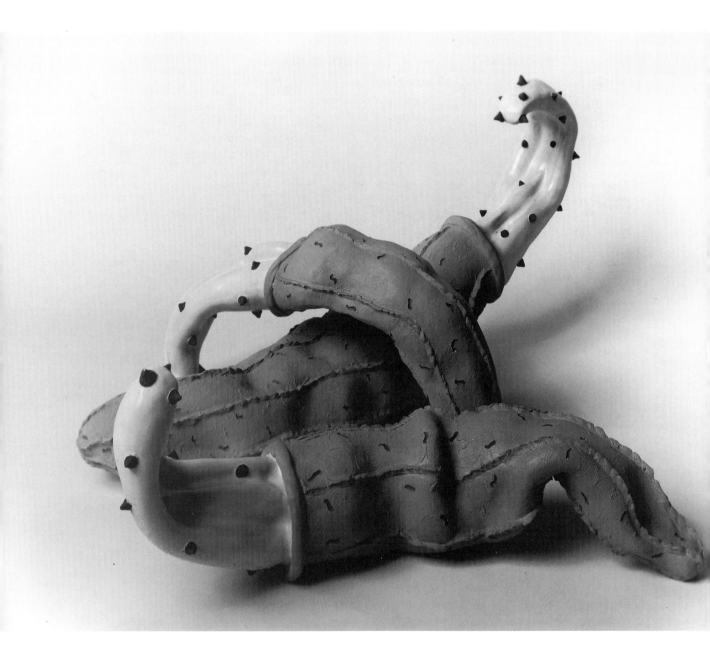

Kim Kirchman, Memories of Bill's Garden, handbuilt and finished with a commercial low-fire glaze and underglazes, 18" × 24" × 24". Kim once explained that: "My friend Bill was on of the worst gardeners I ever knew!"

Metropolitan Musings: A Wall Tableau

With 2 or 3 other individuals, stake-out a small area of wall space and with clay create a bas-relief (low relief sculpture), at eye level, of a real or imagined urban setting. Store fronts, alley entrances, street scenes, the interior of a bookstore or coffee shop, anything that your mind, emotions, senses and imagination might want to play on and graphically depict for twenty minutes would work.

Do the works by the American painter Edward Hopper come to mind? How does the art work of Charles Simonds relate to this exercise? This same theme could also be used to create a diorama: a miniature three dimensional scene. It could be done inside a cardboard box, on a scrap of plywood, on the top of a table or in another environment.

Sharon Hubbard, Window Steps, the slips, underglazes and glazes are sprayed and painted on a cone 5 porcelain clay body, 4" × 16" × 19".

Mark Chatterley, Diving, 6 feet high.

Play, like love, requires intimate trust. Through trust we can venture into unknown areas, we can experience what initially was unknowable, and we can emerge with an expanded understanding of self.

Through play we also develop our capacity to know freedom. Through freedom creative initiative flows. As you may now have come to realize, play releases our expressive self, takes it outside of us, and brings us into the world as a more creative persons. Truly creative people, especially those we call the visionaries: the artists, are able to pass beyond their inhibitions and, playfully merging with the energies of their unique spirit, move to the frontier of the senses. Isn't this what art is, an expression of union between free initiative and the human spirit?

Play—clay (playing—claying), where one ends and the other begins is now up to you. Can you transfer your sense of play to clay . . . to living?

Jeff Shapiro, unrefined & unglazed clay, playfully formed and wood fired, 24" tall.

David G. Wright, pitcher creatively made from more than one thrown form, 8" tall.

3

Handbuilding

There are many ways to give shape to clay. Yet there is no one absolute, best way. Just as each of us are unique there will be creative differences in how we choose to work with and fashion clay forms.

As your participation will eventually reveal, much of what ceramics is about is set in motion by simple human nature. A lot of what anyone knows about working clay comes from a personal, often private, hands-on encounter with the medium itself. Still, especially in the beginning, there is no substitute for a good teacher and inspiring classmates in a positive studio-classroom setting.

To help you feel your way into the remarkable process of creating with clay, this chapter presents the basic handbuilding methods as possible starting points. Each method is explained in basic terms and presented as an area ripe for a lifetimes worth of pleasure and exploration. However, the redirecting of a traditional technique into a new form is sometimes more self-expanding and ultimately a more personally meaningful transcendence of expressive limits than mastering its disciplines. Such a simple twist of the imagination, on your part, could result in the acquisition of a whole new set of personal techniques that the clay community has not seen before.

A personal involvement through touch is a profound and powerful experience in understanding.

Nancy Selvin, Still Life with Three Bottles, raku fired clay, copper and slate. Her work is often composed of a grouping of clay objects minimally framed or pedestaled by non-clay materials. 9" × 9" × 16".

As ceramists we cannot survive without certain fabrication techniques. We employ them and can enjoy them, but we should not seek to cultivate technique without also tending to the imagination. Creativity, like technique, is an equal part of the building process. It's what provides the work with emotional truth; the grandeur of what makes us feel deeply.

Successful involvement with handbuilding is connected to a relationship between the acquisition of and the application of technical skills. Technique and method are not enough. They are the tools, not the content. They are only the servants of art, not its master. Because in the end, as in the beginning, our clay works are affirmations of personal thoughts, feelings and perceptions. They (we) portray the inner workings of the heart and mind that circle the lives we live and as such should not be overcome or seduced by any one technique. Although this text inevitably has to teach the technical, always aspire to follow your creative instincts. Creativity for many becomes a life-time quest. It involves the use of known skills and techniques in uniquely personal ways to make forms that are, for the sake of categorical clarity, sculptural or functional, contemporary or traditional, cerebral or visceral, art or craft and so on until, for better or worse, the need for object distinctions is behind them and they come face to face with the living connections given to their own distinguished path with clay.

As a kind of personal gymnastics the creative process leaps and tumbles between different modes of awareness: intuition and logic, knowledge and feelings, imagination and perception; confusion and certainty. It stops us from thinking and living on automatic pilot and allows us to see new ways and to fuel new beginnings. Ultimately each of us has to live through its mysteries, play in its truths and bring resolution to our clay work through the uniqueness of our own being.

Marilyn Levine, CMN, stoneware and mixed media, 9 1/2" × 20" × 10 1/2". The soft leather-like surface of this slab constructed bag is embellished with oil paint.

Eva Monson's pots bear the textural imprints of her disciplined caring and the joy of her spirited touch. It should be noted that three weeks prior to the weekend Eva pinched these forms she had never before worked with clay.

PINCHING

Pinching is the technique of shaping clay by pressing it between the thumb and fingers. The resulting forms can be sculptural but more often than not take the traditional clay shape of the hollow vessel. For me, the Japanese tea bowls most symbolize the fundamental spirit of pinching. At their highest level of evolvement they reflect an unprecedented balance between artistic and human consciousness.

Pinch pots, on the average, do not receive much attention in the world of ceramics. They are often looked at as training exercises for beginning students, when in fact such initial thinking could not be farther from the truth. While it is true that pinching is often the first contact many people have with clay formation and that many of these early efforts can look crude and out of control, pinching is, none the less, where clay and person find their most intimate state of coexistence. Nowhere is the contact with the clay more direct and qualitative, and nowhere are forms more organic and convincingly beautiful. Not only is this process symbolic of elemental connectedness it is physically capable of gifting both pot and potter in its unfolding.

In many ways the potter who chooses to create forms by pinching is one who understands how to be patient, aware and to perceive what is needed. Because the pinching experience is slow and deeply meditative by nature, it is a fertile ground for maintaining a moment-to-moment awareness of our ever evolving capacities as creative human beings.

This students sits with the first 3 pots she has made in her young life. I wonder how much awareness she has of the spiritual journey that has just begun?

Making A Pinch Pot

With a small ball of soft, well aged clay held in the palm of your hand, slowly press the thumb from the opposite hand into its center. Rotate the ball as you work, firmly pushing the thumb deeper into the clay until a one-half inch thick bottom is created. Do not attempt to widen the opening at this time. To keep from losing control, the hole should be no wider than needed for the thumb to do its work. This is called *opening*.

Making the opening in a ball of clay with the thumb.

The Walls

To shape the walls and to hollow out the interior, gently squeeze the clay between the thumb and middle fingers of the same hand. Start your pressing at the base of the pot with the thumb on the inside and the fingers on the outside. After each pinch, or press of the clay between the thumb and fingers, and while it is still being supported in the palm of the other hand, rotate the clay slightly and pinch again using the same pressure. Slowly and consistently pinch your way all around the base and eventually move upwards, rhythmically pinching and thinning the clay through the course of several revolutions. As you advance, also try to keep the opening at the top narrow and the clay along the rim extra thick for later shaping. If you don't limit the size of this opening the rim may want to flare out and crack.

Shaping the wall by pinching the clay between the thumb and fingers.

Sometimes it is helpful at this stage to further thin and shape the walls by applying a stroking motion to the inside surface of the pot. To do this, place the pot on its side in the open palm; using the fingers of the other hand, reach all the way down inside and firmly press the clay at the floor into the palm with the tips of the fingers and move upwards; rotating the vessel. The repeated movement of the fingers toward the rim stretches the clay into a new shape while beautifully smoothing out the interior surface. Again, rotate the pot after each stroke and keep the opening at the top small. If you are unable to continue the stroking motion from the center of the floor all the way up to the rim, come only half way up on your first rotation and follow up where you left off with a second round of stroking.

By now the shape of your pot is fairly well roughed-out and in need of some fine tuning. If it is still too thick, repeat any of the pinching or stroking maneuvers to make the walls thinner. To maintain symmetry and a uniformity of thickness, remember to repeat the thinning movement all of the way around the form. At this stage the pot could be placed upon a piece of paper and set on a table. The paper prevents it from sticking to the table top and is used as a turntable, allowing the pot to be easily rotated as it is worked. Any surface cracks that might occur as the clay is being stretched can easily be burnished closed by rubbing them with the back of the finger nail or, if they are small, removed by sanding or scraping later.

The Rim

To finish the rim, pinch, rotate and shape the extra clay left around it until it too is of an even thickness and in harmony with the body contour of the pot. Thin clay parts dry first, and pots dry from top to bottom, so the rim may be slightly dry and stiff. If so, place the pot, rim side down, upon damp crumpled paper towels for several minutes to soften it. If the pot was uniformly pinched and is fairly symmetrical the rim should have a natural, undulating flow to it in which case nothing more need be done to it. If, on the other hand, one side is decidedly higher and a perfectly level rim is desired it will have to be trimmed with a knife and the cut edge rubbed smooth. As a final statement rims are extremely important to the overall presence and integrity of a pot and require a heightened sense of consciousness on the part of their maker.

The Bottom

It is often said that a pot should weigh as much as it looks like it should weigh. If, after thinning the walls and the rim, the pot is still heavier than its appearance suggests, you may want to make the bottom area thinner. Prior to doing this it is helpful to wrap damp, wadded-up paper toweling around the lower wall surface of the pot and to place another piece inside the pot to cover the base. The damp paper keeps the bottom third of the pot soft while the upper walls and rim are allowed to dry and stiffen.

With the bottom half wrapped in wet paper towels the top half of the pot can dry.

Before the rim is allowed to dry it should be thoughtfully adjusted to its final form.

Students speed-drying the top half of their recently pinched pots in the sun.

Thinning the bottom without first letting the rim become leather hard can cause distortion. However, once the upper half is firm and capable of holding its shape, the unwrapped base of the pot can be held and supported in the palm of one hand and thinned out by the pressing fingers of the other hand. Once the bottom is thinned out, and given its final shape, place the pot on its rim to dry.

The floor of the pot is thinned by extending it down; into the palm of the hand.

The Outside

The inside walls of the finished pot will be relatively smooth and even. The outside surface of the pot, however, will be somewhat rough and uneven. More likely than not there will be surface cracks. This organic irregularity is the result of pressing and stretching the clay from the center outward and resembles the texture of tree bark, which also originates from an expanding movement of growth from the center.

If the natural quality of the pinched exterior appeals to you the pot is finished. If more refinement is sought, the surface can be cleaned-up while still in the leather-hard state. For this the flexible metal rib is the ideal tool.

It easily conforms to the contour of the pot and its super sharp edge quickly removes surface irregularities. Still, even with this tool, it can take from ten to twenty minutes to bring refinement to the contour. As a bonus, if the clay is heavily groged, a scratchy yet often pleasing surface texture will also occur. If not, a similar texture can be created by sanding the walls with coarse sandpaper when in the bone dry stage.

Using a flexible metal rib to even out and refine the outside contour of the pot.

The finger marks have been removed from the outer walls of the pot and the surface scraped clean with a metal rib. A rasp or file could also be used.

For a smooth surface with a sheen the wall is burnished with the back of a spoon. If the clay gets too dry to burnish try applying a thin application of cooking oil.

For a smoother appearance, the scraping with the metal rib can be followed-up by burnishing with a stiff, yet somewhat flexible, smaller rubber rib. The rubber rib, sometimes called a finishing rubber, is a useful tool for smoothing out and erasing minor surface scratches. After ribbing with a rubber rib, surfaces often develop a reflective sheen. For a more highly polished look, the burnishing can be done using the back side of a silver spoon, a smooth pebble, or the blade of your fettling knife. Originally, burnishing wasn't done as much for surface enhancement as it was to compact the clay surface and make it waterproof. By forcing the larger clay particles into the surface and smoothing over their impressions with the finer particles, a surface is tightened and made to shine. To maintain a shiny surface pots should not be fired much beyond 1800° F: as firing temperatures increase, surface gloss decreases.

There are any number of exciting ways to further treat or decorate surface and to approach the finger pinched form. If you find this way of working pleasurable and enjoy your time spent pinching, I most warmheartedly suggest that you seek out a book by Paulus Berensohn titled *Finding One's Way With Clay*. It is refreshingly human in its self-shaping virtues and is all about making pinch pots. It will awaken you, and thus your clay.

Barbara Walch, Three Bowls, the largest bowl, in this stacking set of three, is 2 1/2" × 7". Using sand colored clay and autumn colored glazes, Barbara pinches clay works that visually alert our senses to the organic forms of the natural world and that deeply echo her spiritual connections to clay and living creatively.

COILING

Coiling is the universal technique of building form with clay coils stacked one on top of another. As an additive process each new coil is aggressively joined to the supporting one beneath it to strengthen the joint. The exact placement of the coils is what eventually determines the shape of the work and whether or not the final form will be symmetrical or asymmetrical.

Jim Kraft, Niche Baskets, coil and slab constructed, 12" × 17" × 7", 17" × 13" × 7". The coils were rolled in mason stains and oxides for color. The pieces are fired with a clear glaze, although most of the glaze was wiped off the outside surface.

As a way of making hollow clay forms, no one technique has prospered and etched itself into the world wide history of ceramics more than that of coiling. Although clay was first used prehistorically for the making of small sculptural figures vested with cultic, mythical or superstitious symbolism, the earliest coil-built pots date back to 7000 B.C. As one of the most ancient yet versatile methods of shaping clay, coiling is intimately tied to many cultures and to clay history. Museums are preoccupied with its examples. Major collections present a full range of works from China, Africa, Greece, Mexico and, most recently, from Peru, when in 1987 the astonishing pottery from the pre-Inca Moche tombs was excavated in Sipan. Presently, the dynamics of America's southwest Indian pottery is a popular example of the contemporary identity of coiled pottery.

Jim Kraft working in his studio on one of several coiled forms simultaneously.

In the histories of our own lives most of us as small children, either in or outside of a school environment, have innocently attempted to join some crudely rolled clay coils together that may or may not have resulted in objects of virtue. Such moments may have had their emotional rewards, leaving many of us comfortable with the activity but ambivalent of the results. What may have been lacking in the crucible of such an experience could have been our ability to envision the wide range of potential this initially simplistic technique possessed. Like many instances in life, there are times when we fail to grasp the mystery of an occurrence or relationship only to come across it again later and see it in a way that allows the experience to become central to our existence. On a similar level, coil building with clay is often neglected and overlooked as a viable or fashionable technique. Encountered later on from a more evolved perspective or with a stronger creative identity, such distancing is often redeemable and the oldest of clay building techniques suddenly has new meaning.

A shift away from simply thinking of coiling in terms of historical significance to an appreciation of the vast influences it can have on contemporary form, allows ceramists greater freedoms of expression. For example, coiled forms need not be symmetrical. As a practical consideration, this single option is ecstasy to someone with an organic sensitivity towards form. Others value the technique for its scale recognizing that, by coiling, any size of pot, large or small, can be built. Still others love to coil for the delicately thin walled forms they are able to obtain. As a relatively slow process, coiling offers a great amount of control and allows for thoughtful development of a form's image as work progresses.

The coiled walls of Montie Mayrend's robust yet elegant pieces are extremly thin.

Ruth Duckworth using dry wall screen to smoothly sand the coiled surface of her visually flowing form.

Mary Barringer, coiled stoneware with multiple layers of slip, fired to cone 6 in an electric kiln, 9″ × 11″ × 8″. The textured surface is visually rich and primitive.

Making Coils

The secret to making evenly rounded coils is to work with soft clay that has been aged and well wedged. For each coil, take a handful of clay and roughly squeeze it into a long sausage-like shape. Place it on top of a wooden table top or a large canvas covered piece of plywood. With the fingers of both hands spread wide, place them both on the center of the coil, side by side, and, using an even pressure, quickly roll the clay back and forth under the outstretched fingers as the hands move apart. Some potters like to roll with the palms only, while others, like myself, prefer to roll from the tips of the fingers to the center of the palms. Repeat this rolling and sideways stretching process in quick, short movements until the coil becomes as thick as the base slab. Several coils may be pre-rolled at this time and covered with plastic for uninterrupted use later.

There are also potters who roll out suspended coils of clay between the palms of their bare hands. As the coil lengthens it hangs down vertically. When the desired thickness is achieved it is immediately attached to the pot. Afterwards another coil is hand formed in the same fashion. Others use coils extruded through metal or plywood dies. Many forming dies are available commercially in different diameters for such a purpose or custom dies can be made for the smaller wall-mounted hand extruders from quarter inch Plexiglas with the aid of a jewelers saw. Some coilers, especially those with professional slab rollers, make large thick slabs from which they cut long strips of clay to roll into coils. The strips need not be rolled prior to use: they can be applied directly as slabs or "flattened" coils.

John Glick using soft aged clay and one of his extruders to make coils.

The Base

Coiled pots need a base or a bottom. Coiled sculptures do not. Since clay seems to possess a physical memory, bases made from spiraled coils have a tendency to unwind during the heat of firing. To avoid these kinds of separations, bases are often made from rolled slabs. The thickness of the slab and the thickness of the coils should be equal. Otherwise, cracking may occur where the wall and the base meet as a result of unequal shrinkage during drying or uneven temperature loss during cooling.

Bases can be flat or rounded. Once the shape for a flat base is determined, it should be coiled or cut out from a rolled slab of clay and placed on a flat surface for support (a small section of stiff plywood, drywall or a throwing bat) and then a turntable in preparation for the coiling of the walls. Paper or a generous sprinkling of grog between the clay and the supporting base will prevent sticking. It is surprising how useful turntables or banding wheels can be. It is inspiring to be able to rotate a work in progress and view it from all sides; somehow knowing that each turn is embedded with the potential to give life to a new idea or a new form. With this same sense of inspiration, the shapes for flat clay bases can be made to vary dramatically. They can reflect and honor the austerity of the classical circular and elliptical form or they can depict an expanded image bank of free form.

Convex bases, however, are generally formed with the support of plaster molds and remain routinely marked by them. Here too, opportunities for image expansion exist through alteration by paddling when the form becomes leather hard. Until the clay inhabits its own strength, support molds are helpful stabilizers of form and give the bottom contour of the work its inauguration, safeguarding the integrity of its contour from the dangers of stress and sagging during the early stages of construction.

The Walls

With a needle tool or an old fork quickly score or roughen the top surface of the base along its edge. This will improve adhesion and make for a stronger joint. If the base is dryer than the coils, dampen the scored surface with water and cover with rolled layers of wet paper towels beforehand. Slip, a mixture of clay and water, can also be applied to the area.

Patricia Gardner joining coils with a wood modeling tool.

The first coil will follow the contour of the base and should be squeezed firmly into place. Although not a necessity, a level working edge can easily be maintained along the top of the pot by completing one row at a time, as opposed to spiraling on up to the next level and stopping wherever the coil ends. After the first coil is in place the following rows of coils can quickly deviate from the shape of the base and dramatically change the overall contour of the pot. Coils placed directly on top of one another will create a straight wall, those placed closer to the outside edge will direct the wall outwards. Placing them on the inside edge will have the exact opposite effect and bring the walls inward.

Scoring between each successive layer of coils is not necessary, but for structural strength each row of coils should be completely attached to the row below as you work. For maximum strength coils should be joined both on the inside and the outside of the walls. The joining is done by dragging clay from the new coil down into an adjacent coil with either the tip of the finger or a wooden modeling tool. The resulting marks can be left, especially on the outside wall, as a unique decorative texture, but the walls are better sealed and made stronger by scraping them smooth with a flexible metal rib. If the distinct identity of the coils is to be retained, however, it's necessary to score and slip the coil joint, but even then the inside walls should be scraped. If the walls become floppy and begin to sag before the pot is completed you will have to temporarily stop and put it aside until it stiffens. The weight of the upper coils can, at times, become too much for the soft bottom coils to support. Be patient and begin coiling another pot while you wait.

The climate of your work environment can have an impact on coiling. If it is warm and dry there may be no need for stopping or waiting for a section of wall coils to firm-up before finishing pots with even large dimensions. Then again, I've watched Dave Roberts, perhaps the finest coiler and rakuist in England, work on eight pots at the same time due to dampness in his studio. If, however, the walls of a pot you are working on show signs of collapsing or you feel as if you're losing the controlling edge, simply give it some drying time. Before you do, wrap the last rows of coils with wet crumpled paper towels to keep them from becoming too dry to receive the next coil when work is resumed.

David Roberts resolving the rim of a leather-hard coiled bowl in his studio.

David Roberts, coil built and raku fired vessels. After being bisque fired, the 17″ diameter top vessel was sprayed with clay slip through which line designs were scratched. After the firing and subsequent reduction, the resulting smoked pattern was revealed by removing the resist slip with a stiff wire brush. The outer surface of the 12 1/2″ high bottom vessel was burnished and textured by carving.

The Rim

Every coil becomes a rim if it is the last coil applied to a vessel. Each forming process generates its own natural style of culmination and embraces its own balance between beginnings and endings, between base and rim. Coil pots often reach their conclusions gently: favoring small organic endings contrasted by full, tumescent bellies. The mouth-like opening may assume many forms, all humbly different but each representing a human act of creativity that attempts to mediate the coming together of an inner and an outer surface. As you the potter perform such a marriage it is important that you respond to all of the related details and demands with attentiveness and care. At times the rhythms of the coiling process and the proportions of the form will carry you playfully along and suddenly, or not so suddenly, gift you with the perfect ending. At other times it won't seem so inevitable and you will be frustrated at having struggled so long in this realm. For each pot made the rim will be different, and yet some characteristics will always be similar. As you will forever be on a rim odyssey for as long as you make pots, a part of your creative conditioning will involve extracting the final statement that the rim will make from the details of the rest of the form and the energy it owns.

Stan Welsh in his studio with large coiled works in progress. Notice how the surface of the terra cotta clay is heavily textured by carving and scraping.

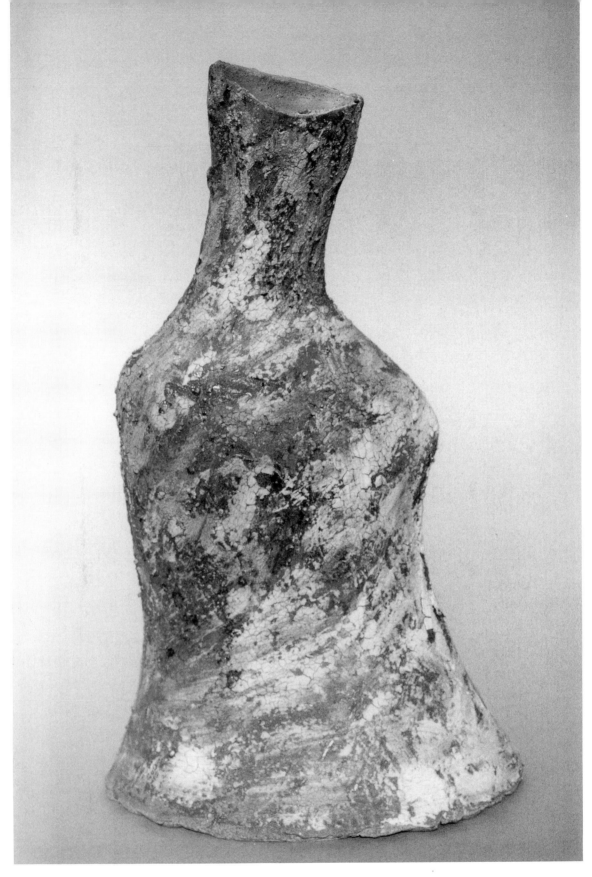

Rafael Duran, coiled terra-cotta form with thick colored engobes brushed over a glazed surface, multi-fired to cone 04, 17 1/4″ × 10 1/4″ × 7 3/4″.

Deborah Masuoka's seven foot tall rabbit heads are constructed from clay coils. The coils range in thickness from 1 1/2 inches at the base to 3/4 inches at the top. These monumental clay pieces took six weeks to complete and, amazingly, were built without interior support walls. Following weeks of controlled drying they were painted with a copper oxide slip, sanded with steel wool to remove the colorant from the high-relief textures, and covered with colored terra sigillatas. For several days afterwards they were slowly fired to cone 04. These single-fired sculptures are very inspiring, yet the power of their presence owes more to the visionary spirit of the artist than to the fabrication technique of coiling.

DRAPE-MOLDING

Drape-molding is a frequently used support technique for giving shape to soft slabs of clay. In this process a rolled-out slab of clay is carefully draped inside a shallow, concave mold and left to dry. If further alterations are planned, such as the addition of feet to the under-side of the form, the clay can be removed after it has become leather-hard, yet still in workable condition.

As a mold-forming process, drape molding is unique and enjoys a special place of respect in the hearts of many handbuilders. Besides being an immense source of relief from the problematic issues surrounding structural support, drape molding is a rich playing field for the imagination. Slabs of clay can be artfully resolved in the most expressive of ways while still flat and unarticulated by the contours of a mold. They can be cut into different shapes and reassembled to form countless design motifs, or decorated in the richest of textures and impressions and given an heroic birth before they are given a final form. Of course, the imagination we bring to the surface treatment of a slab need not be overly ambitious. Our response and our approach can be less imposing. The simplest of forms can find profound strength in the relationship that exists between the rim and the shape of the walls.

Joan Rosenberg-Dent, Hocus Pocus, porcelain form with removable parts, 18" in diameter. Joan uses the bowl's interior as a space and surface to juxtapose multiple sculptural elements of a linear nature with bold design patterns of vibrant color.

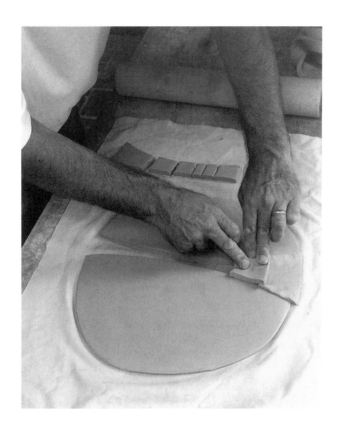

Working out a design by cutting into the clay slab and reassembling cut sections from the back side.

Using a metal rib to clean-up the seams and smooth out the the back side of the slab.

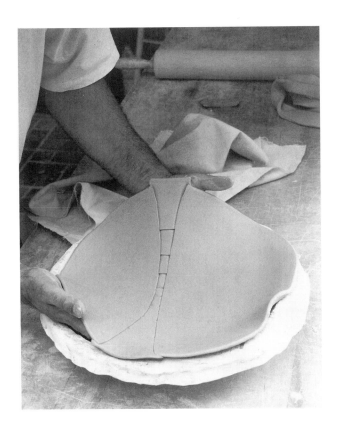

The inverted slab being carefully draped inside the plaster mold.

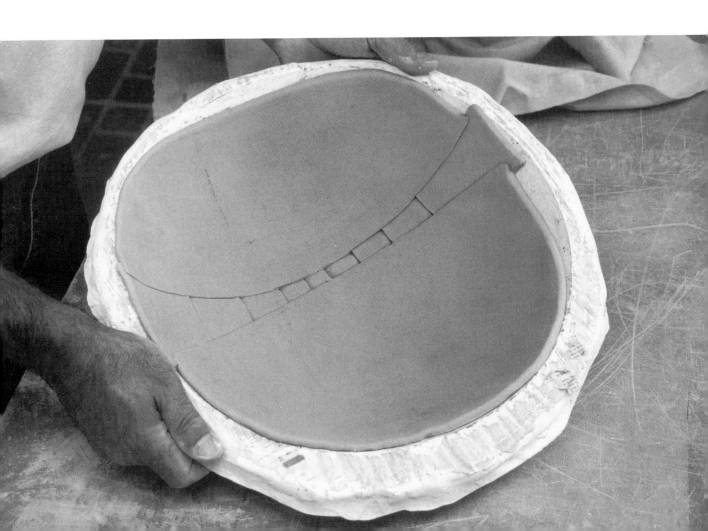

Making A Plaster Drape-mold

Molds for forming clay are generally made from a gypsum plaster. Sometimes called pottery plaster, casting plaster or plaster of Paris, this material is favored for its remarkable ability to absorb moisture: a physical phenomenon that effectively allows the clay to separate from the mold as it shrinks during drying.

The mold itself is made by casting a pre-existing shape in plaster. Bowl shapes work exceptionally well and since molds are used repeatedly, you might consider choosing those that reflect the clean lines of classical shapes and disqualifying those with exaggerated foot rings or texture patterns. The important thing to realize when selecting a form for a drape mold is that it be shallow and slope gently. Otherwise it will not receive the clay sheet without causing wrinkles or other unwanted deformities. To allow for easy removal, forms for casting should be free of undercuts to eliminate any need for two-piece or multipiece molds. A mold I frequently work with, and am personally fond of, was cast from an inverted Chinese cooking wok after the handles were removed. Remember, it's always the outside contour that is cast. A shape similar to the cooking wok could have also been thrown on the potters wheel out of solid clay. For nonsymmetrical molds, clay shapes can be modeled or built-up by hand and covered with plaster.

To cast a bowl, place it upside-down on newspaper and brush-coat it with commercial mold soap. A release agent such as Vaseline, deluded Murphy's oil soap or a spray-on product such as furniture polish or *Pam* could also be used.

In a flexible rubber bowl, made specifically for mixing plaster, add the molding plaster to room temperature water in a ratio of approximately 1 1/3 pounds plaster to 1 pound of water. U.S. Gypsum, a major American supplier of plaster, recommends using slightly less water when mixing their No. 1 Casting Plaster which is 65 parts of water to 100 parts of plaster by weight. Sprinkle the plaster onto the water until a substantial island forms above the surface. At this point the water is becoming saturated and the mixture should be left to slake a few moments prior to mixing. During this soaking phase sprinkle shredded nylon fiber in for additional mold strength. With fingers spread apart place them below the surface and vigorously move them about, all the while being careful not to break the surface. The agitation created by the movement of the fingers breaks down any existing lumps and causes unwanted pockets of air to surface. The resulting mixture should be smooth but not thick; if too watery, work in more plaster. Thin, watery mixes produce soft casts with weakened compressive and impact strength.

Mixing plaster in a flexible rubber mixing bowl.

Plaster strength is also directly dependent upon the mixing time. The longer plaster is mixed the more dry strength it will have . . . longer mixing also shortens the setting time. You want the final consistency to be pourable but not wet to the point that it runs off the sides of the bowl. Plaster sets up rapidly. Don't hesitate—once the mixture is ready put it over the bowl. With your hands, quickly slush on a thin slurry coat over the entire surface. Once this first coat is in place, carefully pour the rest of the plaster on the bowl, Scoop up any plaster that slides down onto the newspaper and keep working it back up onto the mold. Continue doing this until the walls of the mold are an inch or two thick and the plaster begins to set. Before washing your hands, apply any left-over plaster to the top of the mold and form a level surface that can later function as a stable base.

If the walls of your mold are too thin, or if you want to strengthen them without making them thicker, cut cheese-cloth or any loosely woven cotton cloth into half inch strips, dip each one in plaster and build up a second coating— much like *papier mache*. It's very important not to wait long between coats. If too much time passes separation may occur. For plaster to set well it should be fresh, as old plaster will set soft and be lumpy. Set up time is also affected by water temperature and the water to plaster ratio. Warm water, like the addition of more plaster, results in a faster setting.

Cover the entire surface of the inverted wok with a thin coating of plaster. As soon as this is done, very carefully pour the rest of the material onto the mold.

To avoid clogged drains, do not clean out your mixing bucket in the sink. Leave any remaining plaster to harden inside the rubber container. Later, all of it can easily be removed. Standing over a waste basket, simply twist the rim back-and-forth and squeeze the walls with both hands until the hardened plaster fragments fall free.

The mold should set and be hard enough to remove the bowl in 30 minutes. Sometimes the bowls free themselves unexpectedly but more often than not they are awkwardly resistant, remaining embedded inside their cave of plaster. The entrapment is frequently the result of suction forces that require repetitive manipulation to relieve interfacial pressures. If the bowl still cannot be separated from the mold, place them both in hot water. Soaking or a blast of compressed air between the plaster and the bowl should interrupt the condensation bond that was formed when the plaster cooled down. If you're very careful, a bowl can be removed even earlier, when the plaster gets hot and begins to harden. At this stage, 10 to 15 minutes after pouring, the plaster is in an expanded state and removal is much easier. Once the bowl has been freed the mold is ready to use as is or it can be washed with a mixture of vinegar and water to remove traces of the parting agent and allowed to air dry.

After the plaster has set, remove the Chinese cooking wok and clean up the edges of the mold with paper towels. The clay for the retention ring should be discarded.

PRESS-MOLDING

In many respects press-molding is similar to drape-molding with the exception that the clay is added to the mold in sections, which are then pressed together in place. Drape molds are shallow with clean, smooth surfaces. Press molds are deep. Their interior surfaces can be smooth or textured. It matters little, since the clay, unlike in drape-molding, is lightly pressed into the mold for joining and can just as easily be worked into areas with texture.

The natural beauty of press-molding, however, is often underwritten by the juxtapositioning of parts. Patterns, ranging from an organic simplicity to a formidable complexity, can be developed piece-by-piece on the inside surface of a mold only to appear later, in their final arrangement, on the outer clay walls. As a construction technique, the clay shapes are joined on the inside of the form and the resulting seams scraped smooth; first with a metal rib, then with a rubber rib, and finally with a damp sponge. The finished interior is often left bare, with a somewhat solemn if not impoverished look. The focus in this process is generally directed toward the development of the exterior, but not always, and particularly not when the clay is soft and forcefully pressed together. Then the design workings of the seams are diffused if not lost entirely in the process, leaving a form's exterior surface aesthetically baron. Sometimes, of course, surfaces are best left plain and undecorated to honor the form's more subtle qualities. Still, a fair measure of decorative richness can be added to both the inner and the outer walls of the form after it leaves the mold: if it is removed in the leather-hard state.

HUMP-MOLDING

A hump mold is a convex support form created by casting the interior contour of a bowl shape in plaster. Soft clay slabs can then be either draped or pressed, piece-by-piece, directly onto the mold. In this forming process the exterior shape of the plaster hump forms the interior shape of the finished clay bowl.

The great disadvantage is that clay left to dry on a hump mold for too long will crack when it shrinks. While there is less stress with low profile hump molds, clay forms should be watched carefully and not, as can be done with press molds, be left to dry without first being removed while still in a leather-hard state.

When the clay becomes firm enough to support its own weight it

David Snabes ribbing smooth the seams of a large form made by joining two conical half sections of leather-hard clay shaped in a plaster press mold.

should be cautiously removed from the hump and allowed to dry slowly. It's generally a good idea to dry the piece inverted, with its rim resting on several sheets of newspaper. This delays your examination of the bowls richly articulated interior yet it reduces rim stress and is therefore worth the wait.

REMOVABLE INTERNAL SUPPORTS

Metal and wooden armatures are often used by sculptors to support modeled clay forms, such as the human figure from which bronze castings can be made. Clay that is built-up on these fixed armatures is *never* fired and must be kept moist to prevent it from shrinking and cracking apart until sectional molds can be made. For ceramists who fire their clay forms, nonclay internal supports become temporary and need to be removed as soon as the clay is firm enough to hold its own shape.

The possibilities are almost limitless when it comes to deciding what can be used to structurally support our clay. We can look for conventional objects and we can look for transcendent solutions. A support could consist simply of crumpled newspaper or an elaborately sewn fabric shape filled with Pearlite or vermiculite. As the form dries the bottom of the sewn support can be untied and the contents gradually released. The same watchful care, I call it "pot-sitting", would apply if the internal support were a balloon. At the exact time that the clay presents itself to us in a self-supporting state we need to let the air out and remove the balloon. Neglected, the piece will fall into a problematic condition.

Stiff cardboard tubes and PVC pipe can be unfailing instruments of support for cylindrical forms. One way to use these important sustainers of form is to decorate a pre-rolled slab of soft clay while it's still flat and on top of a table. With the fettling knife make a straight cut to define the bottom edge. After wrapping the tube with newspaper to prevent sticking, turn the newly imprinted side of the slab face-down. Place the tube on top of the slab and carefully roll the clay around it. To complete the joint, cut the slab just ahead of where the leading edge touches it and continue rolling until the seam is closed. For the completed joint to look neat and to be well sealed, press firmly down on the extended ends of the tube as if you were pressing down on the handles of a rolling pin, and roll the seam against the table. The rolling of the seam stretches the clay into a wider diameter than that of the tube, thereby eliminating any concern for shrinkage cracks. Still, leave the cylinder to stiffen in a horizontal position and add a base later, after removing the tube. This building technique is sometimes referred to as *soft slab construction*.

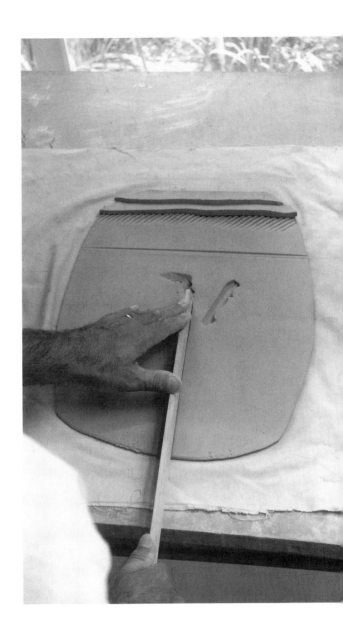

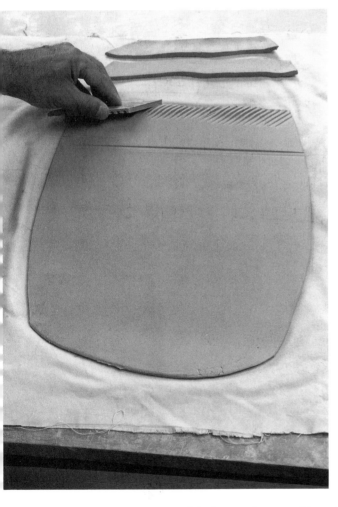

Textural design marks pressed into the clay slab prior to shaping it around a tube.

Shrinkage cracks would be a major concern, however, if the seam of the cylinder was not rolled out but simply cut and attached in place. When cylinders are made in this manner, the tube is tightly gripped by the clay as it dries and, were it not for the newspaper lining, could be extremely difficult to extract. The importance of separators, such as newspaper, cannot be stressed enough when using foreign objects as temporary supports. Without them clay becomes helplessly impaled and the supporting objects utterly unremovable.

Every material and process is subject to certain restraints. With clay, shrinkage is a major character trait that must be acknowledged to give your handbuilding the governance it needs. It's also important to recognize the role of the drying process: don't let it go unattended. As clay dries it will shrink 5% to 10% and in some bodies as much as 15% If the drying does

The bottom and right side are pre-cut straight prior to being wrapped on the tube.

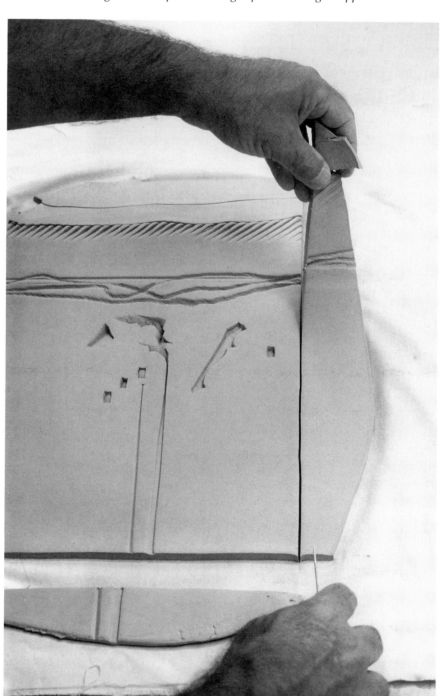

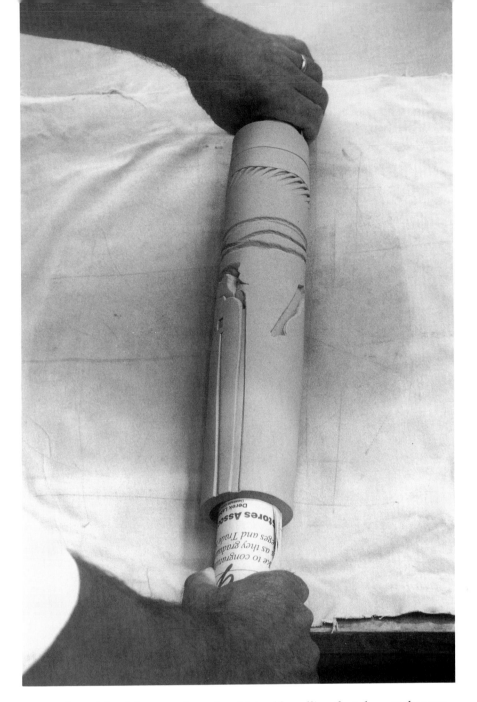

Two edges of the slab are overlapped and joined by rolling the tube over the seam.

not take place slowly cracks may develop. If it does not occur evenly forms can warp. Forms with joints or with walls that vary in thickness are especially vulnerable. Dried too fast, they can virtually break apart. Thin edges and appendages need special attention and should be covered with moist paper towels, occasionally sprayed with a misting bottle, or be painted with a wax resist. Bath towels or lengths of terry cloth purchased from a fabric store are excellent materials for covering wet clay projects and slowing down the drying process. Dry cloth towels absorb moisture while still, unlike plastic, allowing for a slow advancement of evaporation or passage of air. Slow drying is not a take it or leave it elective, it is a valued reality crucial to the success of our work.

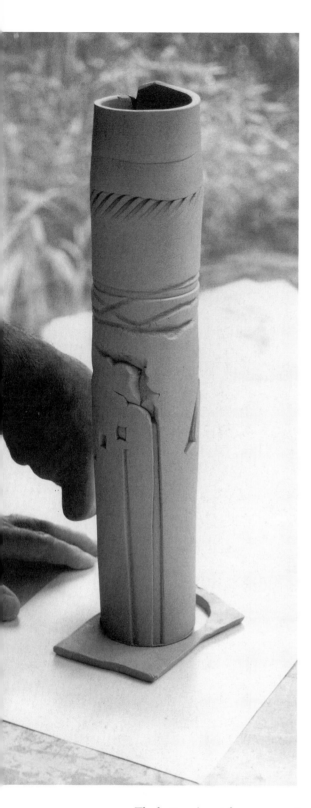
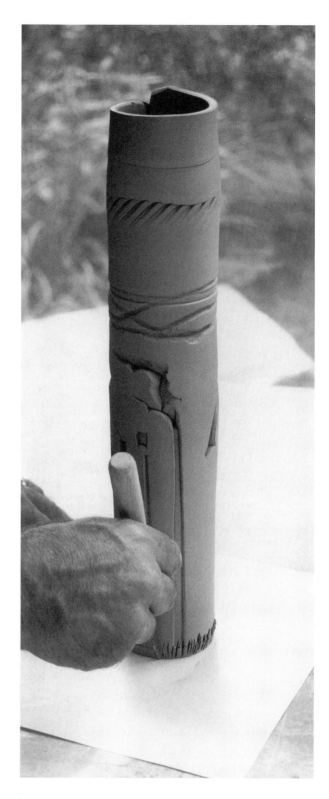

The bottom is cut from a separate clay slab and aggressively joined to the wall.

112   THE SPIRIT OF CLAY

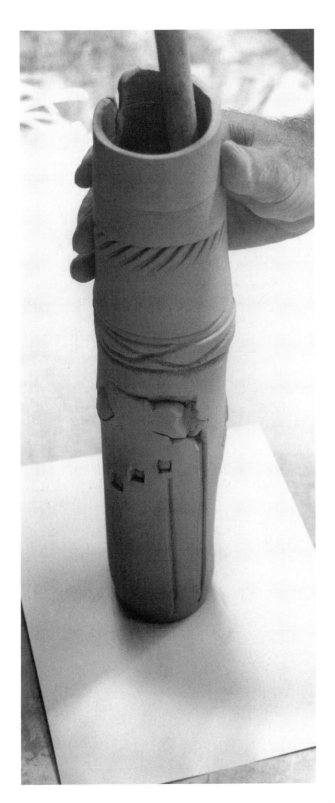
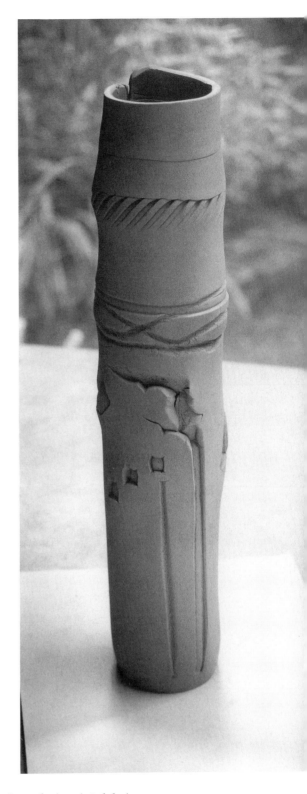

A dowel rod is used to press out and visually activate the imprinted designs.

STIFF SLAB CONSTRUCTION

Stiff slab construction is the process of creating form with leather-hard slabs of clay. The slabs of clay are formed, dried slowly and joined with slip. In historical terms it is a relatively young technique and, by comparison, it is also much more specific than the more amorphous techniques of ceramic sculpture.

As a teacher and artist I have a great deal of respect for stiff slab construction. It is an important part of contemporary ceramics. I have often acknowledged its significance by telling students that if I were allowed to teach only one forming technique that it would be this one and that with just this little piece of profound knowledge, and an open imagination, they would be able to successfully work in clay the rest of their lives. Once you see how teasingly simple it is, you'll probably be pleasantly surprised.

Slab Preparation

Prior to raising the curtain on this mainstream technique we need to go behind the scenes and look first at how slabs are prepared. You can quickly make a slab by throwing clay onto the top of a table with a sliding motion. With each toss the clay is stretched into a flattened shape. To prevent the upper surface from tearing, the slab should be carefully flipped each time it is thrown. Structurally stronger slabs, however, can be made by rolling the clay. Using either a rolling pin or mechanical slab roller, clay can be pressed into a tighter construction material. I use the term construction material here in both a suggestive and a literal sense because building with stiff slabs of rolled out clay is akin to building with lumber and sheets of plywood.

Clay compressed on a slab roller is of a uniform thickness. To achieve similar results with a rolling pin, two lengths of a wooden dowel rod need to be placed along opposite sides of the clay; eventually the rolling pin will make contact with them, creating a sheet of clay that is of a uniform thickness. A 1/4 inch diameter dowel will produce a 1/4 inch thick slab, a 3/8 inch diameter dowel will make a 3/8 inch thick slab and so on ... remember, the larger the form, the thicker the slab.

David Hines using flat slabs of stiff clay to simultaneously create four wall sculptures.

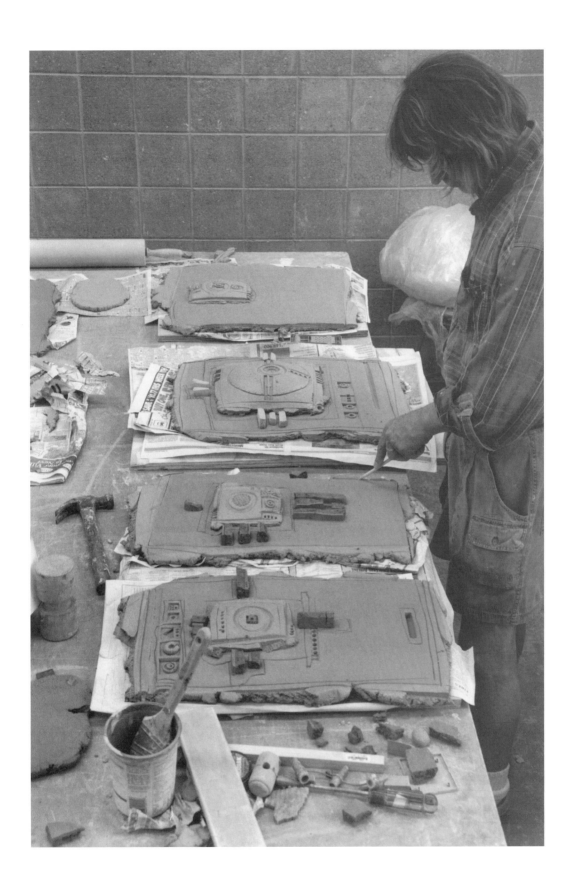

Slabs should be rolled out on pieces of clean canvas and not on newspaper or thin cloth. Newspaper tears and flimsy pieces of cloth cause wrinkles to develop on the surface of the clay and weaken the slab. Canvas prevents the clay from sticking to the surface you're working on and, most importantly, allows the slab to be easily moved around. Sometimes a piece of canvas is also placed on top of the clay to keep it from sticking to the rolling pin. When leveling out clay with a rolling pin it is a good idea to start from the center and work outwards, turning the canvas and directing the shape of the slab as you go. Rolling in different directions also reduces warpage. Clay has a physical memory and even machine made slabs benefit from a subsequent rolling and stretching in opposing directions. Occasionally you may want to lift the slab to release cohesion and reposition it on the canvas to make rolling easier. If you don't mind the resulting surface texture, sprinkle a little sand on the canvas before laying the slab back down and notice how freely and quickly the clay moves! The sand, resembling miniature ball bearings, temporarily reduces friction.

Two things I want to draw your attention to are: 1) be sure to make larger slabs than you think you'll need and 2) make extras. Some artists, such as John Mason, have been known to cover a portion of their studio floor first with plastic and then with one large slab of clay created by overlapping and joining several smaller ones together. Once such a slab has had sufficient time to stiffen it is covered, again in plastic, and returned to whenever building material is needed, much in the same way one returns to a pantry or to a warehouse for supplies. Of course, hardened slabs can also be stacked for storage. Secondly, dry your slabs carefully. This means slowly. Slabs allowed to dry fast will warp. Many handbuilders cover the clay with thin plastic in such a way as to provide partial air movement along the edges and leave their slabs on the canvas to dry. They should also dry on flat, smooth surfaces, such as scrap pieces of thick drywall or gypsum board. Before using a slab it should be dry enough to stand on edge without slumping or be innocently handled without imprinting. In the leather-hard state, you have the best of two privileges: the greatest amount of control and the least amount of anxiety. Privileges we don't often get to enjoy simultaneously while working with clay.

Kathryn Allen, Prairie School Vase, stiff slab built and raku fired, 25″ × 6″ × 6″.

Joining Stiff Slabs

Using a fettling knife and a flat metal framing square, cut the shapes you will be assembling from the center of your leather-hard slabs. If the finished dimensions of your project are critical you will need to allow for shrinkage and joint overlaps by cutting the pieces oversize. If, on the other hand, you take dimensioning less seriously, forgo the calculations and simply put the knife to the clay.

Many slab builders prefer to cut, or plane with a small surform tool, a 45° bevel on the edges of the slabs they will be joining. Others put their trust in the overlapping butt joint where the end of one slab is joined to the face of the second slab. In either case, the mating surfaces need to be softened with a thin coating of slip, preferably made by mixing water with the same ingredients used in the slabs. After painting on the slip, thoroughly and aggressively score the area with a needle tool. For faster results, use a metal fork or serrated rib. As an alternate procedure, you could score first and paste second but this sequence doesn't work the slip deep enough into the surface of the clay.

When using a butt joint to assemble 2 slabs let one edge extend beyond the union.

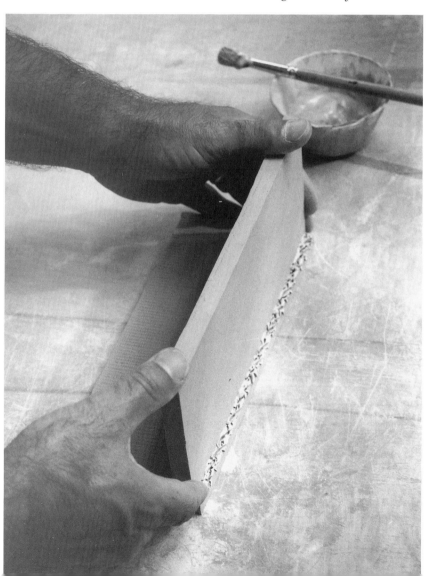

To further strengthen a joint a coil of clay can be worked into the inside corner.

To complete the construction of a butt joint, firmly press and wiggle the two slip covered areas together, leaving one edge slightly extended. Don't be timid! This is a no-nonsense moment. If you fail to successfully integrate these two surfaces now, they will come undone later.

To finish the corner, carefully remove the over-extended edge with a fettling knife. Cut it flush with the surface of the adjoining slab. To straighten up the joint and remove any cut markings or irregularities, scrape it clean with a flexible metal rib. To erase the seam line and remove any grog outcroppings, follow up by burnishing the area with a stiff rubber rib. The ribbing will leave a very sharp corner, one too sharp for glaze to adhere to. To prevent a bare line of unglazed clay from showing through, go over this corner with a damp sponge and soften it.

Cut the extended slab flush with the surface of the adjoining slab.

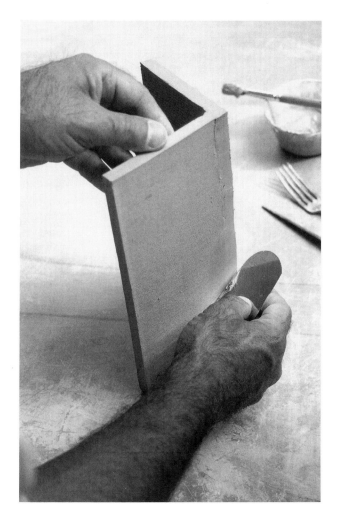

Use a flexible metal rib to square-up the corner and scrape the seam level

Use a rubber rib to apply a smooth surface finish and to erase the seam line.

Run a sponge or chammy along the corner of the joint to soften the angle and prevent glaze from being pulled away from a sharp edge.

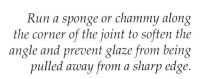

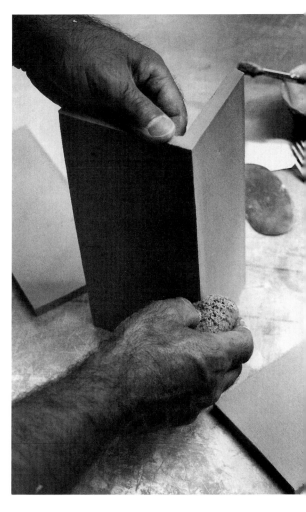

Curing

Curing is a temporary process of conspicuously slowing down the dehydration of the material and preserving its dampness. Semi-dry slabs of clay, recently assembled with a wet slurry, cannot simply be forgotten and left out to dry. For these types of joints to survive the drying process they need to be cured. If the moisture content is maintained at a relatively stable level for several hours, overnight or longer, the dryer clay is able to absorb and assimilate the water from the slip. If this clay, which has already started to shrink in size, is not granted assimilation time it will continue shrinking, pull away from the wet slip used as the glue, and the joint will separate.

Tom Coleman, slab-built tea pot from Manly Tea Pot Series, 16" × 24" × 4". The piece was first glazed fired to cone 5; re-glazed with a thick application of his "Mud Crack" overglaze (50% magnesium carbonate, 20% nepheline syenite, 20% Ferro Frit 3134 and 10% Gerstley borate) and fired to cone 3.

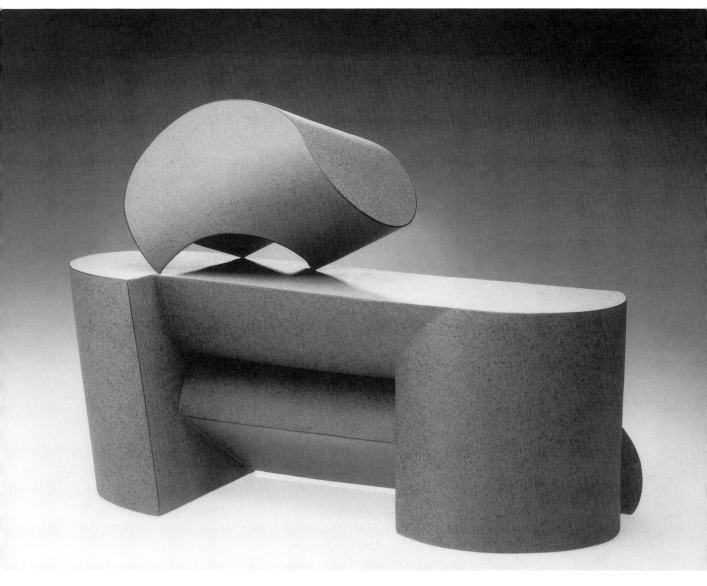

Anne Currier, Rollway, 14″ × 22″ × 9″. Anne's superbly crafted slab-built forms appear almost machine-like in their surface uniformity and cleanly assembled edges. As geometric forms of volume they also articulate a relationship with movement as they silently curve, roll and lyrically flow within one's visual space.

Joints can be equalized and kept from cracking in one of several ways. They may be continuously misted with a spray bottle. They may be painted with a wax-resist. Or, they may be tightly wrapped in plastic, with or without first being covered in wet paper towels. After a period of controlled curing, the work should be casually covered by a piece of plastic that hangs loose and is open near the bottom to permit slow and even evaporation.

SLIP CASTING

Slip casting is a process used to reproduce identical forms by pouring liquid clay into a plaster mold. Because plaster absorbs moisture, the clay touching the surface of the mold starts to stiffen and form a replica of the mold's interior. The longer the liquid clay is left in the porous mold the thicker this clay deposit becomes. When a desired thickness is obtained the excess slip is poured out and the remaining deposit, which is now a clay duplicate of the mold itself, is left to dry.

Successful casting slips are difficult to prepare and many ceramists prefer the reliability of low-fire commercial slips (many containing 60% talc and 40% kaolin and/or ball clay) over home-made slips. Except for heavily grogged or highly plastic throwing clays, almost any existing studio clay body can be converted into a casting body. High-fire porcelain slips and low-fire talc slips both have their niche here but if slip casting remains an avant-garde vehicle for an evocative vocabulary of images, then the stability of the low-fire slips, fired at less stressful temperatures, will continue to reign supreme.

With traditional handbuilding bodies clay particle cohesion is extremely important, but with casting bodies it's necessary to keep those same particles dispersed and suspended in the water. Casting slips contain, on the average, 20% less water than ordinary clay slips and only 20% more water than handbuilding clay. To achieve the viscosity of a pouring slip, without an excessive amount of water, casting slips are deflocculated.

Deflocculation is the separating of clay particles to achieve maximum fluidity with a minimum amount of water. A liquid deflocculant such as Alcosperse 149-C, sodium silicate "N" or Darvan #7 and soda ash, a powder, can be added to the clay ingredients in amounts ranging from 0.2% to 0.4%. If much more is used the clay particles settle and will not remain in suspension. Alcosperse (from the ALCO Chemical Corporation) is much preferred as a dispersing agent over sodium silicate, both are more fluid than soda ash and can be used on their own. Soda ash, although not as durable in the greenware state, can cause pin holing on the surface and should not be used alone. Used together, however, clay and a deflocculant, when combined with less than 40% water, should provide a very stable slip. If a casting slip can contain a large ratio of clay ingredients to a small ratio of water and still remain fluid, its density will reduce shrinkage and make for a strong clay shell.

Prior to use, the deflocculants should be dissolved in a small amount of hot water. When making a casting slip, the dry ingredients should slowly be added to this wet mixture and stirred continuously. After mixing for several hours, the slip should be covered and allowed to season a day or two before it is screened. After screening, grog may be added or the fluidity improved by the addition of water or vinegar. At this point, the viscosity of a casting slip can be accurately checked by weighing to determine its specific gravity - the clay to water ratio. Excluding the weight of the container, a single pint of slip should weigh-in at 29 ounces; a liter at 1775 grams. If the slip weighs more add water.

Slip molds, whether they be in one, two, or six pieces, generally have some form of reservoir or riser built into the top of them to accommodate an extra supply of liquid. Shortly after a mold has been filled it begins to absorb water and the level of slip drops dramatically. As this occurs the mold needs topping off. In twelve minutes, or when the wall has reached a proper thickness, the remaining slip is poured out and the mold turned upside down to drain. After several minutes it is turned upright and the clay is left to dry for twenty minutes or until it shrinks away from the walls. Once it starts to become leather-hard it should carefully be removed and the spare clay, which forms the pour spout and the riser, trimmed away with a fettling knife.

Below is Victor Spinski's slip casting body that was engineered with the expertise of William M. Jackson II who pioneered the use of Wollastonite, Alcosperse and originated Boroflux for the commercial slip casting industry and the porcelain casting body Susan Beiner's used while working in the Artist-in-Industry program at the Kohler Company factory in Wisconsin.

Spinski Casting Body	Cone 04-01
131 lb.	Hot Water
1.13 gr.	Epson Salts
3.40 gr.	Soda Ash
2.83 gr.	Magnesium Hydroxide
453.50 gr.	Boroflux C-13
79.00 gr.	Alcosperse #149
. . . mix 5 minutes & add:	
75 lb.	OM4 Ball Clay
25 lb.	Velvacast Kaolin
200 lb.	Talc (Nytal 100HR)

Beiner Casting Body	Cone 6-9
2.5 gal.	Water
2 oz.	Sodium Silicate
10 gr.	Soda Ash
. . . mix 5 minutes & add:	
12.5 lb.	OM4 Ball Clay
12.5 lb.	Edgar Plastic Kaolin
12.5 lb.	Flint
12.5 lb.	Potash Feldspar

The first additives are mixed together in the water for at least 5 minutes; afterwards the other ingredients are added and mixed for an hour. At this time, depending on the hardness of the water, the slip may need to be adjusted by the addition of more deflocculant until the specific gravity is 1.75. After sitting for one day the slip is again mixed and adjusted. On the second day, following further mixing and adjustment, the casting slip is passed through a 30 mesh sieve.

1   *For molds with enclosed walls two spouts are needed for an even fill: one for slip and one for air exchange. The funnels hold extra slip to compensate for mold absorption.*

2   *After the clay casting shell forms and reaches a desired thickness, Susan Beiner pours out the remaining liquid clay slip and will leave the mold to drain upside-down.*

3   *After draining upside-down for five minutes, Susan Beiner's 4-piece vase mold was turned upright and the cast clay shell was allowed to stiffen for twenty minutes before the clamping straps were taken off and the top of the plaster mold was removed.*

4   *With the top and now the two side sections of the mold removed, the leather-soft clay shell is carefully lifted from the base section of the mold.*

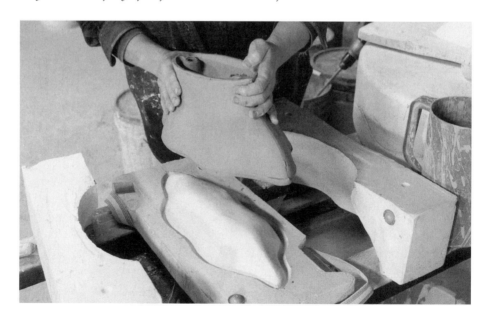

5   The glazed and fired vase was made from the same mold as the leather-soft one. When the clay stiffens and becomes leather hard the pouring and venting channels will be removed from inside the concave foot along with any projecting casting seams.

Making A Casting Mold

To make a simple two-part mold of an object to be reproduced in clay first make sure that it contains no undercuts to inhibit its removal from the plaster and then decide where the dividing line will be. Start by building a thick clay wall perpendicular to the object along one side of this line. The entire piece, and the clay wall itself, can be supported by a solid bed of clay if necessary. Surround the object, and the clay parting line containing the pour hole, with a casting retaining wall (Formica covered particle board works best) and coat with a parting agent. After the plaster has been poured, and after it has set, turn the piece over, remove the clay, carve out two concave locking keys and repeat the process of applying the releasing agent to the other half of the object, as well as to the mold, and cover with plaster. When set, open the mold by carefully prying the two halves apart along the separating line.

The procedure is the same for making multiple-part molds, as shown with Susan Beiner's three-piece cup mold and two-piece saucer mold on the next two pages. The cup and saucer being cast were made from builder's blue insulation foam and covered with spackling. Between each of the three coatings the spackling was carefully sanded to refine the form's contour.

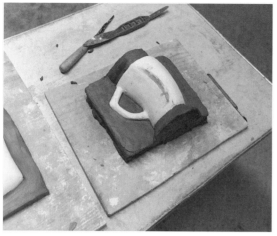

1   *Clay divider around foam cup*

2   *Securing mold frame around clay seam*

3   *Pouring plaster 1" above cup*

4   *Casting second half of cup mold*

5   *Making key lock with a dime*

6   *Casting indented foot of cup mold*

7   *Removing foam cup from mold*

8   *Removing mold soap with white vinegar*

Two cup and saucer sets slip cast from the plaster mold illustrated in the previous photographs. Susan Beiner glaze-fired one cup and saucer as they apeared after being cast, and altered the other set with the addition of several slip cast parts. Approximately 100 additional cups and saucers can be cast in these molds before they deteriorate.

THE MYSTERIES OF CREATIVITY

The mysteries of the creative self are intimate and closely allied to the mysteries of love, health and happiness in that they center around positive self-esteem as a fundamental element of human evolution. To have a truly successful and happy relationship with clay, as with a friend or loved one, we must not only be consciously aware of who we are and what we are doing but also happy and confident with that awareness of self. It is the one indispensable key to creatively meeting the challenges that continuously present themselves to us.

Our belief in ourselves is the immune system of the spirit. It energizes and empowers our thoughts and actions by providing the psychological strength and healthy resilience to prevent life from becoming a frightening experience.

When self-esteem is low, a confining fear dominates all that we do. Insecurity and uncertainty become expansive and the safety of the known and the familiar is embraced. In such a noninspiring state change is avoided and inactivity courted. Creatively, this is a toxic and invalidating existence where personal values, aspirations and feelings cannot be honored yet alone expressed.

High self-esteem, on the other hand, is a highly motivating force. When our self-esteem is strong and positive we seek to experience life (on all levels) in a more active and fulfilling manner. Creatively we seek to express the joy and bountifulness that lives within us. In this sense creativity is a celebrative signature, an affirmation, of your self-assurance.

When we believe in ourselves, not just sporadically or in various degrees but to the very center of our being, we become more compassionate and respectful of just who it is that we are. With this magnitude of self-acceptance not only are we able to be more assertive in expressing ourselves with the handbuilding techniques discussed so far, but we are able to do so in cherished ways that are highly creative. Positive feelings of self-respect, in addition to allowing us to live more creatively, allow us to also live more purposefully and with greater personal integrity.

Self-esteem and integrity are the "heart-and-soul" of creativity. If yours is a little weak at the moment or if you have secret fears of inadequacy and you recognize the virtues of a healthier sense of self, working in clay is one way to begin the journey to a more fulfilling existence.

The road to a greater sense of self through clay is not always easy and it cannot be traveled quickly. Why? Because your non-physical experiences of the human spirit must be translated to the physical world before they can have any permanent influence of a transforming nature. Nevertheless, the road of technical knowledge and the practical application of the physical senses must first be traveled . . . and you have already come this far. I know the road, but it is you who must travel it now. If you're ready to continue and to find new pleasures in the self and pride in your achievements read the final handbuilding category on sculpting and carefully work your way through the chapter on throwing. Given time, you, and your traveling companion clay, can reach altered states of being that are not without meaning, a wonderful state where self-awareness, inner harmony and creative consciousness exist as natural and inevitable qualities of your wholeness.

Elizabeth MacDonald, Pears, 7" × 5" × 3 1/2". Her work is both formal and organic; both delicate and rough, expressing a personal passion to create intimacy within a context of extended time and space.

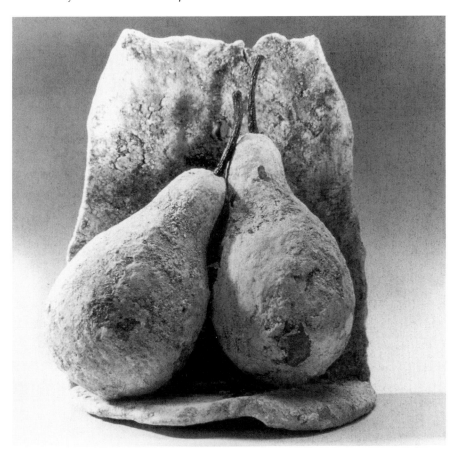

Carroll Hansen, low-fire sculpture made from thinly rolled slabs of clay, 20 1/2".

134　　THE SPIRIT OF CLAY

SCULPTING

Sculpting is a process of giving shape to clay by modeling, carving, or the use of any number of other construction techniques or combination of techniques. As a catch-all term generally associated with ceramic forms that were not dictated by functional use, it encompasses alternative ways of working with a quality of feeling that shapes a visual relationship between clay and space.

When it comes to sculpting clay there is no one correct or authoritative way. Fingers can be the only tools used or machines, such as a pug mill outfitted with dies, can be mechanically used to extrude large hollow shapes. Non-clay materials such as metal, wood, cement, plastic, glass, wire or mechanical fasteners can be creatively employed to extend the limits of clay as a sculptural medium. The first forms that I made out of clay as a child, as well as my son Matthew and my daughter Wendy, were sculptural. With an essentially playful aesthetic, all three of us initially sculpted people. The earliest forms in the history of ceramics were sculptural in the vivid shape of fertility symbols.

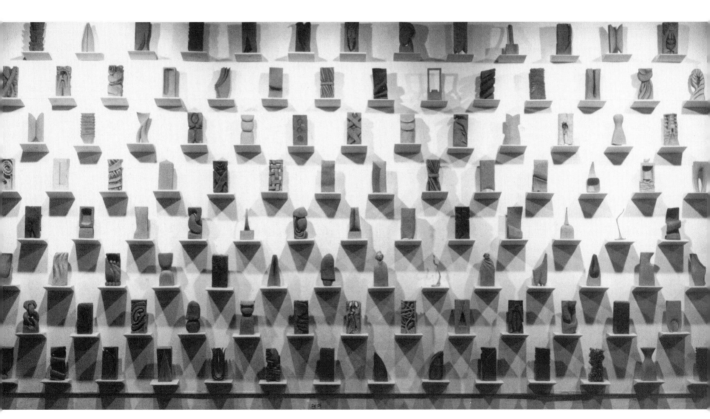

Caroline Court, Brick Wall-Variation #3. Each individual element is unique unto itself, and was carved from a solid piece of clay the size of a standard 2 1/2″× 4″ × 8″ red house brick.

Nancy Selvin, Ledge With Bottles, raku and mixed media, 4" × 2" × 6".

Clay is a valuable and natural sculptural medium. Physically, it is responsively quick. Spiritually, it is capable of sustaining the human psyche. Approached with an open mind, sculpting becomes a wonderful way to retouch a quality of excitement that comes with the widening of a frontier. The sculptural use of clay gives our sensibilities a pioneering path to travel. Functioning as a carrier of a new type of spirit-force, sculpting can endow clay with fresh and exciting possibilities. Ceramic artists who work sculpturally and who utilize fabrication techniques that are of their own innovation, and not found in any textbook, are the ones who are most likely to reshape our thinking. It should be no surprise that the ceramist as sculptor will be one who alters the direction of ceramics much in the same way Eve Hesse altered the direction of sculpture.

Mark Chatterley, Woman With Familiar, 7'.

There is a freedom inherent to sculpting with clay. A freedom to conceptualize, to engage those issues which are personally central and not traditionally peripheral to the experiences of the individual. Historically, individuals following their own interests and utilizing a personal approach to their clay work, have been influential in redefining ceramics. Peter Voulkos played a major role in this area in the late fifties. He almost single handedly altered the course of American ceramics by extending the role of clay as a craft medium containing space to clay as an art object occupying space. So revolutionary was his approach to the vessel and his use of clay that art critic Harold Rosenberg identified it as "unfocused play". Other iconoclastic artists such as Ken Price and Robert Hudson in the seventies and John Roloff and Viola Frey in the eighties further expanded the concept of sculptural ceramics as an art form.

Few ceramic sculptors have been as controversial or dominated the art scene as extensively or as long as California artist Robert Arneson. Arneson had a unique and humorous way of bringing us face to face with personal, societal and global issues, including the threat of nuclear war, by way of his larger than life portraits. Modeling clay sculpturally, he taught us how to see, through his insight, past the faces of life; into different states of human understanding.

These larger-than-life heads by Robert Arneson began as slabs of clay (with a 40% grog content) that were pressed into sectional molds made of plaster.

Robert Arneson, California Artist, low-fired ceramics, 78″ × 28″ × 28″. Robert Arneson, who more than any other American laid the ground work for ceramics as a contemporary sculptural medium, often used autobiographical commentary and the self-portrait as a resource for his work. While there are ceramists who create traditional forms from traditional images as well as those who create personal forms from traditional images. Others, like Peter Voulkos, work with a personal image and a traditional form (often the plate). But what made the role played by Arneson so uniquely important was that both his images and his forms were personal.

How do we find our way with clay as sculpture? What issues do we address, what techniques do we use? Questions and confusion may prevail. The answers, well, they may lie in different realms for each of us . . . if we trust in our *own* process and remain open to life many of them will make themselves known. Still, others may have to be found by stepping forth and boldly participating in the creative process with all that we can bring to bare, working through the unknowns until we grow into resolution.

Though each of us will pursue our own unique forms of expression, clay is a constant. It feeds our spirit and grounds all of our undertakings. Clay connects us to a community of simple yet shared disciplines. Common to each of our concerns are certain technical realities that by and large direct us all to hollow-out exceptionally thick forms, to dry clay thoroughly and to fire kilns slowly. Still, the mechanics of clay do not dominate the imagination. Sculpturally, the material invites each of us to privately find our own way with it. In the "Great Lakes State" the tourist industry has a "Say YES! to Michigan" motto. In ceramics we need to say YES! to our own spirit and work, irregardless of the technique(s) used, with the same human qualities that guide our life.

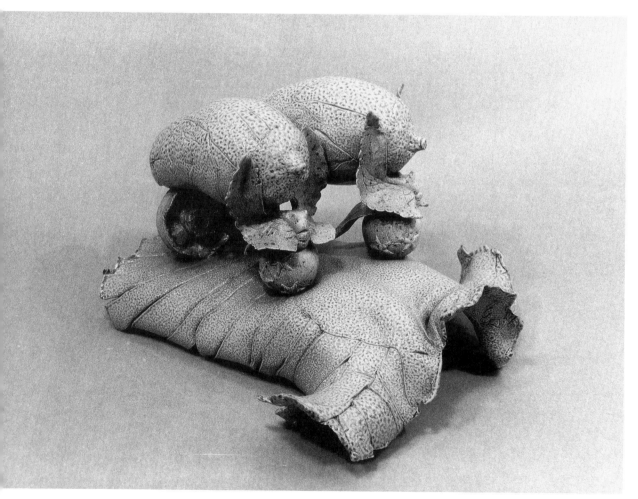

Adrian Arleo, Annunciation, clay, glaze, terra sigillata, wax encaustic, steel rods and epoxy, 22" × 38" × 7". Adrian's primal images metaphorically convey universal states of being and the intimacies of relationships. They evolve from personal feelings into sensuous clay sculptures that are fluid and texturally fertile.

Denis Deegan, salt-fired sculpture assembled from pairs of ceramic egg plants, star balls, wheels and angel fish mounted on top of a torso base, 16" × 13" × 10".

Paul Soldner, #932, low temperature salt-fumed sculpture made from slabs and altered wheel thrown forms, 36" × 26 1/2" × 22".

Paul Soldner
working on a
sculpture.
Often, he will
form and
texture his clay
by stomping
directly on it or
on a piece of
plywood placed
over it.

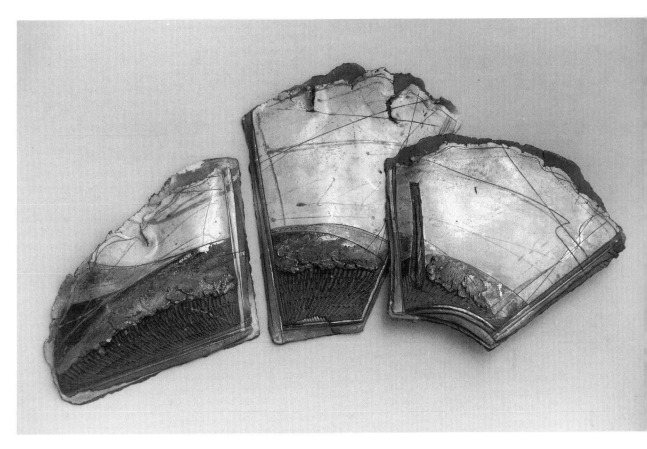

Gail Piepenburg, Full Moon, slab constructed raku wall triptych, 51″ × 25″ × 3″.

Gail Piepenburg incising a design into a leather-hard clay diptych to heighten the decorative interplay between the organic textural elements and the rolled surface.

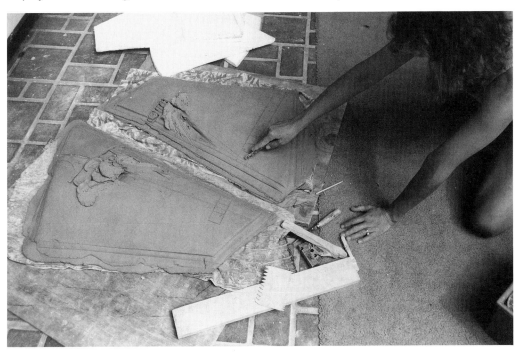

Eva Monson creates 40–50 air channels within the solid clay figures (with a length of brazing rod) leading to a hollowed-out cavity in the base of her sculptures. These channels allow moisture trapped inside the thicker clay areas to dissipate during both the drying and the firing of the clay. The penetration openings left on the exterior surface are covered over with clay.

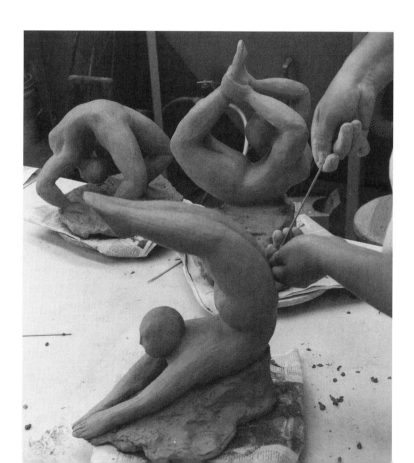

The deepest roots of creativity are spiritual. For clay work to remain vital it must, more than any other element, be nurtured by the spiritual capacities of our being. Our spirit (that deep energy of personal passion we bring to life) is our most precious asset. We must do everything we can in life (from eliminating stress to eating the right foods) to take care of ourselves: to ultimately care for our spirit. If our spirit is astray (or worse, not yet found), if the energy of its birth has not been felt or if it is simply in ill health, we can do everything right; have everything, and still remain separated from the divine wholeness of our very own existence.

Our wholeness is the reverent spirit of clay. What's so ironic here, is that the clay, and our engagement with it, in turn, brings out the vitality of our own spirit and makes it visible.

Our clay work becomes a voice of our wholeness. While the work may exist as a tangible song of our deeper self it is still a gift from our spirit (our sacred source). Like any work of art, ceramics is a creation of the spirit. Clay work is not just an extension of the human spirit it is the heart of it. It not only *expresses* our spirit it *is* our spirit. All that remains for us to make our creative passions a reality is to pursue them. Not in a way that means life's traditional responsibilities have to be abandoned, but in a way that is honorable and personally meaningful.

Robert Piepenburg, Tide of Time #L20-7, raku sculpture, 11" × 9" × 7 1/2".

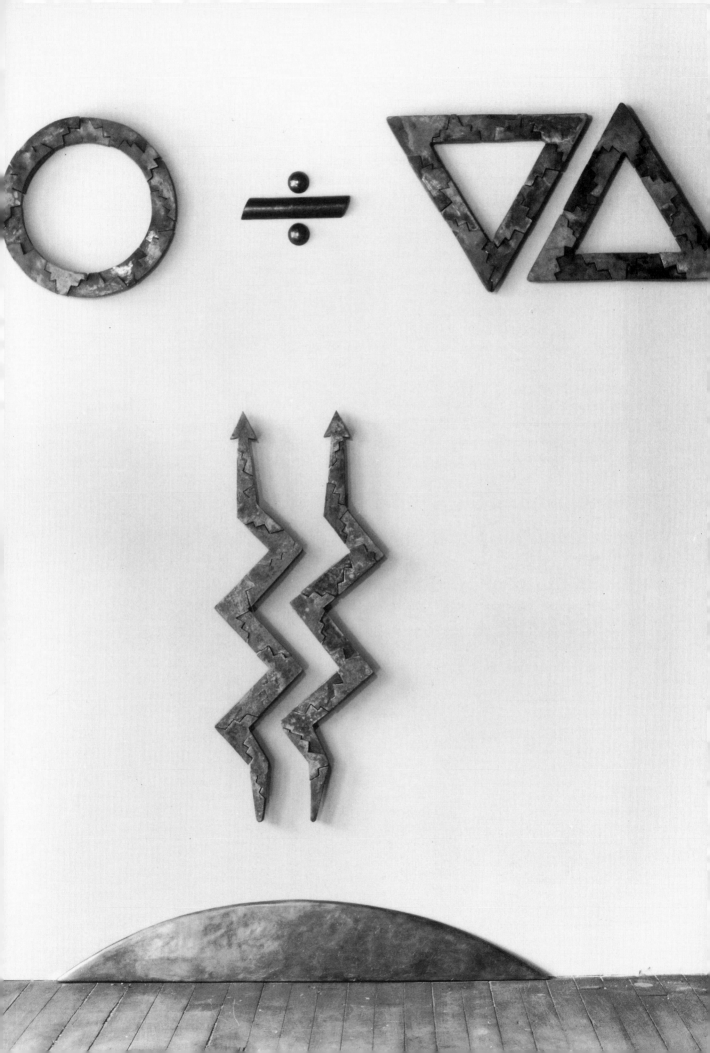

CREATIVE RESOURCES FOR CLAY WORK

In art there is a delicate balance between concept and technique. All to often the structural scaffolding of technique is reinforced, misidentifed or assumed to be the primary ingredient of value in an art object. When, in fact, it is primarily a reflection of craftsmanship, of physical skills. This chapter has dealt with a majority of clay fabrication techniques, and it is important to recognize these, but it is also important to recognize that the professional role of technical skills is to serve the creative imagination by skillfully presenting the artist's concept, and by doing so in expressive ways that are inspirational and heart-felt.

Concept is the art. It is the birth place of the creative object. As such, the true value of an art work is more dependent on its conceptual content than it is on the brilliance of its technical packaging. While it may be relatively easier to communicate, demonstrate, learn and evaluate technical processes it is important to conclude this chapter by indicating some of the sources available to ceramists for discovering personal beginnings for the direction of their clay work.

The origins for one's creative concepts are often deeply personal. By their very nature they are intuitive and subtly spiritual in content and far more capable of driving a work of clay than technique. To find the content and directional meaning for your own creative clay work you will have to trust in your own ever-growing gifts and be ever-ready to journey into the unknown, beyond the exploitative boundaries of material success and historical conformism.

Sandy Happel, 4 raku fired heads that push against the constrictions of life, 12" high.

Ana England, Divide, raku fired symbols, sawdust fired division sign, 108" × 88" × 2 1/4".

Mobilizing Resources

The following resource categories are presented as ideas for fusing the dynamics of your own interests with the origins of your clay activities.

<u>Love:</u> Out of your feelings of love for someone special you can create clay works of great caring and quality of workmanship. Let your knowledge of that individual guide and inspire the shape, design and texture of your forms. Using the love source to direct the making of pottery that will eventually be given to a loved one is very satisfying.

<u>Ecology:</u> There are many threats to the ecological balance of our precious ecosystems. Destructive drift net fishing, reduction of the ozone layer, deadly toxic wastes, loss of the rain forest, nuclear testing and overpopulation are just a few of the issues that can be recognized and expressed through clay with the hope of expanding public awareness to the seriousness of these harmful problems. The destruction of The Great Barrier Reef, the disaster of the *Exxon Valdez*, the threats to Florida's wet lands and the massacre of our natural landscape through clearcutting by industrial foresters are powerful conceptual themes for handbuilding projects.

<u>Endangered Species:</u> Artist's often use their work in the service of wildlife. Many tragic forces, both visible and invisible, globally threaten the survival of many living things. Your concern for the welfare of dolphins, whales, Grizzly bears, coyotes, elephants and countless other life forms can be addressed in your clay work and conveyed to the world. As another alternative, choose to celebrate the life of animals in your work.

Kay Clement preparing to wrap one of her smaller dolphin sculptures with wet paper towels and plastic. This work is still in process and needs to be kept from drying until she returns to finish it. A great amount of Kay's human energy is passionately dedicated to addressing the plight of the world's whales and dolphins.

Eva Monson, lidded raku form based upon Jean M. Auel's book The Clan of the Cave Bear.

Books: I have often reminded my children that if they could read they could learn and do anything. Reading is important to our lives. Books exude images. For the artist, they are an unlimited source for resource images. Imagine the substantial themes for clay works to be found by simply reading Shakespeare. To implicate matters enormously, imagine the innumerable images for directing clay that might be found in books on history, anthropology, science, romance, social issues, mysteries, travel, myths and legends.

Environment: If you feel a spiritual relationship with the earth and her great oceans, if you care about plants, animals and sea life, then you may want to embrace those feelings in your clay work. Trees, for example, are no less than wondrous—what could you make with clay to strengthen that realization?

Ancient Civilizations: History provides a rich legacy of mythological and folklore themes to work from; the awesome temples, columns and sculptures of Greece, Egyptian hieroglyphs, burial tombs and temples, are all filled with centuries of symbolic imagery. The 1000 year old Giza pyramids, for example, are one of the ancient world's seven wonders. Medieval life, with its castle strongholds and knights in armor, beckons the imagination to take off in flights of fantasy.

Ancient Cultures: Australian aboriginal art is a timeless display of dots, designs and color that every visual artist can learn from. Their spirit poles, like the carved masks and totem poles of The Northwest Coast Indians, invite personal responses that are deeply moving and powerful starting points for new aesthetic directions.

Tony Hepburn, Spring, unglazed clay and wood, 36" × 30" × 12". In this sculptural still-life the jug is classically rendered while the water sprinkling can and boots are physically fashioned in a playfully rich and freely uninhibited manner that miraculously honors both process and material.

<u>Still-life:</u> Many artists, and students of drawing and painting, create two-dimensional works of art based upon the compositional relationship of selected objects. Freely working with leather-soft slabs of clay one could easily create some imaginatively sculpted and exciting ceramic works based upon a still-life made up of 2 to 5 objects. Interesting arrangements of bottles, an old baseball mitt, a toaster and a teddy bear, for example, could prove to be stimulating resource materials.

<u>Stamps:</u> Create a ceramic sculpture or relief tile piece that incorporates the dynamics of the combined images found on stamps. Select 3 postage stamps for the visual and conceptual nature of their design. These images should be reinterpreted or redefined in a way that is personally significant to your aesthetic identity. As an additional strategy consider incorporating the elements of texture, geometric shapes and negative/positive spatial relationships.

Diane Stewart using a Q-tip to put the finishing touches on a leather-hard relief tile. The design was modeled from a basket still-life containing fruit and flowers. By working on a section of open metal shelving the tile is able to dry evenly from both sides and reduce its chances of warping.

Raymon Elozua and Micheline Gingras, Oasis Drive In, cone 04 terra cotta clay and oil paint, 32″ × 36″ × 22″.

Architecture: Stiff-slab construction techniques can be used to create clay pieces with an architectural presence. Clay, used in relationship with classical and geometrical elements of architecture, can be used to create shapes that translate as building but abstractly exist as sculpture. Pieces could symbolize (in spirit, form, dimension and commentary) architectural volume (walls, roofs, etc.) and incorporate one or more of the following structural details: window, door, archway, stairs or column.

Fairy Tales: I once had a student who, just after learning how to work with stiff slabs of clay, read her daughter a bed-time story of *The Three Little Pigs*. Immediately, she became inspired to build a clay piece depicting the brick house, complete with open windows revealing the pigs inside. On the roof was the big bad wolf with one leg inside the chimney. The piece retold a story from childhood and I immediately envisioned a one-woman exhibition of her clay work (dedicated to her daughter) based upon children's stories. What type of clay creations could you summon forth from the tale of *Jack and the Beanstalk, The Giving Tree, Rumpelstiltskin, The Tortoise and the Hare* or *The Wizard of Oz*?

Steven Wieneke, raku wall sculptures with images of architectural fragments, 10" × 14".

<u>Poetry:</u> Poems are loaded with images. Images that can touch, arouse and seduce every human emotion. They are written with a respect for the reader's intellectual ability to fill-in the blank spots, to transcend the words with a heart-felt consciousness, and enter the stirring and beautiful mysteries of life. To bring a new vision to the direction of your work as a ceramist, patiently seek out a poem and read it three times. Set it aside and, without any internal coercion, let an image speak to you. Once that image is clearly received, set out to find your way to realize it in clay. An alternative approach involves the selection of one line from the poem to be used as the title. The content of the piece should then be infused and committed to the identity of that line's substance.

<u>Dreams:</u> Every person is said to have at least three dreams a night. Dreams are unconscious images formed from subconscious feeling. Frequently they are without any rational spatial structure or sequential time continuum. If the experience of this autonomous phenomenon can be remembered it can provide subjective material for good, if not nutty and wild, clay work. Surrealist painters, notably Salvador Dalì, successfully used dream associations as a resource for improbable compositions. If Dalì had been a ceramist, how would he have dealt with the images of drooping watches seen in his most famous painting "Persistence of Memory"?

<u>Word Images:</u> Make a list of 50 words. Include words such as *airplanes, horses, baggage, mythology, insects, texture, buildings, identity, wheels and turtles.* Select three of the words from this list. Using the images that these three words encompass, create an innovative clay piece. The images worked with here are important, not for *what* they are but for *where* they take you.

Jeri S. Hollister, White & Kawai Tribute, cone 04 earthenware with slips, 21" high.

Jean-Pierre Larocque, Untitled #7, from a beast of burden series, soda fired with low-fired slips and glaze, 36" × 25" × 14".

<u>Sacred Objects:</u> No clay object is without importance. All are projections of their creator. When we make something in clay we give of ourselves and the creative sincerity of our touch is worthy of respect, of reverence. With clay we can personally choose to make specific objects sacred: dedicated or devoted to the affirmation of a person, a primal event, a commitment or a heart-felt belief. One such object could be a small clay altar. The altar piece could be made to honor the existence of your own creativity in service and communion with your creative spirit. It could celebrate your cherished bond with clay, symbolizing the self-fulfillment unveiled, imbued or received by working with it. The altar, as with any work of art, should be made by reaching into the spirit and, when viewed or meditated upon, should lead your feelings back to the spirit inside of you. The piece itself could incorporate provisions for a few articles that are personally meaningful and/or the burning of a small candle, toxic experiences written on small scraps of paper, a favorite incense or some of nature's aromatic plants, such as sage, cedar and sweet grass, that Native Americans traditionally used in their ceremonies as purifiers or as a communication medium for carrying prayers. As an additional resource to working intimately with clay in ways that can serve to remind us of our own uniqueness, Adriana Diaz's book, *Freeing the Creative Spirit*, offers some ritual guidance and meditation methods into the sacredness of the human and creative spirit that could prove to be inspiring.

The student that fashioned this altar (with stick incense and candles) for the top of her bedroom dresser, manifests a capacity to commune with clay as well as the self.

Penny Truitt, slab-built raku form with foot. Classically trained as an archaeologist, Penny is a full-time studio artist who's clay work is inspired by the physical and emotioanl forces of the American Southwest. Her work is to be respected for its spiritual exploration and viewed as both internal and external landscape. 5 1/2" × 6 1/2" × 17 1/2".

Good teaching, like successful learning, is a connective process. When it comes to teaching and learning throwing, many connections of strengthened significance are made by observing others. In this connection the use of half-circular ware tables is helpful to the generative needs of throwing students. The arrangement engages the activity of throwing in a shared place and with a common spirit of openness where one can continuously observe, learn and find support in a multiple variety of relationships.

4

Throwing

Throwing on the potter's wheel has become synonymous with ceramics much in the same way painting has become with art. Ceramics is, of course, an art but when the word "art" is mentioned, many people don't think of ceramics, drawings, prints, or sculptures . . . they think of paintings. Likewise, when they hear the word "ceramics", images of pots thrown on the wheel immediately come to mind.

Ceramics and throwing are intimately related, even if there are an infinite number of other ways to make clay forms without throwing them. The wheel is a tool, just like a rolling pin is a tool, except that it has, for a number of reasons, become the favorite tool by choice of a great number of people who enjoy working with clay.

The popularity of this 4000 year old method of shaping clay is anything but unusual. Beyond the fact that it is a fast and efficiently productive way to make symmetrically round objects, it has a spiritual presence. Whether people identify it with a history that reveals primal truths or see it as a mysterious balancing force holding previous cultures in place as they make their present ones possible is a matter for human imagining. Perhaps there is another kind of linkage present, one that arises from an inner place alive with passion. A place that touches somewhere extraordinarily close to the core of who we are.

Peter Voulkos, America's most preeminent ceramic artist and a gifted master with the potter's wheel, adeptly throwing a large plate with the aid of a wooden rib.

Maybe it's not extraordinary for everyone, but for some working with the wheel is a connection to a primary creative life source and as such helps explain how people everywhere, like the attraction of children to Walt Disney's Magic Kingdom, can easily become engrossed in watching an accomplished thrower work on the wheel. After all, throwing is an incredible display of humble innocence filled with a measure of self-confidence, self-control and self-knowledge.

A PSYCHOLOGY OF THROWING

Throwing on the potters wheel is not easy. It may look easy when the person at the wheel is skilled, but if you are just starting out your initial efforts may prove to be frustrating, if not humiliating. Eventually, however, you will learn to throw . . . everybody does.

A good teacher, of course, is indispensable. With proper instruction, less wheel time will get wasted and fewer harmful habits acquired. And, as with learning anything, you learn best that which you really want to learn.

Paths to knowledge are also pathways to personal growth. In the beginning, throwing is a bumpy technical path covered with anxiety. Once the physical skills are committed to memory and the anxieties left behind, the process smoothes out. Your attention can then be given to the aesthetic development of form and your path is free to become a spiritual one.

As a thrower you mature to the extent that you integrate your technical knowledge with your inner, spiritual self. If this exchange does not occur your pots will be inconsequential. Stuart Shulman knew that the potter's spirit, like the clay, was a part of every pot when he said, "A pot made without soul is just some clay around a hole." He understood the value of unity through integration and the meaning of its unfolding connection to wholeness.

Without unification it's not just the forms that suffer. More importantly, the human spirit is left restless and in a state of unfullfillment. It's not enough to simply be aware of the need for harmonious development—you need to make it happen. Just like you might need to exercise every day to feel and to stay healthy. To connect with the potters wheel you may have to undergo some personal changes. You may have to become less resistant. Transformation is a yielding process. Clay finds its center on the wheel and grows into form only when it is flexible; it's evolution could not occur if it were hard and unyielding.

People, like social institutions, evolve and change when they no longer are able to achieve what they once did or meet their current needs. The process might be subtle or it might encompass a broader area and be quite dramatic. It could involve a simple change of perception or it may entail a radical restructuring of a compromising living situation that stands between one's being and one's becoming.

Byron Temple's, Bamboo+2, lidded stoneware jar unmistakably exemplifies the spirit of its maker while serving as a vivid expression of how one's spiritual state can shape the clay, 4 1/2" × 4 1/2". It should come as no surprise that ceramic form, if anything, is a display of spirit. Our spirit, our clay spirit, is not only reflected in our pottery—it directs it, and, as with all great works of clay, outshines and outranks technical talents.

If jobs, relationships, or any other of your environment's circumstance tamper with your identity or sensibilities they need to be examined, as all of life's experiences are interconnected and direct our personal reality, including how we relate to clay. If our life is such that we can relate to its various aspects out of love, desire, commitment, excitement or what have you, then that is what is going to be given back to us. It will show up in our spiritual state as a self-fulfilling signal of who we are. How we perceive ourselves is important, psychologically, to how we perform on the wheel. Believe it—we grow and glow with self-affirming perceptions.

Initially, the learning aspect of throwing is so heavily technical that it may frustrate one's spiritual need for expression. Each person has a different apprenticeship period to live through when it comes to acquiring throwing skills. If psychologically there are identification problems with some aspect of this process a person is forced to return and to confront it time and again until it is worked through. For various reasons certain individuals find such challenges difficult to face. Many years ago I had a college student ask for a withdrawal near the end of the semester fearing that he would harm his grade point average as a science major by receiving a low mark, based upon his disappointing efforts at learning throwing. It often happens in ceramics, that students come closer to the core of their identity than they might want or are prepared to. How? Work, in general, is central to our well being because it objectifies. It allows us to come out of self and be in the world. For this student, his work was not up to his personal standards and he was suffering from a wound to the heart of his identity. Work in clay, because it penetrates the imagination so deeply, allows us to value ourselves in the world. Likewise, if one feels good about their work they are going to feel good about themselves. In this sense ceramics is a crafting of self and the pots a reflection of that self in the world.

Brian McGrath's thrown and altered raku bowl exerts a strong spiritual presence. While the indelible indentations complement the smoothly ribbed surface, they also speak of personal explorations of the senses, 10" × 12 1/2".

The place of work in life is as significant as the choice of work in life. In this respect, the student was also struggling with a conflict between a former commitment to a career in science and a new love for clay. The struggle was a painful one.

When the semester ended his thrown pots were no larger than door knobs. Two weeks later, when the next term started he was back, only now he was throwing forms 10 inches tall. Without touching clay in the interim he was able, psychologically, to move from a place of caring about what he was going to be in life to a place of caring about what he wanted his life to be. Creativity, like love, is a moving force and through our involvement with clay we gain new insights about ourselves, our potential and our options. When the boundaries of self knowledge are expanded, especially

Trish Bode creates tall pots by joining two separately thrown forms.

through encounters alive with love and spirituality, transformations of a truly significant nature are possible. Fortunately for this student, he was able to recognize the suffering that results when people remain estranged from the truth of their own humanness. By courageously taking responsibility for his spiritual well being he trusted in his newly found potential and, you've guessed it, he became a professional potter. Two years later, on a Thursday I'll never forget, he made 500 cups on the wheel. Today he's still throwing, but only mornings and only for ten months out of the year. His pottery sales are in the six figures annually and as to his happiness, well, you've guessed that one right too.

Another student, equally as inspired with feelings and motivation for learning how to throw, had a harder time and consequently took a much longer time finding her way. Three semesters of faithful work on the wheel passed before she gave herself permission to disentangle a path to wholeness and genuinely throw a pot. As a teacher, I've literally been with thousands of students as they learned throwing. When this particular student finally brought it all together her thrown forms were hauntingly beautiful, in total response, as a ceramic print-out, to profound changes in her personal life.

The subtle point being made here, as you approach learning on the potters wheel, is that your starting point may be off the wheel.

To affect movement between a physical material and a nonphysical perception, the spiritual powers of each need to touch or live each in the other. Such companioning is not throwing, it is loving throwing. Loving the wonderful gifts, the exciting opportunities for personal evolution. When, at last, we invite awareness and expression to become as one, we not only become the creators of our pottery, we create ourselves.

So, if you're just starting out, with grandiose expectations for duplicating a memorable pot seen, perhaps, in a prestigious gallery on your last visit to Taos, New Mexico and your clay continues to obey the laws of gravity, don't despair.

Don't flee the studio . . . some do.

Don't leave home, family or friends . . . you may need them.

Sure, it's tough. It was tough when you first learned to ride a two-wheeler or play that squeaky clarinet. Even learning to tie your own shoe laces may have been arduous but you eventually did. History is full of men, women and children who have bravely learned to throw on the potters wheel. Each had to start somewhere, and they did it. Now it's your turn.

I could attempt to interject a little humor, just now, to keep you from being too grown-up and from taking this whole throwing thing too seriously, by letting my artistic ego say that you're lucky—you have this book. But I won't. Nah. Won't need to. You'll do fine on your own. Right . . . ?

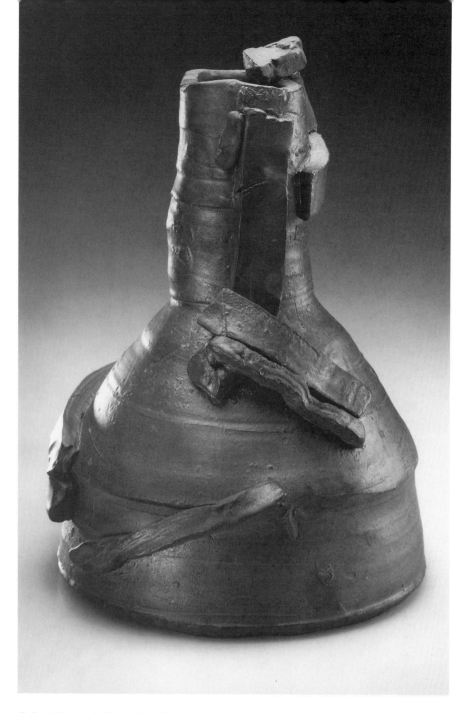

Robert Turner's Form 93-10, is forthright and unrestrained in its use of clay. The playful additions and freely ribbed surface, undauntedly tactile and bold, make for a ruggedly vigorous and hearty statement. Sandblasted stoneware 6 3/4" × 14".

THE WHEEL

For throwing pots the wheel is a necessity not a luxury. A luxury, and a genuinely helpful one at that, would be a professionally earnest video tape on throwing. But a good wheel, the right wheel, is something to be appreciated. Each wheel is unique in how it feels and responds to the user. Certain ones will immediately be comfortable to work at, others will seem difficult to relate to or take time to become acquainted with. If it is not operated from a standing position, frequently, an attached seat or bench can be adjusted to fit the thrower. However, many contemporary wheels are sold without seating, requiring individuals to provide their own. If a stool is used, one needs to be chosen that is not too tall or awkward to sit at: neck, shoulder and back strain, from leaning forward for long periods of time, can be reduced if the natural seating posture isn't overly distorted.

Today's pottery wheels are generally operated electrically or by kicking with the foot. Some are equipped to be used either way. Earlier wheels were often operated by assistants in a variety of unusual and farfetched ways. Shoji Hamada, one of Japan's former living national treasures, used to operate his wheel by hand with a short stick while seated, ankles

Robert Turner in his Alfred, New York studio with works in progress.

crossed, on a platform level with the top surface of a large wooden throwing head. When the rotation of the wheel slowed the stick was inserted into a hole near the periphery of the rotating head and made to spin faster.

Kick Wheels

Kick wheels are usually operated from a sitting position by using either one or both legs to put a large flywheel, weighing 90 to 115 pounds, in motion. The circular flywheel is rotated by kicks from the sole of the shoe. Movement from the entire body is required to make the kick and to transfer the energy necessary to both initiate and maintain the rotation of the wheel. To prevent this unwanted body motion from being transmitted directly to the work, the hands should not touch the clay until the kicking is finished and the feet are firmly supported by the frame of the wheel. Kicking near the shaft, and not on the rim, saves both time and energy by increasing the transmission ratio of force to axle torque. In the beginning a great deal of torque is required to bring a wheel up to centering speed. Once in motion, the wheel is frequently given one or two short kicks to maintain or set a desired speed; it should not, however, be allowed to stop or slow down much between kicks.

Another type of kick wheel is the single-foot treadle wheel or, as it is sometimes called, the English "crankshaft" wheel. Although not as common today as it once was, this European design was favored by the late British potter Bernard Leach, who, like Hamada and Voulkos, is a legend in the world history of clay. Depending on the design, these wheels can be operated from either a sitting or standing position. The short-lasting momentum of the relatively small 60 pound flywheel, coupled with its limited speed, required a continuous and rhythmic kicking of the treadle during the entire throwing process, a characteristic many of today's potters find unappealing.

Electric Wheels

The simplest application of the electric motor as a power source for pottery wheels is in the form of a single speed motor, with a small yet thick rubber tire on its shaft. The motor, mounted on a hinged bracket and attached to the frame of a traditional kick wheel, is pressed with the foot until the rubber tire makes contact with the rim of the flywheel. When the desired speed of rotation is achieved, the foot is removed and the motor lifts away.

A more sophisticated and efficient application of electrical power is in the form of the variable speed motor. Today's self contained and commercially manufactured wheels use such motors in combination with a number of hidden cone, belt and pulley drive systems to quickly and easily modify

Barbara Brown throwing the first of a series of lids. As technical proficiencies increase corresponding forms can be thrown in a relatively short amount of time.

or consistently maintain the rotation speed of the wheel head allowing for a wide range of speeds while still providing an impressive amount of torque.

Electric wheels are very popular with beginning students as well as the professional potter. They may not provide the same sensory feelings of control associated with working on the kick wheel but they do make throwing easier. Through the simple use of a hand lever or foot pedal, the wheel head can smoothly and quietly be set to rotate anywhere between 0 and 200 RPM freeing the potter from the mechanics of kicking and allowing the focus of attention to be directed to the clay.

A spun-metal form attached to a flat wheel head for holding plaster throwing bats.

Bats

Bats are removable discs placed on top of the metal wheel head to allow for easy removal of finished work and for repetitive throwing. Made from a wide variety of materials, such as plaster, particle board or non porous plastics, there will not be many times when you'll not want to use them, unless, of course, you're trimming or throwing off the *hump*—making several pots from a large centered mound of clay.

The advantages of developing a bat system are many. By throwing on top of the bat rather than the wheel head you'll be able to immediately remove a wet pot without directly touching it and thereby avoid the ever-present potential of damaging or distorting its shape. This is just as true for the small simple forms as it is true for the large complicated ones—just as true for the beginner as it is for the professional. If you don't use a bat, you'll unconsciously begin to make heavy pots with thick bottoms to survive the lift-off; a throwing habit that contradicts other wheel skills. You'll also be less inclined to refine skills or expand the scale of work if you're overly concerned with successfully taking it off of the wheel. One of the advantages that I especially like about this safeguard system is that it allows me to bring a stiffened pot back to the wheel, re-center it and stretch the wall into a new and thinner form without a fear of it collapsing.

There are several ways of attaching bats. Many wheels come with two holes pre-drilled, 10 inches apart, for receiving bat pins. Bats can be commercially purchased to fit them, or two holes, 10 inches on center, can be drilled in those you make yourself. I use a system in which an aluminum dish-like shape, spun by a professional metalsmith, and screwed to my wheel head, holds pre-cast plaster bats made in mold. The sides of the bat, like the sides of the bat ring, are tapered slightly and make for a perfectly centered friction fit. A temporary system can be made from a thick, flat disc of soft clay thrown directly on the wheel head. By adding grooves or by creating a slight depression at the center it can be dampened with water, and a bat stuck to it. Prior to adhering the bat with a quick downward rap with a fist it should be centered on the clay. The bat is removed by breaking the suction with a wood modeling tool. And by reshaping the disc the clay pad can be used over and over again. One gentle reminder: clay sticks to every thing but plaster. If you're throwing on top of a non-plaster surface always pass a cut-off wire under your pot while the wheel is slowly turned. This will separate the pot from the bat and prevent the bottom from cracking.

Using a tightly held cut-off wire to separate the bottom of a slowly turning pot from the bat it was thrown on. With plaster bats the drying clay freely separates on its own and this procedure is seldom necessary unless the same bat is needed to make another pot. With non-plaster bats a wire must be passed beneath the base of the pot to prevent it from cracking due to the shrinkage that occurs during drying.

The virtues of centeredness can just as easily shape the person as they can the pot.

CENTERING

Centering is a coming together. According to Tom Rauschke, "Centering is a bringing of order to chaos." It is a state of yielding containment. And, as a place of achieved union, it becomes a quality of stillness in motion. Throwing is center oriented. The transformations that are possible with clay as it maintains its center has a direct counterpart in the life of the potter. The center is the source, the fountain of potency, the seed of growth. From it all forms flow and evolve.

In throwing we center the clay by centering ourselves. And, ironic as it my seem, there will be times when the clay centers us as it finds its own center. Both spin in relation to the other like lovers, both becoming one in their intimacies of being. Before any marriage of true substance can exist, before you center the clay, take time to find your own center . . . everything else will then come together.

To physically prepare the clay for centering, throw a wedged ball or cone of soft clay down on the center of the dry wheel head with a great amount of force thereby compacting and flatting the base of the clay and avoiding future cracking. If the clay lands slightly off of center, quickly pat it in place with the open palm of both hands, centering as much of it as is possible. The rhythmic movement of the clapping will begin to give you a sense of the clay's center and posture it for easier centering once the wheel is in motion.

If you are right-handed, set your wheel turning so that it rotates in a counter-clockwise direction at a fairly high speed (the instructional text and photos found in this chapter describe a throwing technique used by a right-handed person working on an electric wheel) and if you are left-handed, and somewhat ambidextrous, you still might want to throw as if you were right-handed. Many people cheerfully do. Right-handed potters work the right side of the clay. The inside wall of the pot is shaped by the fingers of the left hand, while the outer wall is controlled by the fingers of the right hand. Spinning in a counter-clockwise direction, the clay enters the hand near the center of the palm and exits at the tips of the fingers, allowing for an impact free greeting and a smooth separation. Were the hands to be placed on the left side of the pot, as it rotated counter-clockwise, the clay would hang-up on the sharp tips of the fingers as it passed.

The image of centrifugal force is useful here. Clay cannot easily be centered on a slowly turning wheel. The wheel needs to be turning rapidly to generate enough centrifugal force to throw the clay outwards. By working with and against this force you are able to center the clay and control its shape.

With the clay rapidly turning and your feet securely planted on the floor, sponge a very small amount of water onto the clay to act as a lubricant for the hands. If the spinning clay looks shiny it's properly lubricated. Avoid using too much water at any one time. It weakens the clay and shortens its throwing life. Besides, the excess will only be unduly thrown off onto your legs if you're not using a splash pan. Brace your forearms against your ribs or on top of your legs and, with wet hands, squeeze the clay from both sides, just above the wheel head, and move them upwards without stopping until they meet at the top. The fingers, held tautly together, will be doing most of the work and can be strengthened by keeping the wrists straight and in line with the forearms. Re-wet the clay and press down from the top with the palm of the right hand and in and up with the heel of the left palm. If the left forearm or elbow is supported by the left leg, be sure to use the strength of that leg to athletically push the palm sideways into the clay. After the hands meet, hold them steady for several revolutions of the clay to feel for centeredness and then release slowly. If the hands are removed suddenly the clay will react by bolting off of center.

In the first phase of the centering movement both hands move "in" and "upward", roughly preparing the clay for centering by mounding it up and in line with the axis of the wheel head.

In the second phase of the centering movement one hand moves "in" and one "downward" to precisely bring the clay to true center. A strong inward force from the hand on the side of the mound is critical in directing the clay to the middle of the wheel head. Use the leg supporting the left arm for additional strength.

The first part of this two-part movement raises the clay up, strengthening its core by bringing it into equilibrium with the central torque of the wheel. The second movement is what actually tames the clay and brings it on center. This compression phase is a power movement requiring firmness and is the only time that you may need to muscle the clay. The downward pressure is actually delivered from the right shoulder, at times requiring the right elbow to be moved up and away from the body. The force that actually centers the clay, however, comes from the left side and is applied by the left hand. To obtain additional strength for the left hand it may become necessary to place the left elbow either into the hip or the side of the stomach and to use all of one's body weight to press into the clay. Both movements can be performed as a single maneuver and, if the clay doesn't need additional lubrication, may be repeated until you're satisfied with the outcome. When you no longer see or feel unevenness, the clay is centered.

OPENING

For the left hand to be inside the pot, and be able to do its work, the centered mound of clay needs to be opened. With the wheel spinning at a slightly slower speed and the mound lubricated with water, hold the right thumb just above the center of the clay and place the fingers from the same hand on the right side of the mound for guidance. Keeping the forearm securely braced on the body, place the edge of the palm from the left hand firmly on top of the right hand. With the fingers riding on the side of the mound, and indicating to the thumb where the exact center is, press the tip of the thumb into the clay. The penetration should be quick and go straight down. If the mound is small, the thumb should stop about 3/8 inch above the bat. If the mound is large, remove the thumb, after inserting it as deeply as possible, and press the tightly cupped fingers of the left hand down the remaining distance. They, too, should come to a stop just 3/8 inch above the bat. With the wheel stopped, the thickness of the base can be checked at any time with the needle tool. Greater stability can always be achieved when the hands are in contact with each other and working together, which is why the hand entering the clay should be assisted and supported on top by the other hand.

Supported by the left hand push the right thumb straight down into the exact center of the clay mound. Continue the downward movement until a base 3/8" above the bat is reached or, after forming a partial hole, remove the thumb and complete the opening with the middle fingers of the left hand.

If the mound of clay is too large for the thumb to reach the floor of the pot remove the thumb and use the fingers of the left hand to go down the rest of the way.

Once the proper depth is achieved, the clay is opened and the floor is formed by pulling the thumb or the fingers outward and away from the center of the wheel. If the mound is small and the thumb is used, this movement will be directly to the right. This could also be done by pulling the thumb either towards you or by pushing it away from you. If the fingers of the left hand are used to widen an opening for a large piece of clay the operation is done near the left side or by pulling the fingers directly towards the stomach with the base of the palm held down (riding the clay just above the bat) to envelope the rim and upper wall.

If the surface of the clay doesn't become dry, and you don't run out of lubrication, the opening may be completed in one continuous motion rather than two stages. To prevent any cracks from occurring in the floor later, when the clay dries or is fired, you should go back over the floor with either your fingers or with a wooden throwing rib to compress the clay. By compacting the clay in this manner, you not only release spiral stress or stretch strains that may have developed, but you clean up and level the floor as well. If stretch cracks appear on the upper rim of the clay as you open with one thumb, adjust your hand position so that the fleshy part between the thumb and forefinger can apply enough downward pressure to remove any rim-splitting fractures and keep the lip together.

With overlapping hands (base of the palms bent down), Steven Hill completely covers the rim and upper wall of the clay as he widens the opening.

Pull fingers away from center to widen the opening . . . by gradually moving the base of the palm downward, to just above the bat, the rim can be covered and compressed to prevent it from cracking as it is stretched and expanded. Also, for additional support, the right hand can be placed on top of the left hand.

A wooden throwing rib can be used to form clean/neat corner between the wall and the floor of the pot.

MAKING THE CYLINDER

If there is a secret to throwing, it's in knowing that all shapes originate from a cylindrical form. Wider pots are made from wider cylinders, taller forms from tall cylinders and so on and so on. With very few exceptions this is true. By first making a cylinder, you create a thin wall of clay that can later be shifted into any number of shapes. This wall of clay supports itself during the forming and thinning stages by remaining upright and, as a result, its posture is secure and in little danger of collapsing. If, on the other hand, you were to bypass this stage and, on your first pull, make a non-cylindrical form by severely extending the clay to a non-vertical position, it would be extremely thick and in need of thinning. In the following attempts at making the walls thinner the clay, because it is hanging out with little foundational support, could easily fall or cave-in on itself. By making the cylinder first you are, like the handbuilder who rolls-out a slab of clay, creating building material to work with. The cylinder or the slab of clay is not unlike the lumber or plywood that the carpenter needs to build with. In this sense the potter, working on the wheel, is a shape shifter: capable of converting a cylinder into an infinite number of shapes.

Use a sponge to gently lubricate the outside and inside walls of the clay wall.

Pulling Up The Wall

Gently squeeze your sponge, as it rides the rim of the rotating clay, to release a thin trickle of water down the inside wall. The outside wall could be lubricated in the same manner, however, I prefer to softly ride the sponge up and down this surface, delicately bathing the clay as it passes, all of the while making sure that I don't wet it to the point where water is flying off. Some potters, to avoid fishing in the water bucket for their sponge, keep it clutched in the palm of their right hand while using their fingers to throw with. Others position it between the tips of their fingers and the clay wall while throwing. If you choose the latter approach, I hope that it's just not to forego a little lighthearted nail trimming.

To raise the wall, begin by locating both hands above the rim (to the right side of center) either with the thumb-part of the palms touching or with the left thumb resting on top of the right thumb for support. Hold the fingers in a cupped position, not straight, and place the fingertips from each hand together. They should feel relaxed yet ready to engage the clay.

For support in pulling up the wall both thumbs should touch or be crossed.

With the wheel turning slower than it was during the centering process, separate the fingertips (while keeping the thumbs crossed) just enough to allow the clay wall to pass between them. Place the fingertips of the left hand at the base of the inside wall and the fingertips of the right hand directly opposite them on the outside wall. Only the tips of the fingers should touch the clay during the lifting process. This way the clay remains lubricated for a longer period of time. Also, it responds better if a single point of pressure is applied. If, however, the inside portion of your fingers (which is a much larger area of skin than the tips of the fingers) were to ride on both the inside and outside wall, they would quickly squeegee off water, begin to drag on the surface and eventually twist the clay off of center.

Once the fingers are in position at the base, apply pressure to the clay with the tips of the middle fingers and bring both hands upwards. By pulling upward at a speed slightly slower to that of the wheel's, you raise the clay by forcing it to pass through the space that separates the fingers;

Firmly but gently press into the base with the fingertips and pull slowly upward.

resulting in a spiraling trail of throwing marks on the wall as your finger-tips pass. If you need to slow the wheel down at any time, you will also want to slow down your rate of movement up the wall so that your finger-tips (which are always held together) are able to continuously ride the same spiral roadway up to the top of the pot. If, for example, the hands were to travel faster than the wheel, the fingertips would jump out of these finger grooves and have a harder time maintaining wall uniformity and centeredness.

If air bubbles appear, stop the wheel and use a needle tool to pierce each one.

Remember, the only form that you are trying to make now is the cylinder. To keep the centrifugal force of the wheel head from throwing the clay outward, greater pressure is needed on the outer wall.

To make the cylinder taller, start at the base, create a slight undercut at the bottom of the inside wall with the fingertips and pull upwards again. The thrill of watching the height of the clay move up and up may safely be described as spiritually liberating. These are charged moments of wonder that, no matter how many pots you may have made previously, are always met with wonderment.

Most of the pressure comes from the outside fingers as they pull the clay upward.

Another way to raise the wall is to indent the outside base of the clay with the middle three fingertips of the right hand. And, with the same three fingertips of the left hand, located opposite and slightly above, pull the hands upwards as well as inwards with a gentle yet even pressure. As they advance, a visible wave of clay is pushed before them, much like a wave of water is pushed ahead of a moving barge, increasing the height of the wall and decreasing its thickness. In the making of a cylinder the left hand is more of a restraining force. Later, when clay is pushed outwards during the shaping process, the situation often reverses and the right hand provides resistance.

The pressure exerted on the clay is greatest near the bottom and gradually tapers off as the top is reached. The completion of each pull should leave any one section of the wall thinner than the wall beneath it and thicker than the wall above it. If, for example, the lower half of a cylinder wall where thinner than its upper half it could easily twist or collapse under the weight. Also, when roughing out the cylinder it's always important to leave extra clay at the rim to allow for future rim design options. After each upward pull the rim can be compressed and thickened slightly. In doing so, not only is extra clay obtained for rim formation but the form is further stabilized and more capable of counteracting the centrifugal force of the wheel.

Slowly and gently remove the fingers from the clay rim at the end of a pull.

To prevent weakening the clay it's helpful to complete the cylinder in as few pulls as possible: 4 or 5 would not be unreasonable. If the emerging cylinder begins to flare-out near the top or become too wide, either from a fast wheel or not enough outside hand pressure, it may be straightened by collaring. At times referred to as coddling, necking or choking, collaring is a restraining process that forces the diameter of the form to become smaller. Properly executed, it can also be used to increase the height of a form or bring it back to centered roundness. Before collaring, the clay must first be well lubricated and spinning faster than it was during your last pull. To collar the cylinder, spread the thumbs and forefingers wide and, with arms securely supported, encircle the base of the clay with both hands, squeeze gently and lift upwards. At first you might be timid and not see much movement but soon you'll gather confidence and achieve remarkable results. It's generally a good idea to follow up each collaring with a two sided pull to alleviate any wrinkling that may have occurred on the inner wall as it was being compressed.

If the cylinder becomes too wide it can be narrowed by collaring in the clay and lifting up.

SHAPING THE CONTOUR

With the clay in the shape of a simple cylinder it is now ready to receive its contour. A contour that will be resolved and set in 1 to 3 pulls.

The shaping phase happens very quickly. Yet, it is this phase of the throwing process that will stir your passions and challenge your imagination for the rest of your life as a ceramist. Once the technical skills of throwing are learned they are never forgotten. In time they become deeply rooted in our understanding and less of a conscious concern so that we can distance ourselves from them and live, with perception and response, in the contours of our forms. It's not just techniques or hands that shape clay, it's the total person. The power of your forms and the presence of their contours comes from you living in harmony with the truth of your being with clay. The technician in you may have made the cylinder but if your final form is to possess beauty and articulate meaning it will be the artist in you that gives it shape.

Grasping the nature of form is a difficult undertaking. It involves a different kind of reasoning that is not always logical. It may relate to quirks of circumstance or personality as much as it may relate to a level of understanding or experience. To rationalize the way contour functions in the overall presence of a form is not an effective way to approach its potency. The nuances of form are extremely subtle and varied. If the pot is the face of the potter, it becomes more useful to consider all of those undertones that motivate our innermost self. By examining the shaping phase of throwing as a reflection of the self we come closer to the exotic mysteries and the unknown secrets that bring spiritual vision into tangible form. Given the happenstance of this connection, our quest for form is a quest for self . . . for our creative self.

We have all experienced the silence of dull, generalized forms. But why were they dozing and what caused them to remain divorced from this high-spirited and powerfully captivating process? Could it simply be that wherever there is no risk, no extra effort, no sense of marvel at what the self is capable of that there is no astonishment?

The actual reshaping of the cylinder is a dance between the tips of the fingers. Their choreography is a masterful play between alternating degrees of pressure and astute positioning. The wall moves outward when the inside fingers exert more pressure than those on the outside and the wall moves inward when finger pressure from the outside is greater. To stimulate more of a flowing curve to the expanding wall, simply shift the inside fingers to a position slightly above those outside. To tighten-up the shape and bring the wall inward, position the outer fingertips above those on the inside and exert more pressure from the outside as you pull up. As the wall is already thin, owing to the thinness of the cylinder, the clay will quickly and easily respond to your movements. When shaping the clay, you'll still need to pull up, however, and not just move up the wall, pressing in or pressing out as you go, if you want the contour to have a strength and energy to it. By simultaneously pulling up and pressing into the wall you will not only make it thinner but you'll have a more sensitive touch and voluntary feel for directing its profile. The tips of the fingers are some of the most sensitive parts of our body. Safecrackers even sandpapered their's for increased receptivity. It's amazing that these small areas can harbor so much feeling and control; that as pin points of pressure they can ultimately influence the shape of all our pots. Kissing, in a rather round about way, has a related consequence. The lips, another small area of touch, can affect a nonproportional range of sensations and complex results in the act of a kiss.

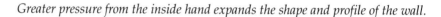

Greater pressure from the inside hand expands the shape and profile of the wall.

Air pockets or bubbles may appear as bumps on the surface of the clay if it wasn't properly wedged. In the initial stages of forming the cylinder these are usually broken, at times audibly, and plowed under by the fingertips during throwing. If any remain or appear during the shaping stage they will hassle the fingertips with each turn of the pot and may cause it to

Greater pressure from the outside fingers shape the shoulder and a narrow neck.

eventually go off center. Contrary to what many believe, air bubbles do not cause that area of the pot to blow-up in the kiln. Moisture causes clay to explode. If clay contains an air pocket, and has been thoroughly dried prior to firing, that air pocket will not burst. On the other hand, were it still damp, the resulting moisture would have expanded to steam inside of the air pocket and, under a great amount of pressure, blow it apart. To remove one of these unsightly tumors from the clay's surface puncture it several times with the needle tool, run your finger back and forth over it to force out any remaining air and smooth the area over with either your fingers, a sponge or by ribbing while the wheel is turning.

A flexible metal rib can be used to make a clean, unimpaired surface as well as a smooth flowing contour with a simple yet powerful presence.

The finger marks made in the clay during throwing often provide a natural and exciting texture to the outer surface of wheel forms and are often left in place. Should you wish to remove them or, more importantly, further refine the final contour of your pot, you can easily do so with a rib. Holding a sponge in your left hand and a flexible metal rib firmly between the thumb and the four fingers of your right hand, bring both hands up the wall, starting at the base, with the metal rib bent to conform to the outer profile of the pot and directly opposite the sponge riding the inside profile. As the rib travels upward, supported by the sponge from the inside hand, it scrapes away the throwing marks, leaving the surface clean and the contour flowing harmoniously from top to bottom. The ribbing process may have to be repeated more than once or be followed by a pass with a rubber rib before the final profile is made smooth and flawless.

Shaping the neck with the aid of a flexible metal rib.

Ken Baskin using the curved edge of a rib to refine the inside contour of his bowl.

Steve Hill using the straight edge of a large wood rib to alter the outside contour.

Sean Najjar using a torch to speed-dry his pot as it rotates on the potter's wheel. When the shoulder area of the clay stiffens a second, pre-thrown, form will be added to complete the top. Electric heat guns are also remarkably useful (standard equipment in some studios) for a quick and serious blow-dry of wet, soft clay. They really make sense when everything is about to collapse or when you're feeling too buoyant to wait for time.

During the shaping process it is important to continuously manage the speed of the wheel. The clay wall is relatively thin at this time and, as a result, very responsive to centrifugal motion. By keeping the wheel rotating at a progressively slower speed, you should be able to maintain control of the clay through this critical juncture and avoid any unwanted distortion. For shapes with a wide flare to them you may even use the speed of the wheel to your advantage.

If the rim becomes uneven during this process it may be cut level with a needle tool. With the clay spinning between the thumb and forefinger of the left hand, pivot the needle on the edge of the thumb nail and cut through the wall of clay, at least 3/8 of an inch below the top edge, until the inner finger is touched. Lift quickly! After removing the uneven clay smooth the lip with a sponge, piece of chammy or your fingers.

Removing an uneven rim with a needle tool.

SHAPING THE RIM

The rim is probably the most important aspect of a wheel thrown form. The way a clay wall ends is a form's final and most convincing aesthetic statement. Once the foot, belly, shoulder, neck or any other contour elements are resolved, the rim is usually shaped to complement them. Although not al-

The rim is formed by pressing the angled right forefinger down on the clay that is supported on two sides between the left thumb and forefinger.

ways, there are times when the shoulder or the belly of a form may need to be redefined, or reshaped, to enhance the rim. More often than not, however, the rim is either formed from the continuation of a pull used in the overall shaping of the contour or during a separate process as a final finishing procedure.

I take rims seriously. As a result of knowing that they are often the key that unlocks the possibilities for a spirited resolution to form—that may still remain hidden in the other elements of the pot—I give the top edge of my clay extra-special attention and do so as a separate shaping process. Although there are infinite numbers of ways to form rims, especially if you leave extra clay in this area for experimentation, there are two strategies that are very universal and unarguably useful.

The first one requires that the a pot's rim be held between the tips of both forefingers and the right thumb. With the thumb riding the top edge of the clay, touching both fingers, as they ride each side of the wall, the rim is securely surrounded on three sides and can gently be turned outwards or inwards to a graceful ending.

The second strategy is even easier to master and very useful when the clay ends up being too thin to bend safely. With the top edge of the clay revolving between the forefinger and thumb of the left hand, press down on the top of the clay with the extended forefinger of the right hand. The downward pressure from this finger, as it receives support from the other two, immediately thickens and defines the rim. By angling the extended finger upwards, the dimension of a bevel is added to the interest of this rim.

Influential rims (rims worthy to be called rims) do not compete with the other integral parts of a pot's form, they originate from them, becoming an uncompromising presence in dialogue with each and every aspect of its existence. As such, you'll always be confronted with the crucial decision of scaling the rim to the body of the form. All too often rims are made too small. They may appear to fit, close-up, but from ten feet away they can fade almost as if they were swept up by an overbearing body contour. In the same way that rims shouldn't be underestimated they shouldn't be under built either. To further influence the quality of a rim many potters use a chammy, a small piece of supple leather, to round and soften any harshness of the edge. The wet chammy can be placed between the fingers and the clay to aid in the forming process or it can be draped over the completed rim to smooth its edge. If you already have the good fortune to intuitively understand the visual and psychological weight carried by rims, you'll have one less intangible endeavor to work through in the world of clay form.

STEPS FOR THROWING POTTERY ON THE WHEEL

1. Throw wedged clay down on center of plaster bat.

2. Rapidly spin wheel counter clockwise.

3. Brace arms and center clay.

4. Bore hole to a depth of 3/8″ above plaster bat.

5. Check bottom thickness with a needle tool.

6. Widen hole.

7. Level and smooth bottom of hole.

8. Undercut inside bottom of wall with fingers.

9. Pull right side of wall up and in with tips of fingers.

10. Recenter and thicken rim by pressing down.

11. Repeat pulling the wall up into a cylinder 4-8 times.

12. Recenter and thicken rim as needed.

13. Shape the cylinder with 1-3 pulls.

14. Level top with fingers or needle tool.

15. Finish rim.

16. Remove inside water with a sponge.

17. Trim bottom with wood knife.

18. Remove bat from wheel head.

19. Invert and trim when leather-hard.

20. Sign name on bottom or side with a pencil.

A basic step-by-step outline to be used as a quick and sequential reference guide for the traditional throwing of pottery on the wheel.

An inside view of a Ken Turner pot showing the distinctive spiral finger marks on the bottom of a thrown and altered raku form, 11 1/2″ × 12″ × 6″.

This student is shaping a clay cylinder (step #13) into a bowl with the aid of wooden throwing rib. Note the use of the large sponge wedged between the tool box and spinning wheelhead to catch excess water. Sponges are useful for controlling throwing water when there is no splash pan to collect it.

TRIMMING

Trimming is the cutting away of excess clay from the base of forms made on the wheel. It is also a reliably compatible and important part of the shaping process. Trimming or turning, another frequently used term to refer to the same procedure, is done with the form centered on the potter's wheel either in an upright or (if leather-hard) in an inverted position; with or without the support of a *chuck*.

Trimming Upright

If a form is tall or large, or if its walls don't flair out too much, or if its floor is relatively thin and doesn't require a foot-rim, it's a good candidate for direct, upright trimming. While it's true that as much excess clay as possible should be removed from the base of all forms during throwing while they are upright and still on the wheel, not all forms can be completely trimmed in this manner. If a form does meet the above criteria, it can often be trimmed immediately after being thrown (cut free with a cut-off wire if it wasn't made on top of a plaster bat) and allowed to dry. The best tool for this type of trimming operation is a long, knife-like, hardwood modeling tool with a thin, pointed blade. Held near its middle, with the right hand, the same way you hold a pencil, grip the tail of the tool between the thumb and forefinger of your left hand and slowly cut into the base of the form.

The blade of the wooden knife is kept parallel to the clay wall as it begins its cut.

Keep the blade parallel to the wall and start your cut at that exact place where the contour of the form disappears into the excess clay. As the tool moves downward, push the tail out and away from the wall so that the blade follows the interior profile and cuts underneath the form. Once the wheel head or bat is touched, remove the tool.

The securely held wooden knife is pressed into the base of the clay, following the interior contour of the form, until it makes contact with the bat.

After separating the trimmings from the bat with a needle tool cut the scrap ring in half and remove with the aid if the wooden knife.

With the wheel slowly turning, insert the needle tool underneath the scrap ring of clay to separate it from the throwing surface. Cut this ring of clay in half to remove it. If the cut was not clean or the wall is still thick, make another cut or hold the blade perpendicular to the wall to scrape away a thin surface layer of clay. The blade can also be used here like a rib to shape the surface and burnish it smooth.

To accurately check the thickness of the wall, pierce it with your needle

The pointed blade of the wooden knife can be used to scrape away additional clay.

tool until the point appears inside the form. Then grip the needle where it enters the outside wall and withdraw it. The distance from the tip of the needle to the fingers equals the thickness of the wall (do not worry about leaving a needle hole in the wall, it closes-up as the clay shrinks during drying). If more clay should be removed but it is too soft to risk further trimming, set it aside until it becomes leather-hard and then trim it with a metal tool—either upright, while it is still attached to the bat, or inverted and recentered on the bat. To achieve uniform wall thickness, a couple of thumb tacks could be placed into the clay wall, from the inside and near the base, and the pot trimmed until the metal tool made contact with the points of the tacks.

Recentering

Leather-hard pots, as well as chucks, can be recentered on the wheel head in one of several ways. Some wheel heads have concentric circles inscribed on their surface that allow for accurate positioning. On unmarked heads they can be quickly drawn in with a pencil as the wheel spins. Another very common method utilizes the needle tool. After first placing the inverted pot as close to center as possible the wheel is rotated and the needle tool, firmly held with both hands, is slowly moved against it until a line-like mark is made on the off-centered bulge of clay. The distance half way between the beginning and the end of this line is the place where the form is farthest away from center. By carefully pushing the form towards the center of the wheel, it is brought closer to being centered. This process is repeated, near the base of the form, until a mark can be lightly scribed all around its circumference, indicating that it has been centered.

A needle tool is used to scribe a mark in the side of the leather-hard pot to locate the precise point where it is farthest away from the center of the wheel.

A much quicker technique for recentering inverted pots, but scary to learn, knocks the rapidly spinning pot onto center. With the edge of the right hand, palm open and facing up, a series of rapid chopping movements are rhythmically delivered to the side of the form. With practice, the rotating clay is promptly centered if briskly hit near the base within a split second after the off-centered area passes. With this technique it's generally a good idea to also support the base of the pot with one or two fingers from the left hand to prevent it from flipping.

Several rapid chops with the side of the hand can quickly bring a leather-hard pot to the center of a spinning wheel.

Steven Hill, Sectional Urn, thrown and altered stoneware. Single-fired with slips and multiple glazes, 20" × 12". The flared base and disc-like rim complement one another. Without this foot the vessel would lack visual balance and harmony.

Inverted leather-hard pots awaiting trimming.

Inverted Trimming

Trimming forms upside down is hazardous to rims. The potential for straining and cracking the rim of any pot through physical handling is great, but the stress placed on the rim of a pot by turning it upside down and trimming it is even greater. Only leather-hard forms that can carry the weight of the pot on a fairly thick portion of their rim's design, rather than an extension of a some thinner lip element, should be trimmed while being supported by their rim.

Prior to turning a pot over for trimming, carefully examine its inner profile and commit it to short-term memory. Forgetting to do this not only makes it harder to trim an outer profile that matches, it also makes it difficult to obtain a wall thickness that is uniform throughout. Once an inverted pot has been carefully centered, firmly hold it in place with pressure from the left hand and use the right hand to press three pieces of clay, spaced uniformly, around the rim securely attaching it to the wheel head.

Three equally spaced wads of clay hold the pot on center during trimming.

The outside diameter of the foot-ring is tooled with a metal trimming tool before the excess clay around the base is removed.

With one of the middle three fingers from the left hand pressing down on the center of the rotating pot to help hold it in place, extend the thumb until it rests on top of the metal loop trimming tool held in the right hand. Linked together, both hands are now in greater control of the cutting tool and the amount of pressure applied to it. The first cut made, with the wheel set at a medium speed, is on the bottom of the pot. Its location is very important as it defines the outer diameter of the foot-rim. For aesthetic reasons, this diameter should often be smaller than initially realized, so bestow this particular decision making process with special thought and feeling.

At this juncture, the rest of the tooling process is fairly elementary. Simply move the blade down the side of the pot, cutting away a layer of surplus clay as you go, until a part of the profile is reached that no longer needs trimming. Continue with additional passes of the cutting tool until the desired wall thickness and completed profile are obtained. To remove any rough looking surface texture, where tooling has disturbed the filler or grog in the clay body, go back over the area with a rib or sponge, held under the tip of your finger, to blend it in with the thrown texture on the rest of the pot's surface.

If you want to maintain a flat, rimless bottom on your pot, and it's too thick as is, trim off the excess until the floor is as thin as the walls. If you prefer a foot-rim, first make a cut inside the foot to establish its inner diameter and tool the rest away. Many potters hollow out the foot by moving from the center outwards, I like to clean this area out by working inward from the foot-rim: leaving an extruded yogurt-like spiral top at the very center. In Japan this type of foot is often called a "spiral shell".

Virginia Cash using a small loop tool to trim away clay from inside the foot-ring.

To check on the clay's thickness, periodically stop the wheel and gently press on the area just trimmed. If there is no give, press just a little harder. If there is still strong resistance, chances are that you can safely remove a little more. If you do, however, feel some flex in the wall, finish with your trimming as soon as possible. Tapping the surface with the finger is an auditory way of checking the thickness of the pot. This method is especially useful on the floor of the pot. With experience you can become super sensitive to the particular kinds of hollow sounds that your clay forms reveal about their physical condition. If, in the removal of a tooled pot from the wheel, you should find the lower portion of it to be, in fact, too heavy or thick for its size, I hope you will feel deeply compelled to retool it. This pot is now a part of your history, and should be read as a positive, and not a careless, contribution of your art.

STEPS FOR TRIMMING POTTERY ON THE WHEEL

1. Look and determine where and how much to trim away.

2. Recenter the leather-hard pot upside down on the wheel by:

    A. Drawing concentric rings on the wheel head with a pencil.

    B. Scratching marks on the rotating foot with a needle tool.

    C. Tapping the spinning pot with the side of the hand.

3. Secure the pot to the wheel head with 3 balls of stiff clay.

4. Define the outside diameter of the foot ring with a metal tool.

5. Trim away excess clay from the foot ring to the side of the pot.

6. Remove trimming texture with a flexible rib or wet sponge.

7. Define the inside diameter of the foot ring with a metal trim tool.

8. Trim away excess clay from the foot ring to the center of the pot.

9. Smooth edges of foot ring with a damp sponge.

10. Sign your name on bottom or side with a pencil.

Sequential guidelines for the traditional trimming of inverted pottery on the wheel.

After trimming is completed, carefully remove the pot with both hands by either gripping it on two sides with open palms or by slowly sliding it past the edge of the wheel head until one hand can be placed inside and the piece turned right side up. Have newspaper ready to set the pot on as soon as it is removed from the wheel. If the pot is large and heavy use several layers of newspaper, each separated by a sprinkling of sand to function as ball bearings, to dry the pot upon. It's usually safer to dry pots upright, as long as the base is sitting on a surface that allows for easy movement during drying.

The rims of large pots should be lightly covered with either a flat piece of plastic (the thin clear plastic wrap used to keep foods fresh clings well) or with an open doughnut-like ring of plastic to slow the drying movement from the top to the bottom and thereby reduce rim cracking from early and uneven shrinkage. A pot wrapped in a terry-cloth bath towel will dry slow and evenly, taking several days.

The opening cut in the center of a plastic covering allows large pots to dry slowly from the center outward rather than stressfully quick from the rim downward.

Trimming With Chucks

Chucks are hallow tube-like forms used for supporting pots during trimming. Thrown on the potter's wheel, their walls are unusually thick and open at both ends. Their outer profile is generally more concave than cylindrical and can be used in the wet, leather-hard or the bisque state. Because their main function is to keep the top of pots, especially those with thin rims and narrow tops, from touching the wheel head and being damaged, they are an invaluable asset and well worth the time it takes to make them.

Trimming Within A Chuck

Closed forms, such as bottles, are trimmed by placing them, upside down, inside of a chuck with a diameter large enough to support it somewhere around its shoulder. If a bisque fired chuck is used, first soak the bottom rim in water so that clay used to secure it to the wheel head will adhere to it. With the bottle inverted and resting on the upper rim of the chuck, level its bottom; either by eye or with the aid of a small pocket level. Next, carefully center the bottle with a needle tool and attach the chuck to the wheel with three balls of clay. Using downward pressure from a finger riding on the center of its base, hold the bottle in place and complete the tooling as you would for any other inverted form.

Trimming an inverted bottle form while supported inside of a bisque-fired chuck.

To use the bisque chuck to trim a number of pots in one sitting you might want to attach it to the wheel head in a more secure fashion by first centering a thin disc of clay, with an upturned edge, upon which to place the chuck. By pressing the upturned portion of the clay around the bottom of the centered chuck it is held fast.

If a bisque chuck is not available for trimming, one can be custom thrown and used while still wet by placing pieces of paper towels over its rim to keep the bottle from sticking to it. After the bottle is tooled and removed, the clay chuck can be reshaped to hold a different size pot for tooling or it can immediately be used to form another pot.

A safer approach to working with a newly thrown chuck is to set it aside for several hours, allowing it to become leather-hard before using it. Once used, it can be wrapped in plastic and stored for future use.

Removing a trimmed bottle from a ceramic chuck.

Trimming Over A Chuck

Open forms such as bowls and plates are trimmed on top of a chuck to prevent rims from touching the wheel head, liberating them from the destructive effects of weight and stress. For this type of chuck to be effective its upper rim should support the inverted pot halfway up its inner wall. If a pot sits too high on the chuck it induces an outward force that can strain and eventually crack the rim.

Clay chucks can quickly be thrown and promptly used to accommodate a wide variety of bowl contours and diameters. Bisque chucks may have to be outfitted with new rim tops. To create a new trimming top for an existing bisque fired chuck, first soak it in water and attach it, centered, to the wheel head. Push a ball of clay, tapered to fit the inside diameter of the chuck, down onto the top rim. Use a paddle, if necessary, to secure it and form a new clay head with a flattened top. With the wheel turning, tool the new head into a flattened cylindrical shape with a diameter roughly matching that of the pot's at a point midway between its base and rim.

Centered and leveled on top of this chuck, the pot can be trimmed, free from worry and harm, in essentially the same way pots are trimmed while held inside a chuck. Because bowls and plates generally have wider bottoms than bottles, it may be necessary to distribute the hold-down pressure from the finger by means of an inverted jar lid. The metal lid is tapped on center and rides between a finger of the left hand and the bottom of the pot. The diameter of the lid used is determined by the size of the foot area.

By trimming bowls over a supporting chuck rims do not become scratched or damaged from contact made with the wheel head and, most importantly, they avoid the risk of developing stress cracks from the torque forces of tooling.

Trimming With The Giffin Grip

The Giffin Grip is a commercially manufactured trimming and rapid recentering tool made from injection molded plastic. It is quickly attached to the wheel head and just as easily popped off for speedy removal. By rotating its top plate, three *sliders* with rubber bumpers are simultaneously moved towards the inverted pot—immediately directing it towards the center of the wheel. Once centered it is robotistically held secure within the grip of the wide rubber pads.

By reversing the three *sliders* within the tracks of the top plastic plate different lengths of metal rods, which serve as extension arms, can be inserted into support holes to accommodate a larger and taller variety of clay forms. To securely hold these forms, bumper pads are attached to the working tips of the metal rods. It is important, however, that the pot is truly leather-hard, otherwise the pressure from the bumpers will bruise or scar the clay's surface during trimming.

John Glick in the process of doing the final tooling on a plate that is being held secure by the three padded sliders of a Giffin Grip trimming attachment which has been mounted on the wheel head of a potter's wheel.

Robert Sperry preparing to add a coil of clay to the inverted base of a plate. Once attached, the coil will be thrown into the shape of a large foot ring.

THROWING TRADITIONAL FORMS

There are a few fundamental groups that most thrown forms originate from. Within each group certain techniques are common, while an infinite number of form variations are possible. It should come as no surprise that these forms can be small or they can be large and still emerge from the same basic skills. Once you start to understand how simple and interconnected these techniques are, you can compliment them with your own gifts and begin to enjoy the spirit of throwing.

Open Forms (Bowls)

Bowls are the easiest forms to make on the potter's wheel. As the most primary of ceramic forms, the bowl is made, in concert with the centrifugal forces from the revolving wheel head, by progressively pressing outward against the cylinder's interior wall. As the grouped fingertips from the left hand draw the cylinder wider, in their movement upwards, the outer wall is supported by the fingertips from the right hand. These outer fingers travel just above those on the inside; thinning and pulling the clay wall into a gently swelling curve. If these same fingers were below those inside, the curve would flare out. With each new pull upwards, the initial form of the cylinder gradually disappears, evolving into the expanding curvature of a bowl. As this curve opens, the speed of the wheel is slowed to maintain control and to keep the clay from being put at risk of collapsing.

Brian Migdal working with the centrifugal force of the wheel to gently open the clay cylinder into the form of a wide bowl.

The rim of this wide bowl is being stabilized and formed with downward pressure from the right forefinger.

As the rim widens, downward pressure from a finger is used to flatten it and to start the beginnings of a thickened lip. Not only does this prevent it from tearing apart, it also stabilizes the upper half of the bowl. The final pass of the fingers should fill out the curve and bring definition to the rim. Ribs could be used to further refine the profile and a chammy employed to turn-down and smooth-out the lip. Prior to removing the bowl from the wheel, the base is trimmed with the wooden cutting tool and the excess clay pulled away.

The throwing of a bowl is simply an extension of those techniques used in the making of a cylinder and the shaping of contours and rims. As the classic open form, it is covered here more as a matter for reviewing than for new insight. Although, I should point out, in case it goes unnoticed, that large bowls are made from cylinders with wider bottoms.

Closed Forms (Bottles)

Bottles are the most difficult forms to make on the potter's wheel. The challenge they present is that of dramatically bringing the clay wall back in on itself, after the middle of the form has been stretched wide, so that the delicate shaping of a narrow neck can be accomplished without it falling in on itself. All this from a single piece of clay. Because bottle forms undergo so many meticulous shaping processes, they should be made with stiffer clay. Harder clays are more difficult to center but they hold their shape longer and allow you to work with thinner walls.

The opening at the top of the cylinder that you are going to make the bottle from should be kept narrow. During the entire throwing process the opening should only be large enough for you to pass your hand through; if it's allowed to become any wider you may not be able to close it back in and still have enough clay left to form the neck.

Starting from the base of the cylinder, shape the lower half of the bottle by pressing outwards with the inner hand. As you come to the upper half press in more with the outside hand, taking special care to leave extra clay near the rim. Without this thicker wall of clay at the top you will not be able to throw a one-piece bottle; the neck would then need to be thrown separately and added to the stiffened body later. The lower portion of the form receives most of the attention at this time. Its contour needs to be resolved before the curve of the shoulder can be determined and the neck coddled. A great deal of aesthetic decision making takes place at this time. Because bottles, stylistically speaking, are the most celebrated carriers of contour, their overall shape is a matter never to be taken lightly as you direct its form.

Satisfied with the expressive detailing of the lower beginnings and the emerging belly of the form, direct your attention to integrating the upper curvature of the profile into one, continuously flowing, visually appealing, silhouette. As these various features fall into place, direct the curve of the wall into a vertical shape as it nears the opening at the top to form the neck. The closing-in of the upper wall area can be done with the fingertips and added pressure from the outside hand but, if achievement is lacking, the wall can be just as easily coddled inward.

Closing-in the top of a bottle form. When making bottles never let the upper one-quarter of the form become wider than is needed for your hand or a throwing stick to pass through. Also, never let this part of the wall become too thin to coddle.

Begin coddling the bottle's neck by using six points of pressure from the tips of both thumbs and forefingers and the first knuckles of the middle fingers. As it narrows, use only the four fingertips and forgo the use of the knuckles. Like the belly of the bottle, the neck, too, should have a natural and gracefully flowing curvature, and not be straight and uninteresting. Hopefully, you'll have enough clay left after coddling to make a strong statement with the rim and not have it end with a whimper. The rest of the form could possess masterful qualities but if the rim is void of a sense of resolve or detail, due to a shortage of material to work with, the final statement will be a compromise. And—surprise!—look like it.

Using the tips of the thumbs and forefingers to apply 4 points of pressure to gracefully narrow-in the neck of the bottle.

Resolve the design and final shaping of the rim while the neck is still somewhat thick and able to support the handiwork.

Bottles are more involved with form than function. If you want yours to make their mark, take time—take extra time—to reconcile all aspects of their contour. Use flexible ribs if necessary. If a shoulder is in danger of collapsing, let the clay dry for a while. . . returning later to seek completion. Don't quit them without first being genuinely satisfied at having given them your all. Finally, remain as fully aware and committed to proportion and size of both the neck and the foot as you possibly can. It helps if you can keep the diameters of each small; smaller than you might at first imagine.

As a culminating act, the neck of the bottle is carefully narrowed and shaped to become an elegant and flowing transitional element between the body and the rim.

Should your attempts at forming a bottle with a stem-like neck fall short, you'll still be in a favorable position to complete a striking form with a narrow opening.

Low Forms (Plates)

The plate, as the classic standard for all open and shallow forms, is fairly easy to throw but requires extra care during formation, drying and firing to deal with the natural stresses placed on its large, flat surface. Wider plates require larger throwing bats. Plaster bats, because they absorb moisture and aid with the drying of the base, make good throwing surfaces, especially when they're in good condition and not marked-up. On a plaster bat the base freely separates on its own, thereby avoiding the risk of being deformed from a cut-off wire passed beneath its floor.

Plates should be thrown with soft clay. Stiff clay would be an unnecessary strain to both the plate and to the potter during centering. Begin by centering the clay into a low wide shape. This is done by slowly forcing the clay down and out towards the edge of the bat with either the bottom edge of a fist made with the right hand, with the heel of the left hand or with both hands cupped tightly together. Centering is a demanding process made even more so with plates because the clay needs to be centered as a wide flat mound. To prevent the clay from stretching and tearing as its outer edge expands, surround it with the fingers or palm of the right hand and round it over near the completion of each outward movement.

The centered mound is opened by inserting the fingers of the right hand into the clay and pulling outward. These fingers should be bunched together and supported on top with the fingers of the left hand. Again, surround and support the clay from the outside as you near the edge to keep it from tearing. Repeat the outward pulling of the clay from the center until

the desired floor thickness is achieved. Do not allow the floor to become too thin (use the needle tool as a gauge for checking it). Pull the clay, accumulated at the outer edge during the opening phase, up into a wall forming a short cylinder. Go back over the floor with the straight edge of your wooden throwing rib to clean-up the surface and, most importantly, to compact the clay. Compressing the clay strengthens it and reduces cracking. If the smoothly ribbed surface lacks visual interest, sponge it down and, with the wheel turning slowly, move your finger from the wall to the center, leaving a pattern of spiral finger marks in the floor as you go.

With the bottom completed, finish the cylinder by thinning the wall and shaping the lip. Prior to bending the wall of the cylinder outwards, trim away the excess clay from the base with the wood trimming knife.

Next, the most dramatic, exuberant and blossoming movement in throwing is about to be accomplished: the transforming of the wide cylinder into a flourishing plate. With fingers and a sponge supporting the outside wall, place the curved edge of a rib against the inside wall and, with pressure from the left hand, push out and downwards. Within a few seconds an entirely new and final form is profiled.

Steven Hill, wheel-thrown and altered stoneware platter with thickly brushed slip and multiple glazes. His single-fired work is always a fresh and lively integration of human sensitivity and technical skill, 14 1/2" diameter.

To prevent this boldly extended and exceedingly cantilevered rim from collapsing, immediately stop the wheel from rotating. With the exception of some additional trimming during the leather-hard stage, the plate is finished. Before setting it aside to stiffen, you may want to go back and slowly work the needle tool or the blade of the fettling knife part way under the outer foot of the plate to help it shrink off the bat later. A rib and sponge were used to develop the wide form of the rim, but the rim could have been turned out flat with just the fingers. A rib, however, does a faster, neater job and as you become more comfortable with using ribs, you'll realize their value as a plate shaping tool.

Dry your plate slowly and carefully. Cover the rim in plastic, but not the floor. Plates need to dry from the center outward. If the rim dries first, which is what will happen naturally if left uncovered, chances more than double for it to crack or warp as it, and not the floor, shrinks. One way to speed-up the drying of the floor is to cover it with a thick layer of dry powdered clay. Plates also need to be trimmed when leather-hard. Invert them carefully to avoid straining the rim and trim over a chuck if possible. If the diameter of the plate is wide, it may need two concentric foot rings. After trimming it should, again, be dried slowly, rim side up, on several sheets of newspaper.

Ken Baskin builds adaptable shelving for his large plates from 3/4" plywwod and bricks.

Used bakery and bread carts are first-rate shelving units and studio ware carts for transporting work.

Peter Voulkos, wheel thrown stoneware plate with a freely scratched, carved and struck surface, wood-fired in Peter Callas's anagama kiln, 4 1/2" × 22".

Ken Baskin with a large plate that he is drying on several layers of newspaper separated by thin sprinklings of sand. The sand acts like ball bearings: allowing the plate stress-free movement during shrinkage.

Covered Forms (Lids)

Thrown forms can be covered with lids to protect the contents placed inside them. Lids may be thrown in one piece, with or without the need for additional trimming, or they can be thrown from two separate pieces of clay, the second piece of clay being thrown on top of a leather-hard lid to form a knob. In general, lids fall into one of three categories: those that fit onto the pot, those that fit over the pot, and those that fit inside the pot.

The flat lid is a good example of one that fits onto the pot. This simple lid requires that a small ledge be made inside the rim of the pot. When throwing the pot, leave a thicker wall of clay at the top and form a flange by pushing down the inside half of the rim with the fingernail of the left thumb. The rim is literally divided down the middle, with the inside half of the rim lower than the outside half. Using the right-angled corner of your wood throwing rib, scrape the surface of the lower, flanged rim level and

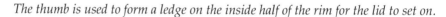

The thumb is used to form a ledge on the inside half of the rim for the lid to set on.

The corner of a wood rib is used to clean up the seat formed in the rim for the lid.

square with the wall, making a suitable seat for the lid. Chammy the upper rim round and measure its inside diameter with calipers.

Flat Lid

The flat lid is made from a ball of clay with a diameter equal to one half the size of the opening to be covered (lids larger than 5″ in diameter run the risk of slumping in the kiln). It is centered, opened flat by pushing down and out just to the right of center. The knob is shaped from the stem of clay left standing and the exact diameter is cut with a needle tool while calipers are held steady above the revolving clay. Thrown on a plaster bat, without any major surface gouges, a needle tool can be run just under the edge of the lid(letting in just enough air to aid with lift-off during shrinkage) and the lip rounded smooth with a chammy. After this little detail, the lid is finished and should be set aside to dry.

A sponge is used to push down and flatten out the clay just to the right of center.

The top of the clay left standing is partially hallowed out and given a beveled rim.

After the top of the knob is completed the stem is shaped with the fingertips.

Calipers are held just above the clay as a needle tool cuts out the lid's diameter.

Cap Lid

The cap lid is one that fits over the rim of the pot. The pot itself need only have a tall, straight-sided rim. No special tooling is necessary, as the lid, in the shape of a straight-sided bowl, fits over and around the outer wall of the rim—a captivating fit. This type of lid is thrown upside down as a shallow bowl form, with an inside diameter slightly larger than the outer diameter of the pot's rim. When leather-hard, it is inverted and neatly trimmed, either on the wheel head or on top of the centered pot. If the diameter of the lid is small enough to be held by an open hand, a knob is not necessary. If it is too wide to easily grip, its center is scored, slipped and a small ball of clay is pressed on and thrown, with as little water as possible, into the shape of a knob.

The cap lid on this small covered jar by John Glick was thrown to fit over a flanged rim, making the sides of both the jar and lid part of a continuous profile.

Flange Lid

The flange lid is one that partially drops down inside the pot. Although they can be made right side up in one piece without trimming, they are frequently thrown upside down as a shallow bowl with a very tall, vertical rim. After being inverted and trimmed, a knob is usually added. Because these types of lids are used most frequently on teapots, knobs not only look good, they function beautifully.

When used on tea pots what was once a tall, misleading, rim on a small bowl becomes a long flange that keeps the lid from falling off whenever tea is poured. The depth of this flange should, at the very least, equal half the diameter of the rim. Flanges for lids not used on teapots do not have to be made as long.

The long flange of lids used on teapots helps in preventing them from falling off whenever the pot is tipped for pouring.

Lids

Flat lids are thrown right-side-up on a bat as a single piece. To prevent sagging they should not be larger than 5" in diameter.

Arched lids are used to span diameters larger than 5". Thrown upside down like a plate the knob is thrown from a ball of clay added to the lid just after trimming the finished curve of the arch.

Cap lids are thrown and trimmed like a small flat-bottomed bowl. The diameter of these lids is usually small enough to grasp with an open hand making knobs unnecessary.

Domed lids are thrown and trimmed like a small rounded bowl with a gallery-like rim which functions as a flange.

Flange lids are thrown upright as a single unit. This type, with its small diameter and deep flange, is used for a tea pot.

Hump lids are usually thrown off a larger "hump" of clay. They are quick to make and require no trimming.

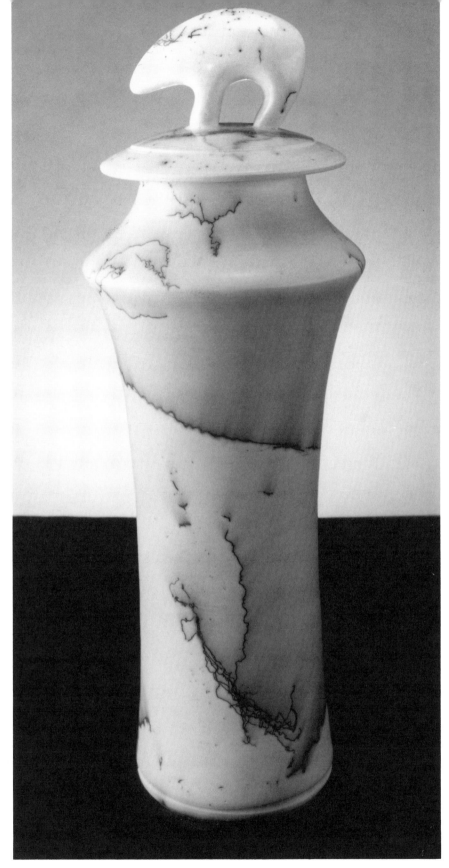

Michael Morier, thrown form with flange lid, 6" × 17". Prior to being raku fired, removed from the kiln at 1500° F and decorated with combustibles it was sanded with steel wool and polished with vegetable oil while on the wheel in a Giffin grip.

CHANGE: THE FUTURE WITHIN

As you begin to cultivate and cherish your throwing skills it becomes enormously exciting to work on the potters wheel.

Why? Because it continually compels us to grow . . . to change.

Granted, learning to throw is a unsettling process that often appears brazenly chaotic and ego threatening. Its beginnings are filled with alternating feelings of frustration and exhilaration, humiliation and prideful joy. But as the challenges are met the initial crisis passes and in that passage changes occur. The outward choices that confront us in this evolutionary process also affect our inner being and the unfolding of future journeys with clay.

The interwoven experiences of throwing on the wheel and personal change represents to me a synthesis of reconnection between the inner and the outer self. When embraced as such we can easily understand and initiate the reshaping of our awareness as freely as we reshape the clay. Awareness and clay—both in motion—are brought to new states of being, to a greater purpose, by the forces of change.

One of the ways that one may personally come through the newness of this somewhat technical and systematic encounter, with the continuous circling of clay, is identity affirmation. To live is to change. To find a way to live that brings and carries spirit into life is to grow through change, manifesting the undefinableness of wholeness.

Your spirit, the internal dimensions of your perceptual understanding, is your real identity. It is every bit as real as the external circumstances of your life. Unfortunately the external dimensions of experience are often allowed to passively dominate identity development. If the intellect, through rational projections, is continuously left to guide, formulate and express your sense of self it makes it difficult for you to access and embrace your inner strengths and to integrate them, in new ways, with every part of your life. In short, it makes it difficult to know who you are and to throw quality pots. Clearly, the spirit is, in so many ways, the personality of your clay forms just as it is of your body or, for that matter, your life—which M. C. Richards calls the "big" art.

One comes to know oneself through a number of personal ways: love, friendships, parenthood, etc. and being creative. One way that one comes closer to understanding life and their own spirituality is in physically working with clay. Because working with clay is, above all, spiritual. It softens the encumbrances of the past, and of illusions, allowing the possibilities of self new discovery . . . new hope.

Secrets. Life's secrets. There are many ways to learn them from life's experiences, whether it be something as simple as throwing a pot or exceedingly radical as seeing the sun set in Botswana. When the spirit within each

Peter Voulkos using his creative energies on a muscular stack piece made from heavy sections of wheel thrown clay. This piece is more about personal process then it is a sculptural presence. In a mysteriously elemental way the piece is him.

of us is activated enough to override the limitations of our intellect, and the indexed restrictions of convention, both our life and our clay work are meaningfully transformed to the point where both have a greater abundance of freedom and fullness of purpose.

Jun Kaneko, brightly glazed ceramic sculptures on display in the artist's studio. After the forms have dried for several months, Jun uses India ink (which disappears during the firing) to layout the decorative patterns on his surfaces. When the designs are completed they are painted in with colored slips, covered with a clear glaze and fired slowly (for weeks) to cone 4.

5

Glaze And Glazing

A glaze is a coating of glass fused to clay. Its chemical composition is slightly different from glass, however, in that a glaze contains an additional amount of alumina (aluminum oxide) as an adhesive, usually in the form of powdered clay, to hold it onto the surface during the firing process. Glazes are often viewed as the mysterious and overwhelming aspect of ceramics. Why? Because the formidable effect they have on the final appearance and function of the surface is astonishing. Also, because they are fraternally associated with chemistry—at times an imposing symbol of what we don't know or cannot control. To progress beyond any estrangement from glazes, it helps to know a few things about the properties of certain materials and the subtle nuances of glaze technology before you begin to experiment with formulating and applying them.

Chemically, the crystalline structures of glazes can be quite complicated yet beyond such intimidating analysis they can be quite simple and delicious—beyond beautiful. Some ceramic surfaces bring on strong emotional responses. There is no rationale needed to find a glaze awe-inspiring. The ironic thing is that they are little more than a skimpy coating of glass melted onto the clay's surface during a kiln firing. Interestingly, they are easy to formulate. Your standard, no frills, utility glaze is formulated from only four ingredient categories—three if you don't count the coloring oxides that generously give glazes their subtly flattering, if not out-right luxurious, punch. The remaining three categories, though far less alluring, are the glass formers, the fluxes and the refractories. The problem is, how do you know which chemicals to mix together and in what amounts? You don't . . . that's what makes it interesting. So, stop worrying, keep reading and be ready to do some experimenting.

GLAZE COMPOSITION

Glazes are composed of four essential ingredients: silica, flux, alumina and colorants. Any glaze formula will resemble a variation of these materials. The formula itself presents each material as both a unit of weight and a percentage totaling one hundred. Many ceramists don't consider the coloring agents an essential part of the basic glaze composition, so you'll often see these oxides and carbonates listed as separate additions to the written formula.

Glass Formers

Ground silica (flint) alone would make a glaze but its melting point is too high (3100° F), so fluxes must be added to the formula to bring down the maturing temperature.

Fluxes

Fluxes promote fusing and lower the melting point of glaze ingredients. The fusing temperature of a glaze can be lowered by adding a flux, or combination of fluxes, to the silica. For low temperature glazes, compounds of frit, sodium or Gerstley borate are used. For high temperature glazes, compounds of spodumene, nepheline syenite or feldspars are modestly substituted.

Refractories

Refractories are materials that are resistant to heat. At high temperatures they are chemically stable and seldom deform. To help the glaze materials remain in suspension, stick to the ware, and remain stable during firing, a high melting alumina refractory is needed. Kaolin (China clay) is the common refractory and source of alumina. Of course, alumina is found in other minerals and compounds, which can also be introduced to prevent running, to promote surface toughness, to reduce *crazing* (glaze fracturing), and to make a surface less glossy but they are not as directly suitable.

Colorants

Glaze color is derived from the addition of oxides or carbonates of metals. Colorants such as cobalt, copper and iron may be used alone or in combination. Combined colors don't appear as raw. If, for example, an iron bearing glaze isn't taking-off, visually, add a little rutile, and you're on the runway to great beauty.

GLAZE CATEGORIES

Glazes may be described in many ways. I've often come up with a few of my own unguarded descriptions, so will you, from time to time; some wonderful, others shocking. Nevertheless, they are often professionally categorized according to the following five characteristics: (1) firing temperature (2) surface appearance (3) firing procedure (4) major flux and (5) fired color.

Temperature

Glazes fired below pyrometric cone 6 (2194° F) are referred to as low-fire or earthenware glazes. Those fired above cone 6 are called high-fire or stoneware glazes. This includes the ever handsome porcelain glazes. The medium temperature glazes that openly straddle the cone 6 fence sometimes go by the stage name of soft stoneware. Most of these hang-out on the cone 4 side.

Surface

A glaze surface may be shiny or mat, opaque or transparent like glass. Crystalline glazes form star-like or snowflake-like patterns on the surface and salt glazes, developed centuries ago in Germany, have a pitted orange-peel surface texture. The astonishingly irresistible lusters, made from metallic salts dissolved in oils, are traditionally applied, like china paints, on top of a previously fired glaze and fired to a very low temperature.

Firing

Wood fired glazes are undeniably the richest of ceramic surfaces. As wonderful as you remember or as spectacular as you imagine . . . the results are mystical. The firing process itself is often an energetic social scene, especially when an *anagama* kiln is involved (the term anagama was first used by the Japanese to describe a long chamber-like kiln built up the side of hill). *Raku* (another term first used by the Japanese to describe a swift firing process) and *salt* firing are two other highly charged procedures that gift the glazed surface in ways that us mortals never could. I think of these processes as romantic and holistic. Because the firing process is often as lively and rewarding as the final surface effects, the procedure has become synonymous with the surface. Glazes applied directly to unfired clay are called *single-fired* glazes. The term *reduction*, as opposed to *oxidation*, is also used to describe a category of glazes. Simply put, reduction glazes are fired in fuel burning kilns whereas oxidation glazes are generally fired in electric, toaster-like, kilns.

Fluxes

Glazes are often categorized by the major fluxing component in the receipt. Terms such as ash, lead, feldspar, frit and now Boroflux are persistently common. A feldspathic glaze, for example, usually contains 50% or more feldspar.

Color

The fired color can be very descriptive when it comes to categorizing a glaze. Celadons and copper reds (even their names are beautiful) have an enviable place of honor in the history of ceramic art.

Steven Hill, Teapot, wheel thrown with extruded handle, slip trailing, multiple glazes, single-fired stoneware, 12" × 19".

GLAZE FAMILIES AND CHARACTERISTICS

To further understand the properties of certain types of glazes and their potential for contributing to the fired finish of a clay's surface, they are grouped here, alphabetically, into individual families that, for one reason or another, share certain characteristics. In theory, a knowledge of these common traits can be helpful but in practice you may witness many discrepancies. In either case, awareness of these various subdivisions should provide you with a great deal of insight and fascinating background information to profit from.

Alkaline Glazes

Alkaline glazes gain their popularity from their beguiling ability to produce the most exuberantly intense colors this side of Persia. They are so called because alkaline compounds are used as the flux. The low-fire glazes use sodium compounds such as borax or soda ash; a sodium carbonate. Sodium dominated glazes are unusually clear and glossy but tend to craze a lot. Also, they are fairly soluble and should be used at once or introduced in a frit form. The high-fire (cone 4-9) alkaline glazes use lithium carbonate and whiting, a calcium carbonate, as major fluxing agents. The high-fire alkaline glazes are less soluble in solution during storage and modestly less colorful.

Ash Glazes

The earliest form of glazing resulted from ashes flying through wood-burning kilns and fusing with the clay body. Today's very beautiful and winning ash glazes are only 30% to 50% wood ash. The two other main ingredients, feldspar and kaolin clay, are sometimes accompanied by silica. A few ceramists simply screen the ash through a 60-mesh sieve. Most, however, soak it for several hours, pour off the excess water, wait for the ashes to dry and screen them through a 100-mesh sieve. One heedful note: this stuff has attitude—it's caustic. Use a mask and wear rubber gloves so the lye does not burn the skin.

Boron Glazes

The strong fluxing boron compound gerstley borate or boro-silicate frits are used in these glossy low-fire glazes. Besides silica, boron oxide is the only other common glass former. Although not as stable or hard as a glaze containing silica, Gerstley borate or a boron frit can be used alone to create an exceedingly respectable glaze. They are very active and bubbly during firing and can become milky in character if applied too heavily. Still, with colorants, these glazes can be spectacular, especially in raku. Gerstley borate or colemanite, a natural form of calcium borate that is no longer available, can also be useful in high-fire glazes, but in amounts less than 50%.

Commercial Glazes

Commercial glazes, mostly low-fire and often better than imagined, can be purchased ready to apply. They are reliable products, conveniently pre-mixed, to save the ceramist mixing time and to by-pass the hazards of handling powdered chemicals. Health wise, if only the lead free and the barium free ones are used, they eliminate exposure to toxic fumes during firing and surface leaching during use. The chemist's for companies like Duncan, MayCo, AMACO and others have succeeded brilliantly in the creation of a cone 05-06 color palette that is, even by today's standards, triumphantly rich and wide spectrumed.

Crackle Glazes

More than anything else, the cracking patterns that form in and on a glaze surface are the direct result of tension created between the glaze and the clay body. During firing and cooling they simply contract or expand at different rates. To a certain degree the size and configurations of these patterns can be controlled by altering the chemical make-up of both the glaze and the clay body recipe. Soda feldspars and soda frits promote glaze crazing. Lithium carbonate, spodumene and boron frits discourage it.

Crystalline Glazes

The formation of light catching crystals in the glaze surface is due to a lack of aluminum oxide (alumina) in the glaze recipe. The aluminum oxide content of feldspars is around 18%, so these compounds are rarely used. One difficult aspect of these glazes is the controlling of the firing or, more specifically, the cooling cycle. It is critical that the cooling temperature be arrested and held at a temperature just above the glaze maturation point for several hours. Without feldspar and with a higher presence of chemicals such as zinc oxide, borax and sodium they are also very runny. Such fluidity is the behavior ceramists welcome least.

Earthenware Glazes

Any glazes in the cone 04 (1922° F) range that are applied to natural, often iron colored, clay bodies that remain relatively porous after firing are often referred to as earthenware glazes. Be wary, however. The term is more synonymous with a type of clay than it is with a glaze composition.

Lead Glazes

Glazes that use lead carbonate, a white lead, and lead oxide, a red lead, for a flux are commonly known as lead glazes. In the raw state they are extremely toxic. During firing the fumes given off are harmfully noxious and on culinary ware they are poisonous. Be assured, not many contemporaries even allow the stuff on their premises. The best substitutes for lead in low-temperature glazes is Gerstley borate and/or leadless frits.

Feldspathic Glazes

Glazes that have feldspar as their major flux are called feldspathic. Generally, these full-bodied glazes contain 50% to 80% feldspar. There are two major types of feldspar: potash and soda. Custer feldspar is the most common potash feldspar—a friendly favorite in high-fired recipes because it produces a harder fired surface. Kona F-4 feldspar is the most popular soda feldspar. Sodium is used in the mid-temperature firing range because it is a stronger flux than potash, although it does promote crazing. In broad daylight it has a more dramatic affect on color than its counterpart. Nepheline syenite and spodumene can be substituted for feldspar, especially if the firing temperature needs to be dropped a cone or two.

Frit Glazes

Frit or fritted glazes can be any glaze which contains frit. Frits are similar to feldspars as both are powerful fluxes. Some anti-establishmentarians even refer to them as commercial, versus natural, feldspars. Whereas feldspars do their best work in the high temperature country, frits do better in the low lands below cone 6 (2194° F) and most specifically at cone 05 (1888° F). Frits are a combination of soluble compounds fired together with silica under strict supervisory regulation and dramatically shattered during a rapid cooling; the resulting small glass particles are ground to a fine powder.

Be assured, fritting offers dependable uniformity and control in glaze making. It also eliminates some of the hazards and problems of working with raw chemicals. However, the important fact is that some of the best looking low-fire glazes, the ones you dream of, are made with frits.

There is still controversy, however, concerning the safety of fritted lead glazes. Fritting decreases solubility. Different frits, fired at different temperatures, are said to be capable of rendering lead or barium insoluble and non-poisonous. Still, leaded frits are toxic. They are dangerous to handle during the glazing process and lead, because it is volatile at high temperatures, could be inhaled during the firing process or become attached to non-lead glazes. One intelligently simple solution: renounce them, walk away and never look back. Besides, there is Boroflux and a significant number of leadless boro-silicate and alkaline frits to work with that leave you free to live a healthy and productive life.

Popular Leadless Glaze Frits And Their Equivalents

FERRO	PEMCO		O'HOMMEL
3110	P-1505		
3124	P-311		90
3134	P-54		14
3195	P-67		
3269	P-2301	25	
3278	P-830		K3
3819	P-25		259

Low-Fire Glazes

This is a generically descriptive title that applies to any number of formidable glazes that mature below cone 6 (2194° F). They are extremely popular not only for their wide range of exciting colors, like the bright reds and oranges, but because they can easily be fired in the all-affordable and ever-available electric kiln.

Zak Zaikine, A Bright Sunny Day, 15" in diameter. Like all the work from Zak's New Spirit plate series, this piece is fired with multiple layers of bright underglaze and a highly fritted overglaze to create gentle images which open our spirit to those miraculous moments that play into our lives and lovingly stay in out hearts.

Luster Glazes

Metallic luster glazes are a combination of metal compounds suspended in an oil base. They are an overglaze in that they are thinly applied with a camel hair brush to an already fired glaze surface that is perfectly clean and void of greasy finger marks. After application, they are fired just high enough for the oil to burn away (cone 018 for most lusters or for gold and cone 019 for the glaringly subtle mother-of-pearl luster) and for the metal to fuse to the surface of the base glaze, but not high enough to reach the melting point of the first glaze. Some lusters, like purple or mother-of-pearl, are very translucent and elegant while the various golds and platinums are austerely opaque.

Matt Glazes

A matt glaze is any glaze that is non glossy. The firing temperature has little to do with this characteristic unless, of course, a glaze is underfired, in which case it will be a physically arid or matt surface. Baring any such accidents or intentional forays of experimentation, larger than usual amounts of a refractory, such as kaolin clay, or a lessening of the flux in the recipe are

Ken Turner, thrown porcelain form with a gold luster glaze on rim, 15" × 10 3/4". The texture was obtained by spraying clay slip mixed with black stain onto the surface with a spray attachment used for texturing ceilings and walls with plaster.

usually employed to generate this glaze effect. Barium carbonate used to be the age-old favorite material that was added to glazes whenever a matt or a "dry" surface was needed. Yet it is incredibly toxic and is often used as an inactive ingredient in rat poison. Sound discouraging? Many health conscious individuals go to great lengths to avoid it. Titanium might be substituted as a matting agent. In large amounts this wondrous opacifier affects more than color. The amount of zinc oxide, dolomite, whiting, silica and especially magnesium carbonate can be increased in a glaze to improve its matte appearance. Some creative sandblasting, after firing, will also relinquish a distinctively matt finish by virtue of its abrasive power. Harnessed by implicit personal intent, sandblasting has the added contextual potential for accentuating the presence of any fired glaze.

Raku Glazes

These glazes in the cone 07 (1783° F) to 06 (1816° F) range are uniquely known for their rich crackle patterns and most recently for their copper surface. Patinas are a dry, matt-like surface formed from a watery thin glaze which is high in copper and low in fluxing agents. Crackle patterns and copper patinas become even more dramatic when viewed against the contrasting gray/black of the smoked clay body. The recipes themselves are unusually simple, consisting primarily of a Gerstley borate or a frit base. Where these glazes come alive, and take on a personality, is in the post-firing reduction process . . . a time of unmatched excitement and challenge for the artist.

Salt Glazes

Salt glazing is achieved by introducing ordinary salt into the kiln just after its been fired to maturity. The sodium instantly volatilizes and forms a thin glaze coating as it combines with the silica and alumina content of the ware. During this process, chlorine gas, a *major* health hazard, is given off. Slips or glazes may be applied to the ware prior to firing but generally the ware is placed into the kiln in an unglazed, greenware state and fired straight through to cone 9 or 10. The resulting surface colors and orange-peel textures are very unique to this form of vapor glazing.

Slip Glazes

These are warm earth colored glazes made from natural clays where the flux is a part of the chemical makeup of the clay itself. Albany and Michigan clays are popular examples of *vitreous* (glassy) slips. Fired at high temperatures, these clays alone can be used to form a glaze. With the addition of other fluxes they can be made to mature at lower temperatures. By adding ball clay in amounts up to 30% the fired surface can be brought from a gloss to a semi-gloss, or to one that is almost dry looking. Colorants are seldom added as most of these glazes are already dark and naturally full of rich, deep tones of reds and browns, but a little rutile is always flattering. Albany clay, a natural self-glazing slip, is no longer obtainable and has been replaced by a synthetic product called Alberta slip. Seattle slip, mined in the state of Washington, is also used as a substitute for Albany slip.

All slip glazes work especially well for single firing. However, to take full advantage of the bonding capabilities of these slips in their natural state, even if the ware is eventually going to be bisque fired, they should be applied to the clay surface while it is still wet or leather-hard. If applied to a bisque fired surface slips may have to be reformulated to reduce shrinkage.

Stoneware Glazes

Any glaze that is fired above cone 6 (2194° F) on a stoneware clay body is referred to as either a high-fire or a stoneware glaze. A high-fire glaze that is clear or translucent and can be fired to cone 9 (2300° F) or higher is often called a porcelain glaze. Stoneware glazes work well for culinary or functional ware by providing a visually satisfying yet safe and hygienic surface for holding and serving foods and drinks. These glazes may be unrivaled for their usefulness, but they are also popular for a meaningful range of shared classic, historical, and yes, romantic reasons. Some of us first fell in love with pots through these enchanting glaze surfaces, and many of us possess significant memories of a Shaner's Red or a Ohata Black or any number of other quite wonderful stoneware formulas that have been secretly or benevolently passed along between generations of potters. Such formulas deserve, if not command, a legendary place of honor and we can only hope they will never totally disappear from the world's ceramic studios.

Underglazes

Underglazes are colors that are applied to the surface prior to the glaze. They include a wide range of colorants, stains or washes that are decoratively applied to bisque ware. Underglazes do not contain glass forming minerals so they are used for color only, and are usually covered by a zinc-free transparent or semi-transparent glaze coat. This (over) glaze is then fired to its maturing temperature, providing protection and immortality. Underglazes come in many knock-out colors: Chartreuse, Royal Orchid, Zinnia Orange and Bright Turquoise. Colors that will throw your eyes slightly off balance while leaving the rest of you fancifully excited to pursue them. No wonder so many ceramists use them with a passion.

BASIC GLAZE CHEMICALS

The raw materials used in ceramic glazes form a rather large and diverse collection of chemicals. Some are pure elements which cannot be broken down into other substances while most are actually compounds, in union with one or more other elements, and are, more often than not, contaminated with various impurities. The ones that are least toxic and the ones that are most frequently used in the formation of glazes are alphabetically listed below. Also shown are some of their basic characteristics, as well as a variety of innocent properties they might contribute when used in combination with other chemicals, glaze types or firing conditions. There are many factors affecting what any one chemical does or does not do to the final outcome of a fired glaze, so view the following information as a general guide and not as absolute or definitive data.

Bentonite

As a derivative of volcanic ash, this very fine-particle, super-plastic clay is used primarily in clay bodies to add plasticity. Added to glazes, 0.2% to 1.5% of this sticky, high shrinkage substance aids particle suspension and reduces settling during storage. It also acts as a binder by helping the applied glaze to stay on the pot's surface after the glaze has dried and to survive that fragile stage of handling it goes through while being placed in the kiln. To be fully effective, bentonite must first be worked into hot water to form a milky slip and passed through a fine mesh sieve several times prior to being added to the liquid glaze. For this mixture to become fully assimilated it should be allowed to sit overnight. To extend the glaze suspension capabilities of bentonite, especially over a longer time period, 0.1% to 0.3% of magnesium hydroxide (Hydramax-B8) should be added. With some glaze formulas, 1% of any food preservative may be substituted as a glaze suspender.

Bone Ash

A calcium phosphate made of ground and calcined animal bone, bone ash is used as the main body flux in English bone china. In high-fire glazes it is used in small amounts with feldspars as a flux. In low-fire glazes it provides a frosty opaqueness and enriches the texture of raku surface patinas. Sold either as a natural bone ash (English) or as tricalcium phosphate, a synthetic and more potent form of bone ash, the particle or mesh size used in glaze making is critical to the final outcome of the fired surface.

Borax

Borax is a very active sodium borate compound used as a strong fluxing agent in low-fire glazes. Borax is often used, in the powdered form, in combination with Gerstley borate to make some raku glazes. Because it is highly water soluble, it should be used immediately or in the more stable fritted form where changes in temperature or moisture content don't affect weight calculations. Besides lowering the firing temperature of glazes, borax softens their viscosity and promotes brilliant colors by making blues, blue-greens and purples brighter. Used in excess borax, as an early melting flux, can cause surface crazing and pin-holing. In some recipes one half the amount of anhydrous (without water) sodium carbonate may be substituted for borax to obtain a softer glaze finish.

Boroflux

Borofluxes (also sold as zinc borates) are very fine grained zinc borate crystals that melt around 1800°F. Developed by William M. Jackson ll and first marketed in 1981, this white ceramic grade flux is available in 2 main composites. Boroflux #1 contains 33% zinc oxide and 41% boron oxide, while Boroflux C-13 contains only 20.2% zinc oxide, but 52.4% boron oxide and the addition 14% calcium oxide. Added in very small amounts to casting slips, it will lower the firing temperature of the clay and increase its strength up to 25%. It also reduces warping, accelerates drying and promotes whiteness. Added in larger amounts (20%–50%) to glazes it out performs some frits by eliminating pitting or pinholing while improving surface sheen and clearness.

Cornwall Stone

Also known as Cornish Stone, this sedate English feldspar is partially derived from decomposed granite rock. As a glaze flux, with a very high silica content (close to 70%) cornwall stone is often used as a substitute for other feldspars as it contains both soda and potash. To help distinguish cornwall stone from the old "DF" form it now has an identifying blue-green tint. This added feature does not, however, affect the final color of the glaze. It is used in both low-firing and high-firing glazes. In some cases cornwall stone can even be used by itself as a glaze. When mixed with other chemicals it can reduce the shrinkage of a glaze in both the fired and unfired state thereby keeping glaze defects, such as crazing, to a minimum. It can also be mixed with cobalt to help soften the electrifying appearance of this expressively raw blue colorant—especially at the higher firing temperatures where its vividness becomes even more potent.

Dolomite

In high-fire glazes dolomite is used in small percentages as a flux. When used in quantities exceeding 15% to 20% it promotes a smooth, buttery matt surface. This is, perhaps, dolomite's most renowned function and useful quality. If chosen to replace whiting, in an existing recipe, dolomite raises the maturing temperature of the glaze. If used in the presence of cobalt it can render mauve to violet red colors; it can give pinkish hues when copper is present. In low-fire glazes this natural calcium and magnesium carbonate acts as a refractory; a figurative walk across the street from where this double carbonate normally resides and works.

Feldspar

Feldspar, sometimes called spar for short, is a mineral that is both available and favored world wide as a flux for earthenware, stoneware and porcelain clay bodies and as the major fluxing ingredient for high-temperature glazes. Although it begins to melt around 2200° F, feldspar continues to remain moltenly viscous to temperatures beyond 2400° F, which helps decreases fluidity and keeps the glaze from running as it is fired. Used as a recipe constituent below 1900° F it functions as a refractory and promotes matt surfaces. Although there are several types of feldspars the two most frequently used in ceramic glazes are potash feldspar and soda feldspar.

Potash feldspar, also frequently referred to as custer feldspar, melts at a temperature higher than that of soda feldspar making for a glaze surface that is harder and more resistant to scratching. Whenever an undesignated feldspar appears in a glaze formula the potash variety is the one that would be commonly used.

Soda feldspar, most commonly known as Kona feldspar, is used when a more sensuous and brilliant glaze color is sought. Although it matures at a temperature 100° F lower than potash feldspar, and decreases the durability of the surface, soda feldspar does enhance the overall color quality of fired glazes. Reds, especially, appear to be visually richer, while blues take on more depth and become less harsh.

Flint

The main glass-forming ingredient in glaze is flint. Also called silica and sometimes quartz, this hard, fine-grained material is more useful than any other in ceramics. In clay bodies flint increases thermal expansion. In a glaze it helps to decrease it. Added by itself to a glaze, or in the form of an alumina-silica compound such as ball clay, kaolin, or one of the feldspars, it combines with alumina to form a tough, glossy surface. Increasing the silica content of a glaze decreases its fluidity, raises its maturing temperature and also improves its resistance to abrasive wear. In matt glazes the silica content is generally low. When making glazes, use the finely ground 325 mesh silica: the coarser 200 mesh is generally added to clay bodies.

Frit

Frits are commercially manufactured fluxes. Ferro, Pemco and Hommel are the leading brand names. As a form of powdered glaze or glass with a wide firing range, they are pre-ground to a 200 mesh particle size and can be purchased dry in either a leaded or lead-free state. Many potters now only use the lead-free ones . . . and with excellent results.

Ferro 3134 is one of the most popular and widely used leadless frits. This sodium-boro-silicate frit, like any frit, is rarely used alone and when in combination with alumina and other materials produces consistently beautiful glazes. Although this frit melts at cone 06 (1816° F), it can be used in glazes that fire as high as cone 6 (2194° F). Mixed with 10% clay or spodumene it produces a good transparent glaze with a glossy surface at cone 04-06. If the clay percentage is increased the surface can be made to appear more matt-like. Like Ferro 3195, this frit contains 23% boric oxide, a very active flux, and bubbles dramatically during the sintering stage of a firing, refusing to settle down until the glaze reaches maturity. Frit glazes also become a milky bluish-green if applied too heavily.

Gerstley Borate

Gerstly borate is a very popular and extensively used low-fire glaze flux. Utilized in place of lead oxide and as a more stable substitute for colemanite, a natural form of calcium borate which is no longer mined, this calcium and boric oxide compound has a relatively low coefficient of expansion. In many glazes this can reduce crazing or fine cracks in the glaze surface, especially if the glaze is not applied thickly. In raku glazes, some of which contain 80% to 100% Gerstley borate, crazing is induced by rapidly cooling the glaze to obtain a decorative crackle pattern. Ten percent added to a stoneware glaze can lower the firing temperature one or two cones.

Lithium Carbonate

Lithium carbonate is an important high temperature glaze flux that minimizes thermal expansion. Calculated into an existing stoneware glaze recipe it can lower the firing temperature by one or more cones. It can also be used with larger than normal percentages of flint to produce a more durable and much brighter glaze surface. Lithium carbonate is frequently added, in the amount of 5% to 10% to low temperature glazes lacking soda ash or borax. Lepidolite is a so-so substitute.

Magnesium Carbonate

An expensive source, in comparison to dolomite, for introducing magnesium into a glaze is magnesium carbonate. At higher temperatures, cone 6 to 10, it functions as a slow-acting flux. At lower temperatures it serves as a refractory. Magnesium carbonate has a strong and positive affect on color. Cobalt blues come alive in its presence sometimes turning to purple-pinks, and, while too much can dirty celadons, large portions can add a satin smoothness to an otherwise unexciting surface texture. In other cases this chemical can promote opacity. If dolomite is going to be substituted for magnesium carbonate it is important to reduce the amount of whiting, if some is present in the formula.

Magnesium Hydroxide

Magnesium hydroxide (sold as Maglite H or Hydramax-B8) dramatically reduces settling and increases the plasticity of clay casting slips and glazes without the need for aging or bacterial action. Less than 0.0125% can stabilize the suspension properties of glazes for many, many months, especially if less than 1% of Boroflux #1 and/or a drop or two of Alcosperse 149-C is added to the glaze.

Nepheline Syenite

Similar to soda feldspar this snappy flux, higher in both alumina and soda than potash feldspar, can lower the maturing temperature by one to two cones if substituted for all or part of it.

Spodumene

As a feldspar, with the largest percentage of lithium, this super active flux can be substituted for other high firing feldspars to lower the maturing temperature of glazes by as much as two cones. This is a good compound to have around if you like vintage, creamy colors and mellow feeling surfaces. Blue glazes are made to appear infinitely more tender with the addition of this singular ingredient.

Tin Oxide

Tin oxide is the most effective and popular opacifier used in ceramic glazes. In amounts ranging from 5% to 10% almost any temperature glaze can be made undeniably opaque. It is also extremely useful as a major color enhancer for both underglaze and glaze colors. For example, as little as one half percent can make copper reds substantially richer and more full-bodied. An important side note related to tin, not only can it give a glaze a pleasingly soft surface texture, it can also give colorants a fresh, summery appearance. Whites, in particular, will have that vanilla ice-cream look, appearing virtuously bright and unblemished.

Titanium Dioxide

A strong and important glaze opacifier. In amounts over 5% it also becomes a useful matting agent and color moderator. Rutile is an impure iron-bearing form of titanium oxide and if used as a replacement, with additional amounts (4 to 8 percent) of red iron oxide, can produce (in a reduction firing) a mottled, galactic spectrum of colors ranging from warm oranges to deep, dark blues. With titanium dioxide whites are creamier, subtler and less bright than they are with tin oxide. Because titanium is also a flux, the mere addition of 1% to 3% of it to an engobe or clay slip recipe will significantly strengthen its matt-like surface characteristics by functioning as a hardener.

Whiting

Whiting is a finely ground chalk compound used as a relatively pure form of calcium carbonate to increase the tensile strength of glaze surfaces. In high temperature reduction glazes it can function as a flux and, in the presence of iron, contribute to the gentleness of celadon colors. It can also assist in the production of elegant reduction reds from copper. Strong, and definitely not feeble, whiting, like many calcium fluxes, can wash out some coloring oxides and instigate some opacity in low-fire glazes. Excessive amounts can also cause a surface to have a circumstantial matt-like texture.

Wollastonite

A calcium silicate compound (47% calcium and 50% silica) that is used to reduce both clay and glaze shrinkage during firing. Wollastonite is an excellent glaze hardener and dramatically increases the strength of clay bodies, making them more resistant to thermal shock. Can also be substituted for flint and whiting in some glazes.

Zinc Oxide

This is one multi-amazing oxide: powerful and spirited, yet beastly and fickle. Just 2% of zinc oxide becomes a strong flux in low-temperature glazes and, for the same reason, must be used sparingly in higher temperature glazes. In amounts from 2% to 5% it can increase the opacity of a low-fire glaze without affecting its glossiness. Still, as an opacifier, it has half the strength of tin oxide; the strongest opacifier in glaze chemistry. In larger quantities (8% to 10%) it becomes a definite opacifier and begins to form a seductive matt surface. Beyond 10% the glaze surface can develop a dry texture. Although it increases surface durability, it helps, even if slightly, to reduce crazing, and inhibits the excessive running of some formulas, zinc oxide has a high rate of shrinkage and I have often found it to be impetuously difficult to regulate. To help reduce the sensitive nature of this metallic oxide, calcined zinc can be substituted, especially if a particular glaze formula crawls too much or if it cracks excessively on the pot while still in the dry state.

When it comes to glaze colorants, zinc has more of an influence than any other single ingredient. Its affect can be mystically beautiful—especially on glazes fired in an electric kiln, which is to say, in oxidation. Coppers are made brighter, cobalts are made softer, while others, like iron, are muddied if not destroyed with authority.

Jun Kaneko, Untitled, brightly glazed ceramic sculpture (with interior support walls) handbuilt from 2-3 inch thick "chunks" of stacked clay, 71" × 53" × 22 1/2". Prior to being glazed, a light colored slip pattern was covered with masking tape and painted with a black manganese slip to create a hard-edge underglaze design.

Zirconium Oxide

Zirconium oxide is a high-temperature glaze opacifier that remains white in reduction firings. Zirconium is often used as a substitute for tin oxide. Known commercially by such brand names as Opax, Superpax, Ultrux and Zircopax, with the exception of Superpax, quantities two to three times greater are needed as a replacement for tin.

BASIC GLAZE COLORANTS

Color in glazes are generally achieved by the addition of metallic oxides or carbonates. The oxides provide stronger color than the cabonates and usually cost much more than their weaker counterparts. When carbonates are substituted for oxides, the amount used needs to be increased if the same color results are sought. Sometimes, the carbonate may have to be doubled to obtain equality. The ingredients of most ceramic glaze recipes are formulated to add-up to 100 grams, or 100 percent. To this total figure of 100, known as the base recipe, the colorants are added as supplemental or extra material.

Just as often as not, more than one colorant is added to a glaze to soften a visually harsh surface, achieve a special affect or create a specific decorative treatment. Still, the color generated from the use of any one metal oxide is the result of many variables—some occurring simultaneously. Color is responsive to and regulated by such factors as the temperature of the kiln, the firing atmosphere inside the kiln (oxidation versus reduction), the chemical make-up of the glaze, the reaction to other colorants and even to the color of the clay body. There are other surprises, of course, that make matters interesting, and take you beyond expectations. The following is a list of the most commonly used metals as colorants and should provide some insight as to their potential characteristics.

Cobalt

Cobalt is the strongest and most consistently stable colorant used in ceramics. Less than ½% (½% written decimally is .005) of the oxide produces a medium to strong blue. Increasing the amount to 1% intensifies and darkens it gravely, especially if zinc is present. A significant rise in firing temperature will also have a similar affect. Used in the carbonate form, a range from 1% to 2% can produce a Matisse-like family of blues. Most ceramists use the carbonate because it's less expensive and, owing to its smaller particle size, easier to work into the glaze mixture. If not mixed and screened properly it can form spots and streaks in contrasting shades of blue. Mixed with red iron oxide, magnesium or rutile, cobalt can be greatly modified and pushed toward shades of purple and plum reds.

Copper

Copper, like cobalt, is tremendously popular as a glaze colorant. It has met no equal since the Egyptians used it before the time of Cleopatra to color a self-glazing clay known as Egyptian Paste. Today rakuists use it to achieve copper lusters and copper matt surface patinas in a firing process known as raku. Copper oxide is one and a half times stronger than copper carbonate but the carbonate is used much more often in glazes. One half of a percent combined with 1% tin oxide produces those historically famous reduction copper reds. Actually they are more the result of a reduction firing followed by a carefully controlled, non-oxidizing, cooling in a tightly sealed kiln. Still, copper is the catalyst if the base is feldspathic and high in soda. In almost any glaze, 1% will generally give a subtle blue-green, 2% to 4% a vivid green, or turquoise blue if the glaze base is alkaline, and a dark black, iron metallic look, if more than 8% is used. When fired to cone 9 or higher, copper vaporizes, frequently leaping onto the surface of nearby forms; coloring them with a slight blush of red or pink color. Unlike cobalt, which could pose a slight hazard to the respiratory system, copper is potentially more toxic and care should be taken to see that it is not touched, ingested or inhaled.

Iron

Iron oxide is an inexpensive, major earth-tone colorant for clay as well as glazes. By adding 1% to 2% of red iron oxide to a glaze (with red, and not yellow or black, being the most common form used) colorants such as cobalt or copper are subtly civilized and made to appear richly elegant in the sense that dinner looks more appealing with candle light. The deeply beautiful blue-greens and impressive grays exhibited in celadon glazes, for example, are the result of small amounts of iron in glazes fired in a strong reduction atmosphere. If more than 10% is used, and the glaze heavily applied, a shinny, imperial black surface may occur. Such high-temperature, high iron content, glazes are also known as iron saturates and as temmoku glazes: a famous Japanese glaze of considerable vintage and a prized orange-brown to black mottled look. If potash feldspar is present in a recipe the reddish iron colors are brighter; if zinc is present they are muddied.

Manganese

As a colorant manganese fires well in both oxidation and reduction. At low temperatures as much as 8% can be used before it becomes unpleasantly dark. At the higher stoneware temperatures it becomes fluid and should be used in slightly smaller percentages. Added to the glaze, either as manganese dioxide or as manganese carbonate (which is the form used most frequently), it produces colors that range from brown-blacks to purples. By mixing it with cobalt the purples become recognizably more beautiful. Mixed with red iron oxide the browns are tempered, appearing less muddied, and the blacks are darker, almost metallic, when combined with copper. Granular manganese dioxide, which is roughly a 60/90 mesh, is used in glazes to create reddish-black speckles on the surface. Added after screening, these granular elements can visually activate an otherwise sober, flat-looking glaze.

Nickel

Used strictly as a colorant, known either as black nickel oxide, green nickel oxide, or in its weaker form as green nickel carbonate, nickel is often combined with other colorants to help tone them down. By itself, in amounts of 1% or less, it can promote some stimulating grays. Increasing that percentage by small amounts can also cause the glaze surface to become more matte. Although it is not a popular colorant, when black nickel oxide is combined with copper in a raku glaze the resulting lusters can be quite dramatic.

Ochre

Closely allied to umber (a natural iron oxide earth stain containing some manganese oxide: known as burnt umber in the calcined form), yellow ochres frequently contain some clay impurities and are used as a colorant in slips and glazes to produce tans, light browns and yellows that are brighter than those made from iron oxides.

Rutile

Rutile is an impure form of titanium dioxide. As a colorant it's a sleeper—not very strong when used by itself. For example, 5% barely produces a light yellow tan in most glazes. What this colorant is, however, is an out and out team player! Its greatest virtues manifest themselves in the presence of other colorants. When combined with iron oxide an entire palette of mottled color is possible. If more than 5% of each is used some wonderfully deep, broken orange-blues are possible in reduction.

STAINS AND UNDERGLAZES

Glaze stains and underglazes are made from the basic metallic oxides and are popular colorants for decorating and expanding the range of surface color. Stains, such as those sold by the Mason Color Chemical Works, are commercially manufactured colors (close to 150 varieties) that are generally mixed into existing glazes and slips in amounts from 1% to 20%. Essentially, stains are a blend of calcined (pre-fired) oxides which are finely ground (150 mesh) and combined with various opacifiers, frits and binders to form a consistent, insoluble (stable when wet) color. All stains fire well at low temperatures in an oxidizing atmosphere but some of the warm colors (reds in particular) burn out and disappear when high fired. Stains also work best in glazes that contain some whiting and no zinc.

While stains are sometimes referred to as in-glaze colorants, under-glaze colorants are applied directly to the clay and then covered with a clear or semi-clear glaze. To obtain the brightest colors possible from underglazes cover them with the most transparent or clearest glaze available such as Duncan's Envision Clear glaze. Underglazes can be oxides mixed with water or commercial colorants purchased in the form of a liquid, paint pan, crayon or pencil. Underglazes are frequently applied to bisque fired ware just prior to glazing but if any sgraffito decorative techniques (scratching through a coating of colorant to reveal the clay body) are going to be used they can be applied prior to bisque firing. Because their formula includes a cohesive binding medium to prevent smudging, it's often helpful to apply underglazes to greenware and then bisque fire, burning off the binder, to eliminate any possible problems with the glaze surface separating do to a lack of assimilation.

The American Art Clay Company (AMACO) manufactures a popular set of lead free underglazes known as their Reward Velvet series. The Velvets are not as brilliant or opaque as their luscious Tru-Tone line of underglazes and obviously take their name from their velour-like appearance when left unglazed, which is partly what these rich and versatile colors were designed for (something to smile at) and how they are most often used. Velvets tolerate the higher firing temperatures, fire true to their color in the liquid state and can be mixed with each other to form an even larger color palette. And, like all underglazes, can be made to appear matt or glossy depending on the nature of the glaze they are covered with.

Nancy Selvin airbrushing a stain onto a taped-out area of the pot's surface.

MIXING GLAZE

Glazes are made by adding the correct amount of each dry ingredient from a specific recipe to water. The dry materials are measured either by weight, in units called grams, or by volume, in the form of cups. If, as might be the case with large batches, a glaze is measured in ounces or pounds it may become important to know that one pound weighs 454 grams. Don't blink. You may need to know this conversion some day and then it won't seem trivial.

Glaze chemicals being weighed on a triple beam balance scale.

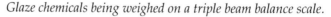

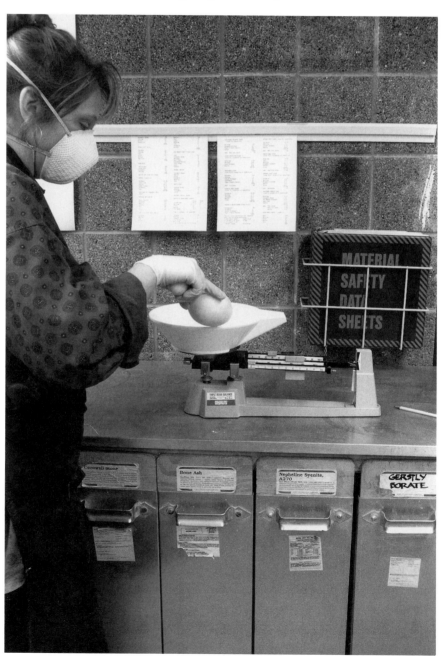

The triple beam balance scale, which weighs out grams in 1/10, 1, 10, 100 and 500 gram increments is the most common instrument in use for accurately weighing glaze chemicals. If the recipe of the glaze being made contains bentonite, which is both a binder and a suspension agent, weigh it out first (after putting on a protective mask) and add it to the plastic container that will be holding the glaze. This container should already hold the estimated amount of water needed for the glaze and the water's temperature should always be hot to help the bentonite dissolve . . . which it has difficulty doing. In fact, some potters pre-dissolve the bentonite the day before they make the glaze by frequently shaking a lidded glass jar of it along with water and left to blend. Others simply find it helpful to dry mix the bentonite with all of the other ingredients to disperse it. Following bentonite, the clays, especially the ball clays, are the toughest to blend and should be weighed and added to the hot water next. The remaining materials, those with milder tempers, can be added last.

The resulting liquid mixture of chemicals and water is blended by hand with a wire whip or, better yet, a commercial paint mixer attached to a variable-speed electric drill. The most effective drill mixing attachment I know of is the stainless steel Turbo Mixer, a giant in its class. It's a simple looking device, a long shaft with a spring-like coil on one end. It does a tremendously quick job of mixing glazes thoroughly. Blended mechanically, glazes are far more homogenous and their ingredients remain suspended for a much longer period of time. As the glaze is being whipped additional water may need to be added to improve its consistency.

A Turbo Mixer attached to an electric drill is used to blend chemicals and water.

Glaze being screened with a Talisman sieve. This uncanny unit fits snugly on a 5 gallon plastic container and, when rotated by hand, quickly works the wet materials through one of the interchangeable stainless screen discs. The 3 nylon brushes that make-up the working end of the handle axis are also removable for cleaning or replacement.

After the glaze ingredients are mixed they must be screened—at times more than once. This is done by placing a 60 mesh bowl sieve over an empty container and passing the glaze through it. Glaze sieves can be purchased to fit onto the rim of a standard 5 gallon plastic container and come in 30, 40, 60, 80, 100, 150 and 200 mesh sizes; if the glaze is not going to be applied with a spray gun the 60 or 80 mesh screening is adequate. More often than not it becomes necessary to help the glaze pass through the sieve by working it back and forth with a large, stiff white nylon paint brush, white nylon scrub brush or a rubber rib.

Immediately re-check the consistency of the glaze after screening. The water content is of critical importance, affecting the success of the application process, the thickness of the glaze coat and the fired results. Some glazes require more water than others. A raku crackle glaze is often thick and creamy. A raku dry patina glaze, on the other hand, is often watery thin. Most glazes, however, work best when they are the consistency of milk and have been set aside for at least twelve hours after having been made to give the ingredients some additional time to assimilate water and undergo chemical changes.

The consistency, or viscosity, can be calibrated with a hydrometer (a specific gravity of 2.5 would be normal) or by dipping one or two fingers into the glaze. When the fingers are removed, the glaze should readily drain off and clearly reveal the outline of the finger nail. If this does not happen add more water or, in place of the water, add a very small amount of Calgon or, better yet, a few drops of Alcosperse 149-C to thin the glaze and thereby adjust its consistency. Should the glaze turn out to be too thin, which seldom seems to be the case, let it sit undisturbed a day or two and then skim off some of the clear water that forms near the top. If you're unable to wait for the water to rise to the top, add Epsom salts (a hydrated magnesium sulfate) to the glaze as a thickener and as a suspension agent.

The glaze needs to be fluid so that it can freely flow and cascade over the contours of the form being glazed. If it's too thick, like Karo syrup, it will form a heavy build-up and an uneven coating. If several pinholes or cracks occur on this surface, the glaze is definitely too thick. From time to time glazes need to be topped off with additional water, especially if they have been sitting for long periods of time or if the lids to the container don't seal well. Evaporation, of course, reveals itself all to often.

Finally, don't drive yourself crazy by accidentally failing to label the container with the correct title of the glaze. And don't make the mistake of labeling only the lid. For century after century, lids everywhere have been known to end up on the wrong jug, jar or barrel.

APPLYING GLAZE

Glazing can be tricky. That is until you get the hang of it, then it's not particularly hard to do at all. If you are new to ceramics, new to glazing, you are bound to feel a little ill at ease. Applying glaze to one of your first works in clay, to your babies, is an uneasy moment-of-truth experience where you more than faintly realize that what you do now will ultimately determine their fate for all of eternity. Well, it doesn't have to be all that dramatic, slightly demanding, yes, but not tormenting. Are you wearing old pants and shoes? For this job you should be.

Glazes are most often applied to ware that has been bisque fired. They could be applied to unfired ware if the clay content of the glaze was 30 percent or higher but *single-firing*, as it is frequently called, can be a somewhat hazardous process resulting in unnecessary breakage. For those that have learned to master the once-fire process it does save a lot of time and firing expense.

If the bisque pieces have been sitting, uncovered, around the studio for awhile—waiting for a stirring summons of glazing courage—they should first be wiped clean with a damp sponge to remove dust and to aid glaze adhesion. Incidentally, bisque ware should be handled as little as possible to prevent the natural oils of the skin from acting as a glaze resist. Some ceramists wear light cotton gloves when unloading and transporting bisque fired ware—especially if the clay is white porcelain.

The foot-rim of a pot is dipped into hot paraffin to resist glaze absorption.

Hot paraffin wax or liquid wax resist, of the room-temperature variety, should be applied to the bottom of the bisque ware after cleaning and continued up the outside walls to a height of 1/4 inch. As you come to know your glazes you'll realize that the non running ones do not require as much clearance. If lidded forms are being glazed, their mating surfaces should also be waxed. Wax is a resist. It helps to prevent parts from being glazed together and bottoms from being fused to the kiln shelf. Under normal conditions a glaze might be fairly stable but should it be applied too heavily or should the kiln overfire, it could become quite fluid and run. Not all bottoms need to be waxed. If a particular form can be held in such a way, during glazing, that its underside can easily avoid being covered in glaze it need not be waxed. Liquid wax can be applied with a brush directly from its container; the paraffin needs to be melted first. For this a shallow electric skillet, with a removable lid, can be used and the bottoms of pots dipped into it. To avoid the fumes from the hot wax the skillet should be located adjacent to some form of exterior wall exhaust fan. For safety, use a very low temperature setting and always turn the unit off as soon as you have finished waxing or if the melted wax begins to smoke. If a constant level of wax, approximating one quarter of an inch, is maintained, pots can momentarily be left to rest inside the skillet. When removing the pot, avoid the temptation to examine the bottom by tilting it sideways. The wax may drip or run on an unwanted area in an unflattering manner. Once this nonsense happens, there is no way to remove the stuff short of running the pot through a second bisque fire.

A design made by hot paraffin is brushed on the surface of a pot as a glaze resist.

Dipping

The most frequently used method for applying glaze to bisque ware is referred to as dipping. For this process to be successful the base of the ware must be waxed.

The half-dip technique is a two step process. If a flat form is being glazed, first dip one half into the glaze, hold there momentarily and then remove and vigorously shake back and forth to remove excess glaze drips. In a minute or so, after the glaze is dry, the other half is dipped. Where the two coatings overlap, and the glaze is twice as thick, there will be a noticeable color change in the glaze after firing. You should consider the decorative aspect of this process carefully when deciding how and where to direct the placement of each glaze coating. Bowls and open vessel forms can be glazed in the same manner. Also, different sections can be dipped in different glazes. If, for example, equal sections of a bowl are dipped into three different glazes there will be three new colors in the overlaying areas to add to and complement the colors of the three original glazes. Depending on the selection of glazes the results could be less than poetic but I have seen some stunning bowls multi-glazed in this fashion.

Bill Beaver and Linda Savell dipping pottery in extra-large containers of glaze.

Glazing tongs can be used to effectively dip small to medium size pots into glaze.

If a pot is relatively small, and if there is enough glaze in the bucket, it can easily be completely immersed with glaze tongs. These tongs or pliers have sharp metal prongs at the end of pivoted jaws that securely grip the pot while barely touching its surface. All that one has to do, while holding the pot with the handles of the tongs, is to smoothly slide the entire piece into the glaze, in such a way that the interior surface is completely covered. Without trapping air inside, calmly withdraw it for a quick twisting and glaze shake off. When the glaze dries, use the tip of the finger to gently rub over the tiny marks left by the tongs and sponge off any glaze that remains on the waxed foot area.

Pouring

If the ware is larger than the glaze bucket, or too difficult to dip, glaze can be poured onto it. Pouring, because it offers such a wide variety of creative options, is my favorite means for applying glaze. By pouring I can immediately and creatively choose where a glaze will or will not go. If I pour one glaze over another, which I do frequently for a richer feast of color, I am able to leave an area unglazed to reveal another glaze or even the clay body itself. When glazing a bowl I can put one glaze on the inside and a totally different one on the outside. I also enjoy the ease of glazing tall or narrow forms, which are prime candidates for glaze pouring. Also, they don't have to be waxed. By simply gripping the inverted base with the tips of the fingers the glaze can be made to uniformly cascade down their walls as they are rotated. To improve the flow of any poured glaze, it helps to lightly wet the pot first with water.

Glaze the inside surface of pots first: this will avoid disturbing glaze applied to the outside. After pouring the glaze inside the pot, quickly swirl it around and nimbly pour it out by rotating both wrists as far as is possible to one side followed by a smooth rotation in the opposite direction. Once the rim is completely coated, shake the pot back-and-forth to remove and prevent dripping.

The classic procedure for pouring glaze requires that the inside of the pot be glazed first. Begin by filling a pouring container, such as a 1 to 2 pint measuring cup, with glaze that has just been stirred. While holding the pot upright, pour the glaze inside until the form is almost half filled. Holding the pot in both hands, swirl it around a time or two to direct the glaze further up the walls. Immediately tilt the wrists as far as possible to one side and begin pouring the glaze out and back into the bucket, uniformly coating the inside walls as the wrists turn. Shake or rotate the inverted pot back and forth to remove any excess glaze. If any drips run down the outside wall or if there is too thick a build-up on the top of the rim itself, sponge the area clean.

If one hand can easily hold a pot upside-down, by the foot, a layer of glaze can be uniformly poured around its outer surface. Rotate the wrist of the hand holding the pot broadly to one side; systematically reverse the direction of the rotation as the free hand pours glaze from a small container down its sides. Once the form is completely covered, remove excess glaze by twisting the pot back-and-forth.

With the inside of the pot finished, you now have several methods to choose from for glazing the outside and none of them require a waxed foot—if you're careful. Pots that can be securely held by the foot with one hand are enviably easy to glaze. Feet or bottoms that are small in diameter can also function as handles to fearlessly hold pots upside-down. Held directly above the glaze bucket in this manner, glaze is poured over the outside of the form with remarkable ease as the pot is slowly rotated by the wrist. If the diameter of the foot is too wide to be held by the fingers, one hand can be placed inside the inverted pot to both support and rotate it while the other hand pours on the glaze. Or, the outside of a pot can be glazed after being placed over a banding wheel. The banding wheel, itself, should sit inside a shallow pan to catch the excess glaze run-off. If it isn't tall enough to hold the pot in suspension above this pan, place an additional object under it to extend its height. Another way for holding the pot upside-down for glazing is to rest its rim on two narrow sticks of wood or on

a metal cake rack placed over the glaze bucket. If the diameter of the pot is wider than the bucket, place the supports over a larger pan. With this method the supports leave marks in the glaze where they make contact with the rim. If possible, even them out by rubbing them with the tip of the finger or sponge the rim clean and re-dip it in glaze.

Glazing the outside of a pot while it is inverted is always advantageous. Whenever a pot, with or without a waxed foot, can be glazed so that the glaze pour runs off at the rim, rather than at the foot, it is in less danger of becoming fused to the kiln shelf. If the thickest glaze build-up is at the rim it has a longer distance to travel and to thin itself out, should it become fluid, before reaching the kiln shelf. If the pot were glazed while in an upright position, the build-up would be at the wax line, which melts away early in the firing and which is located just 1/4 of an inch above the shelf. Should the glaze run for any number of reasons, this pot would almost certainly become attached to the kiln shelf.

Spraying

If your forms are too large or awkward to glaze by either dipping or pouring you might want to use a spray gun. If you are having difficulty applying glaze evenly and desire a more uniform coating you definitely want to use a spray gun. There is an explicit connection between spraying and control in glazing. With practice, glaze can be sprayed on with great uniformity and accuracy. It can also be sprayed systematically, so that there is a gradual build-up in thickness from one area to another, resulting in a subtle gradation of color. In fact, an entire series of lively effects such as stenciling, highlighting, fading and airbrush detailing are creatively possible with this procedure. With understanding, spraying becomes a simple, fast and a qualitative method for applying oxides, slips, stains, underglazes, glazes and over-glaze lusters to clay.

The interior of forms with openings too narrow for spraying should be glazed first by pouring and then externally by spraying.

Almost all forms are sprayed while on a banding wheel. To prevent drips or an uneven build-up of glaze the ware should continuously be rotated as it is sprayed. Likewise, the gun, too, should always be in motion. If the glaze is sprayed indoors a well ventilated spray booth should be used; if it is sprayed out-of-doors the wind should be blowing on your backside. In either situation, take the necessary safety precautions—and, absolutely, wear a respirator.

The spray gun, which is powered by compressed air pressure, need not be overly expensive or complicated. The simple siphon-type spray guns, where the air blows directly over the top of the siphon tube coming from

Using a siphon-tube spray gun to glaze a large bowl.

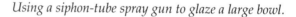

the storage container, are hassle free and easy to clean. To keep the orifice from becoming clogged the glaze should normally be passed through an 80 or 100 mesh sieve, but with this type of gun a clogged particle can instantly be dislodged by simultaneously running the fingertip across the top of the siphon tube and the air orifice. Again, seldom does one directly come to know something without having to first work through certain physical experiences. Spray glazing is like that. Initially everyone seems to underspray their work by over-estimating the thickness of the sprayed-on glaze. In this context, spraying is strikingly deceptive. To achieve adequate coverage, more often than not, twice as much glaze will need to be sprayed on as was originally thought or deemed necessary.

Work that is going to be once-fired or single-fired is frequently spray glazed. In the leather-hard state, and even as bone-dry greenware, these pieces are ideal candidates for spraying; the process that transfers the least amount of moisture to the clay body. I can still remember the first time I observed Steve Smilove spraying his greenware pottery. Attached to his spray gun, in place of the standard glaze-holding canister, was 6 feet of flexible tubing, the end of which he would expeditiously place in different buckets of glaze, located on the floor all around his spray booth, to rapidly spray 3 or 4 separate glazes onto the same pot. Short of genius, there was absolutely nothing special about it.

For rhythmic variety Heidi Ciofani will partially wrap a pot with twine, spray it with glaze, remove the twine and spray it again with a glaze of a different color.

Brushing

Many self-mixed glazes cannot be successfully applied with a brush. Because they usually don't contain the sophisticated suspension media of their finely ground commercial counterparts they simply are not as brushable. Individual brush strokes are often shockingly visible after firing—especially if the glaze is opaque. Also, the larger the surface area covered the more offensive the marks can become. Transparent glazes, on the other hand, are somewhat more brushable. Low-fire commercial glazes, because they contain gum binders, are very brushable, so much so that three thick coats are needed for them to work. Raku glazes are also appropriate for brushing. As one of the exceptions, these highly versatile glazes can produce profoundly clean results if a wide, soft-haired brush is used to uniformly apply one or more thin, flowing coats.

The main point to remember here is that glaze is not paint. It does not look or behave like paint. It is one color in the bucket, a different color after firing. It is one texture on the bisque ware, a different texture as fired ware. If a glaze is going to be applied with a brush, let it be applied as linear decoration: as line. Applied in a lively manner, perhaps with the thin soft point of a Japanese brush, it can be a fresh, clean addition to the ceramic surface either under the main glaze coating or on top of it. Disappointing point isn't it? . . . I, too, like to paint.

W. Mitch Yung, Oval Jar, Majolica/Earthenware, 8" × 9 1/2" × 14 1/4". Majolica is a term, dating back to the 13th century, used to describe the tin-glazing and decorative painting of terracotta. Basically the clay is covered with an opaque glaze followed by the direct brushing on of colored oxide designs and a final coat of clear glaze. Painting colors onto dry raw glaze gives them a wet-wash look.

Paula Rosensweet preparing to apply 3 coats of a cone 05 transparent clear commercial glaze with a brush to her footed plates made with colored clays.

GLAZE TESTING AND DEVELOPMENT

The Basic Glaze Recipe

When two or more glaze forming minerals are combined to form a ceramic glaze the resulting composition is traditionally put into a formula or recipe framework where each of the elements are indicated as percentages. The recipe for the transparent gloss glaze appearing below is a standard format for writing a base glaze.

Transparent Gloss C/10-R

Custer Feldspar	35%
Flint	30%
Whiting	20%
Kaolin (EPK)	15%
	100%

The C/10-R refers to the firing temperature and to the atmosphere inside the kiln during firing: cone 10 reduction. Cone 10 is the equivalent of 2345° F and a reduction firing is one where the amount of oxygen available for combustion is reduced. This is the opposite of an oxidation fire and greatly affects the color of the clay and the glaze. The four ingredients make up what is known as the base glaze. They are listed in percentages and should add up to a total of 100. These percentages can also be expressed as grams.

If the percentages, or weights, of the combined ingredients do not add up to 100, the total for the recipe can be brought to a balance of 100 by dividing the amount of each individual ingredient by the sum total of all of the ingredients.

Colorants to a glaze are often, but not always, included in the recipe as a separate addition. This addition is expressed as a percentage of the total sum of the base ingredients. If, for example, you wanted to change the appearance of the glaze from a clear transparent to a light-green celadon you could try adding 4 percent of red iron oxide. By multiplying .04 (4% written as a decimal) times 100 (total base weight) you will be able to see that for every 100 grams of base glaze you'll need 4 grams of red iron oxide. Likewise, if you wanted to make its appearance less transparent you could add 11% tin oxide as an opacifier to the base. This would amount to adding 11 grams of tin oxide to every 100 grams of glaze base: (0.11 x 100 = 11 grams).

Developing A Base Glaze Recipe

There are several ways to formulate a new glaze recipe. Existing recipes can be altered, one ingredient at a time, until a totally new glaze base is developed. Glazes can also be created using the capacity of different oxides to unite and interact with one another. One such approach is the *molecular unity formula*. It is a technically complicated system of calculation that uses the chemical formula and the molecular weight of oxides in a three part formula for placing them according to molecular equivalents, or ratios of molecules, rather than parts by weight. I, personally, am ill-at-ease with this method and feel more comfortable with a process modestly known as *limit formulation*.

Limit formula glazes are created by selecting ingredients from the three foundational groups of glaze chemicals (the glass formers, the fluxes and the refractories) in amounts based upon their specific limits of operational effectiveness in a glaze. The amount of each ingredient chosen, not including the colorants, should lie somewhere between the upper and lower limits of their relative usefulness. Their combined total in the recipe should equal 100 and because these limits are approximations, and not absolutes, should be referenced for guidance only. Following is a list of basic glaze materials and their limits by percent when written into a formula.

Glaze Materials: Possible Formula Allowances By Percent

Ball Clay	0–50 %
Bentonite	0– 2 %
Bone Ash	0–10 %
Boroflux	0–50 %
Cornwall Stone	20–70 %
Dolomite	0–10 %
Feldspar	20–70 %
Flint	0–40 %
Frit	0–80 %
Gerstley Borate	10–80 %
Kaolin Clay	0–30 %
Lithium	0–40 %
Nepheline Syenite	10–50 %
Spodumene	10–50 %
Talc	5–20 %
Whiting	5–40 %
Zinc Oxide	0–20 %

Yoshiro Ikeda, Enigma, coil-built and oxidation fired to cone 07, 20 1/2″ × 20″ × 7″.

When assembling ingredients for a glaze formula in this manner, pay special attention to the firing temperature and to the type of surface finish you're intending to achieve. Glazes maturing at the higher cones will require more feldspar or nepheline syenite as a flux; those firing at lower temperatures will use gerstley borate in larger percentages. Gloss finishes will require larger amounts of flint; matte surfaces rely on larger amounts of alumina or clay; harder more durable surfaces need whiting, bone ash or dolomite. Although this process may initially appear invitingly simple, assembling ingredients still relies on trial and error and many of your test results will need to be remedied by further adjustments and testing.

If you're still a little in the dark and uncertain as to what each chemical contributes to a glaze or what happens to it when fired to the temperature you're firing at, you might want to mix each one of them individually with water and fire them on separate test tiles. By doing so you'll be in possession of a set of references for visual guidance—enabling you to make immediate and more knowledgeable comparisons between the surface qualities of the various materials when fired.

Triaxial Blend

A system known as the *triaxial blend* is a graduated method that can be used for developing a base glaze from only three ingredients.

The triaxial diagram seen here is laid out to blend 3 ingredients (Ferro Frit 3124, Edgar Plastic Kaolin and Flint) in 20% increments—with the hope of developing a cone 05 glaze base. An extended version (using parallel lines to depict ten instead of five spatial segments) could just as easily have been set up to represent 10% increments.

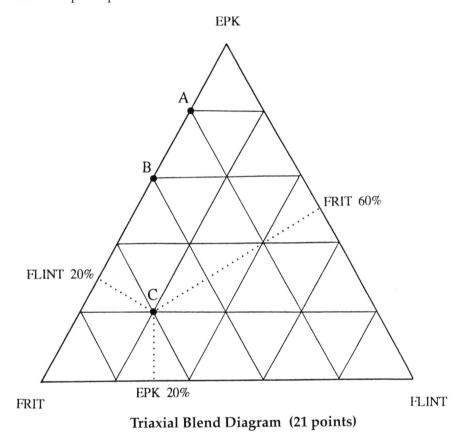

Triaxial Blend Diagram (21 points)

Points along the three legs of the triangle are a blend of two components. The glaze at point A is 80% Frit and 20% EPK. The glaze at point B is 60% Frit and 40% EPK and so on. Points inside the triangle are a blend of all three components. The glaze at point C is 60% Frit, 20% EPK and 20% Flint. The percentages were found by counting the spaces up from the leg of the triangle, the side of the triangle opposite the corner bearing the component name, to point C.

Glaze Test Tiles

Whenever a new glaze is formulated or a new recipe acquired it should first be tested. Testing gives information that is pertinent to your individual situation. It informs you as to how the glaze works with your chemicals, on your clay, in your kiln and with your personal glazing habits. A glaze that works one way in one studio may work differently in yours.

Testing of glazes is usually carried out on small clay forms. Uniformly made, and prepared in advance specifically for such purposes, these clay forms are commonly known as test tiles. Their shapes are infinite. The ones you make should be thrown, handbuilt or extruded from your own clay, and should be shaped to reflect the surface and texture of your own work. They should also be stable and be at least 3 inches tall to clearly reveal how the glaze will both look and perform on a vertical surface.

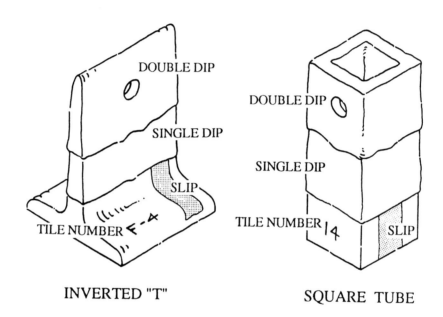

INVERTED "T"   SQUARE TUBE

Extruded Glaze Test Tiles (2 Examples)

Once the tiles are made, and become leather-hard, brush on a wide band of white slip and a band of iron oxide slip. Others, such as a copper slip or black slip, can be added or substituted but be certain to leave plenty of the clay surface uncovered to see how the glaze performs on the clay body itself. Using the wide mark of a lead pencil as an engraving tool, number each tile and write your name on either the back or underside. This identifying information can also be added later, after the bisque fire, with an underglaze pencil or with the sharp point of a small bamboo calligraphy brush and a cobalt-iron slip. As a final consideration, use a fettling knife to bore a good-size hole near the top of the leather-hard tile so that it can be hung on a nail or strung together, necklace-like, with others on a piece of cord.

Glaze test tiles being cut from a circular wall of leather-hard clay that was thrown on the wheel. Following the cutting the fettling knife will be used to bore a hole near the top of each piece for hanging on a nail or stringing on a loop of twine.

Glazing The Test Tile

Before going further, make sure the test tiles are bisque fired. That done, proceed to weigh out 100 grams of base glaze for each test conducted. Mix the glaze in a cup with water until the desired consistency is obtained and pass it through an 60 mesh sieve. Pour the test glaze over the upper two thirds of the tile. As soon as this dries, pour a second coat over the top third of the tile. This single and double coat of glaze will show how it looks when applied thick and when applied thin.

Immediately record the test in your glaze journal or ceramic notebook. If there is room to record specific glaze information on the unglazed area of the tile, do so with the fine point of a round oriental brush and a dark signing slip. After the tile is fired, complete your notes on the test by recording the results. Include such descriptive data as fluidity, translucency, color, texture and defects. I now use a "four star" rating system and give it serious credibility during future evaluations.

Color Testing

When everything about a newly tested glaze base appeals to you, consider adding oxides for color.

The color possibilities from metallic oxides or carbonates, alone or in combination, in a single glaze base can be tested systematically by using a method known as the *50/50 dry blend*. It is a procedure for testing a set number of colorants, of certain percentages, along with all of the possible cross blends between any two of them. The row running across the top of the stepped chart seen here is the base line. It should show five different colorants of various percentages or the same colorant as five different percentages: either way the choice is yours to make. The remaining rows show all of the existing 50/50 blend combinations of the original five colorants chosen.

Make 500 grams of the glaze base, dry mix it thoroughly and add 100 grams to each of five individually labeled cups (the size of this test chart could be easily extended but for 15 tiles 500 grams of glaze is sufficient). To each of the five cups add the assigned percentage of color and once again thoroughly mix and screen the dry ingredients.

If tile #1 were to be glazed with a mixture containing 4% red iron oxide (4% expressed decimally is .04) and tile #2 with a mixture containing 8% titanium dioxide, tile #6 would be glazed with an equal mixture of 1 and 2; or a new glaze containing only 2% red iron and 4% titanium—because the amount of glaze base has been doubled, the percentage of coloring oxide is now reduced by one-half. To create this blend for tile #6 either weigh out 20 grams of glaze from cups 1 and 2 or take a level teaspoon of glaze from each cup and combine them with water. Adjust the consistency, sieve and pour the blended glaze onto the appropriately marked test tile.

Remember, if the firing of test tile #6 is successful and you want to mix a large batch of this newly colored glaze, add only one-half of the tested colorant percentages (from the top row) to the base glaze.

50/50 Dry Blend Glaze Color Test

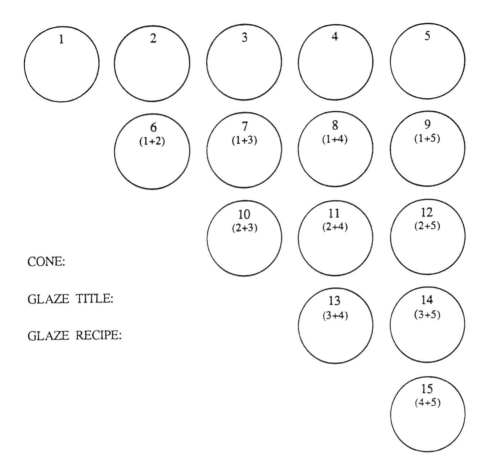

CONE:

GLAZE TITLE:

GLAZE RECIPE:

Following is a selected listing of single colorants, including percentage limits and color possibilities, that can be quickly referenced as a source of information for testing:

Cobalt 0.2–1.5% Light to dark blue, slightly greenish-blue when zinc is around.

Copper 1.0–3.0% Greens and some turquoise, reds to some purples in reduction.

Iron 1.0–10.0% Light yellow to reddish browns, gray-greens in Celadon bases.

Mason Stain 5.0–20.0% Black #6600, soft gray to dark black.

Manganese 1.0–5.0% Soft reddish to strong plum-blue browns, some purples.

Rutile 4.0–12.0% Pale yellow tans to mottled orange-browns, some white-blues.

Tin 2.0–10.0 % Translucent whites to strong opaque whites.

Titanium 4.0–10.0% Light ivory-cream to a mottled gray-blue.

The straight *line blend* is another and somewhat simplistic way for testing the results that occur when two glazes, either with different bases or the same base but with different colorants, are systematically combined.

TEST TILE:	#1	#2	#3	#4	#5	#6
Glaze A	0%	20%	40%	60%	80%	100%
Glaze B	100%	80%	60%	40%	20%	0%

Line Blend Test

In the 6 point line blend shown above, test tile #2 would be a test blend of glaze A (20%) and glaze B (80%). If both glazes were made from the same low-fire base and A contained a yellow colorant and B a red colorant, tiles #2 thru #5 would test out to be four shades of orange. And if, for example, the line were extended to include an 11 point blend, and the glazes were combined in 10% increments, the test would now yield nine colors of orange.

To systematically test the blending of three colorants in a base glaze use the 21 point triaxial diagram seen in the section "Developing A Glaze Recipe".

Only now place *three* colorants, such as rutile, iron, and copper at each vertex. Substitute rutile for the EPK, iron for the Frit and copper for the Flint. You'll be making 21 tests, so mix up 2100 grams of your chosen glaze base and place 100 grams in each of 21 individually marked disposable cups. Assuming you decide to test the color combinations in one gram increments (divisions of one percent), test each colorant at 6%. To cup A add 5 grams (5%) iron and 1 gram (1%) rutile. To cup B add 4 grams iron and 2 grams rutile. To the cup representing point C add 3 grams iron, 1 gram rutile and 1 gram copper. After all the cups are filled add water, mix, screen and apply to the test tiles.

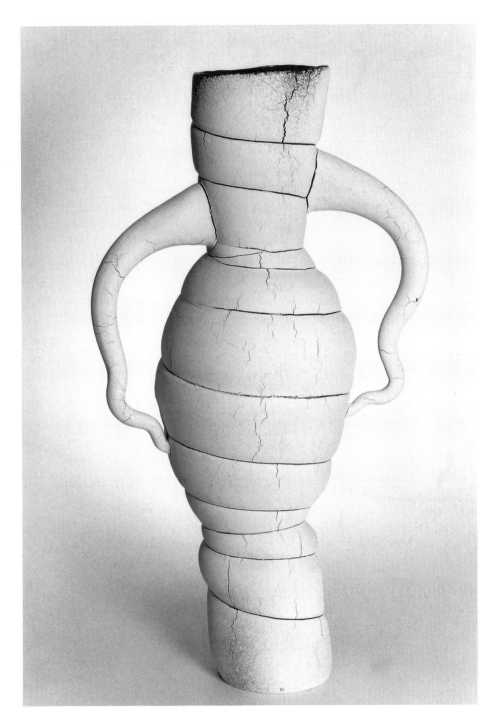

Susan Crowell, Untitled Vase, thrown and altered porcelain, 24" high. Susan bisque fires her large vase forms to a high temperature for vitrification. While still warm from the kiln she applies a cone 05 black glaze followed by a thin coat of terra sigillata. Where the terra sigillata swims apart, as it dries and shrinks, crack patterns of shiny glaze appear when the vase is fired the second time.

GLAZE PROBLEMS AND ADJUSTMENTS

Glazes have always amazed me, full of intensity, of lip-licking splendors, appearing both luxurious and serviceable to my senses. At other times they have been exceedingly mysterious and, without question, full of trouble. True, they have brought much satisfaction but they have also brought on times of disappointment where I have humbly been made to scramble for clues, causes and cures. What I have learned from these experiences is that many of the most agonizing faults were not a direct result of defects in the glaze formula, but in how it was applied and how it was fired. There are many other factors that also affect the final outcome of a glaze: the clay it's fired on, the temperature of the bisque fire, its location in the kiln, or even how the kiln itself was stacked. As another despairing example of what can go wrong, twice this semester, at the college where I teach, we were faced with faulty batches of glaze. After some careful investigation it was discovered that one batch was incorrectly weighed and that the chemical make-up of the flux in the other had been altered by our supplier.

Running

Fluidity is a very common problem. Glazes that easily run and fuse the pot to the kiln shelf are the cause of much duress. If the running is not the result of an overly thick application or an over-fired or over-soaked kiln and it cannot be made less viscous by reducing the content of the fluxing agent or by adding flint and more clay, it should simply be replaced.

If this fluid glaze runs this much on a 4" cup, what would it do on a 12" vase?

Crawling

Crawling is a descriptive term given to glazes that roll back or bead up leaving patches of bare clay. The causes can be physical such as an accumulation of dust on the bisque ware or the build-up of body oils and/or hand lotions through excessive handling both prior to and during glazing. On other occasions glaze will crawl if the bisque is underfired, if the glaze is made too thick, if the clay content is too high or if it is applied too heavily and/or forced to dry at an accelerated pace. Heavy applications of slips or underglazes can also cause the covering glaze surface to pull apart.

Chemical causes for crawling are the result of either too high a percentage of ingredients, that either shrink a lot, such as ball clay, zinc and bone ash or that function as opacifiers, such as tin and zircopax. The use of calcined zinc as a substitute for zinc and the use of kaolin in place of the overly plastic ball clay can help reduce shrinkage.

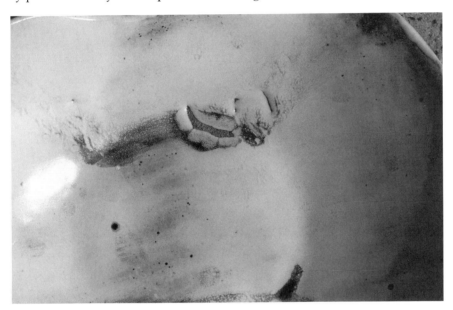

The glaze inside this bowl crawled as a result of too heavy an application.

Pitting

Pinholes or small craters in the fired surface generally result from the glaze melting to soon and entrapping gasses from the clay body before they escape or if the glaze is not fired long enough. The active sintering or bubbling phase that a glaze goes through as it melts and matures takes time to settle down. If this time is cut too short, by firing the kiln too fast, the bubbles are unable to smooth themselves out.

If a glaze is not fired high enough, or if it is applied to thick, similar defects in the surface can result. If a glaze is not under-fired and some pitting still occurs the addition of just 2 percent of Boroflux or Gerstley borate will have an effect that will not go unappreciated. Materials with a lower viscosity such as soda feldspar, nepheline syenite, spodumene or whiting should also be added. By lowering the percentages of one or more of the highly viscous recipe ingredients such as flint, clay or an opacifier, all of which are chemically slow to respond and subsequently slow to heal surface irregularities, a noticeable improvement in the glaze will also, hopefully, occur.

Roughness

Glaze is essentially glass. If it is applied too thin, which is not uncommon if the glaze is sprayed, or if you are simply new to glazing, there will be an insufficient amount of material available to form a glassy surface and the roughness that is often felt is the textural surface of the clay itself. If the glaze is not thoroughly mixed just prior to use, a similar grainy surface will result from all of the glass forming chemicals being left, out of suspension, at the bottom of the glaze bucket.

Underfiring will make any glaze surface feel less than smooth. On certain sculptural forms such a dry or coarse surface may be desirable and intentionally planned for. If, however, a glaze is properly applied and fired to its correct temperature and it still has a rough, stony feel, it may be in need of additional flux. By increasing the percentage of flux already in the recipe or by adding some gerstley borate the glaze may be adjusted to melt at a desired temperature without having to be fired to a higher cone.

Crazing

A term given to an extensive network of very fine cracks, often barely noticeable, that occur in a fired glaze. Crazing often results when the glaze cools and contracts more than the clay body. In raku this crackle phenomenon is highly valued with the glossy glazes and is often obtainable by putting the glaze on thick and by waving it back and forth, with tongs in the open air, after it is removed from the kiln and just prior to being smoked inside a closed reduction container. The cold air causes the hot glaze to go into thermal contraction and the smoking visibly defines the crazing.

To prevent high-fire and utilitarian glazes from crazing the ware should be allowed to soak awhile once the kiln reaches maturity. Afterwards it should be cooled slowly. This prolonged heating both hardens the clay and allows for the glaze, if thinly applied, to become chemically assimilated by it.

Adjustments to the glaze recipe can also be made to reduce crazing.

Additional amounts of flint, especially the finely ground 325 mesh size, can be added to increase expansion. Small or additional amounts of clay, talc and zinc will have somewhat of a similar effect. In the same somewhat seriously scientific vein, by lowering the percentage of soda feldspar, or by replacing it with a substitute such as spodumene, the recipe will be less likely to craze.

Shivering

Shivering is the peeling away or flaking off of fired slivers of glaze. Shivering usually occurs at the edges of rims and throwing marks or near areas of high relief; especially if the glaze is reduced too soon or too severely in the kiln. It is primarily a result of the clay body contracting at a greater rate than that of the glaze. Because shivering is the reverse, basically, of crazing its remedies are opposite. Instead of aiding expansion the goal becomes that of decreasing it by reducing the percentage of flint and increasing the percentages of soda feldspar or frit.

Todd Johnson, High Frontier, earthenware with low-fire glaze, 6 1/2" × 7" × 7".

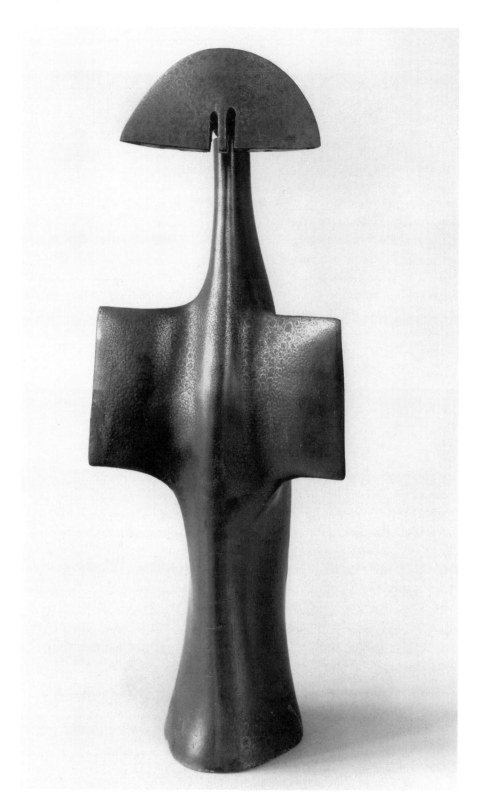

Ruth Duckworth, #2261290, glazed porcelain, 23″ × 8″ × 7″.

David G. Wright, Hoof Cup, glazed stoneware, 3 1/2″ × 4 1/2″.

David G. Wright, Slug Mug, glazed stoneware, 4 1/2″ × 5″.

RELATED SURFACE TREATMENTS

There are many exciting ways to bring suitable finishes to the clay surface other than by glazing. Many of these strategies carry a marvelous spirit of their own yet remain interconnected to the glazing process. This relationship is unique and, in the promise of possibilities, some of these special procedures are being given recognition here.

Oxides

Oxides mixed with water and brushed onto unglazed clay are a popular way to add decorative color to ware. Applied to a heavily textured area of unfired clay, the oxide wash can be wiped clean, so that the color remains only in the deeper recesses of the texture. It is easier to wipe it off the high-relief areas of greenware with steel wool than it is to wipe off the same surface in the bisque state with a sponge. The steel wool takes off a thin layer of the dry clay, so the results are quicker and cleaner looking; worthy of quiet celebration. Afterwards the surface may or may not be covered with glaze. If it is going to be glazed, any excess oxide that remains unfixed after bisque firing can be washed away with running water before glazing. Always allow a bisque pot that has become wet to dry slowly and thoroughly before applying glaze.

It is important that oxides be applied somewhat thinly if a coating of glaze is going to be placed on top of them. Otherwise, thick applications of oxides, especially cobalts, can cause glaze to flake off or crawl during the firing. The physical properties of these natural oxide stains can be improved by adding a little ball clay or a borax frit (such as Ferro 3134) and 1%- 3% bentonite.

Red iron, copper and cobalt are the oxides used most repeatedly. Coloring oxides are frequently applied locally (with a sponge-like piece of high density foam cut to a geometric shape, with a self-made long-haired brush, and an oriental calligraphy brush or with an air brush) to achieve a decorative effect on a limited part of the pot.

Slips and Engobes

The terms slip and engobe are often used interchangeably—even by the most intelligent of minds in the ceramic profession. They have their differences, of course, but until you know and understand a few incidentals pertaining to each, confusion will be involuntary.

Generically, the term slip refers to clay in any number of liquid forms. To some the term is only synonymous with casting slip: liquid clay which is poured into plaster molds. In attempts to avoid confusion and to develop a more definitive description for liquid clay when it is used for surface decoration as opposed to a casting body, the term engobe often appears. Generally, if a surface finish contains mostly clay, and very little else in the way of chemicals, it is referred to as a slip. If it contains less than 50% clay and 10% or more flint, usually in combination with a flux such as a feldspar or a frit, it is called an engobe. And, if an engobe formula contains less than 25% clay you may want to start thinking about calling it a glaze. Still confused? Well, another explanation I find to be refreshingly helpful states that an engobe is used to cover the whole pot while a slip only covers a small portion of it.

Suzanne Stephenson applying thick slip to a leather-hard plate form.

Suzanne Stephenson, Dusk Water Rock, terra-cotta plate formed from a slab thrown on the wheel over a plaster hump mold, 3" × 27" × 27". Clay slips and colored vitreous engobes were applied to leather-hard clay and fired to cone 03.

300   THE SPIRIT OF CLAY

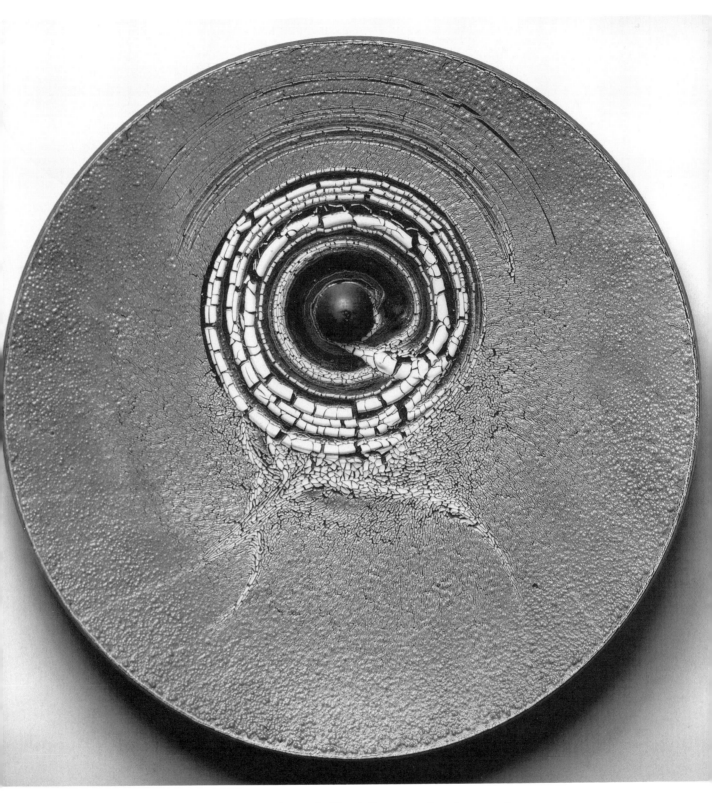

Robert Sperry, Untitled #991, 4 1/2" × 27". The richly textured surface was obtained by applying a thick white clay slip over a black glaze that was fired to cone 7. As it dried, the clay slip shrank dramatically on the surface of the smooth glaze. The slip was permanently affixed to the glaze by refiring the piece to cone 5.

Slips do not become vitreous or appear glossy in the way some engobes do. Used decoratively slips are used to create backgrounds for glazes much in the same way unpainted surfaces, such as walls and ceilings, are primed prior to painting. When used in this manner they are applied with a flat, and extremely wide, thick-haired Hake brush (made from the softest of sheep hairs) and usually in the form of several thin uniform coats, while being rotated on a wheel, to avoid too thick a build-up and flaking. Slips, like engobes, are often used, either subtly or dramatically, to texturally activate a surface. Yet the largest and most underlying role slip plays in visually transforming the appearance of ceramics is when it is used facially to add a stirring element of color design or linear Chinese brush work to the surface.

Brush work has its own imperishable worth, its own meaningfulness, when laid down naturally in a spirit of invisible hope and love. It can be loaded not only with sensory delight but with one's maturity and sense of being.

Robert Sperry applying white clay slip to the fired black glazed surface of a plate.

Steven Hill applying a thick clay slip to a plate just thrown on the potter's wheel.

The universal formula for a high-fire white slip is the same as that for porcelain: equal parts of kaolin clay, potash feldspar (or nepheline syenite), ball clay and flint. Usually some bentonite and borax is included to aid adhesion. For stronger whites or greater opacity tin oxide or zircopax can be added. By using metal oxides or carbonates, such as red iron, manganese and cobalt, or certain commercial stain mixtures capable of surviving the higher temperatures, the color can be successfully altered.

For a good fit and even shrinkage, decorative slips should be made from the same clay the pot is and should be applied while the pot is still wet. Slips can be adjusted to fit leather-hard clay by substituting calcined clay for part of the clay content or by adding frits, flint and feldspar to the mixture. For bone-dry surfaces the amount of clay should be reduced to less than half of the total formula to compensate for shrinkage, and the quantity of fluxes and binders increased. The clay content of slips used on bisque ware should not exceed 30 percent.

Steven Hill decorating and scraping through a wet layer of slip with a wood rib.

Terra Sigillata

A creamy clay slip known as *terra sigillata* is another, more refined, example of a low temperature slip glaze. Fired between cone 010 and cone 06, this slip is made from fine grained earthenware clays, such as Cedar Heights Redart or ball clays (for a white finish) that have been thoroughly mixed in distilled water, with or without a defloculant (Soda Ash, Darvan Dispersal #7, Alcosperse #149, Tri Sodium Phosphate or Calgon), and allowed to settle in a glass container for at least 48 hours. After the heavy particles have fallen to the bottom the clear water at the top is carefully removed and the very upper most portion of the mixture, the visible layer containing the finer clay particles in suspension, is siphoned off and used as the slip glaze. An alternative procedure would involve removing the top layer of water (with the lighter particles still in suspension) 5-8 hours after the initial mixing and placing it into a separate container where these lighter clay particles can settle to the bottom and form an exceptionally smooth terra sigillata . . . the remaining water is left to evaporate.

Prior to spraying or brushing several thin coats onto a leather-hard pot this smooth, extra-fine, slip can be colored with oxides or Mason stains. Once on the pot, and while still leather-hard, it can be polished with a soft cloth or plastic bag for a harder finish. To create a surface sheen with even more depth, it can then be burnished with the back of a metal spoon or a smooth stone. Following the firing the original shiny surface can be reactivated and brought to life again by warming the piece and applying clear shoe polish.

Historically, the ancient Greeks were the masters of slip glaze decoration on clay vessels. As far back as 1000 BC Greek pottery was being painted with clay slips. In Athens, between 700-530 BC painters were using black slips to paint animals and people in scenes depicting daily life, athletics and mythological legends onto orange-red clay backgrounds. From 530-400 BC this decorative motif was reversed. Figures where then portrayed in red on a background of black slip. The beautiful red-browns and sensuous blacks on the Greek pottery from these Classical periods are very famous examples of terra sigillata surfaces, yet these painters of pictures on pottery, who were more famous then the figurative sculptors of their day, established their place in the history of art with the phenomenal discovery of foreshortening. Up until this break-through moment in time, just prior to 500 BC, the figure, at it's best, had always been represented as an unalterable profile or silhouette.

Jill Bonovitz, earthenware vessel with terra sigillata surface texture, 4 1/2" × 25".

Slip Trailing

The process of adding a raised line-like design to the surface of the clay is known as *slip trailing*. By using a compressible rubber bulb with a needle-like nozzle, the wet slip is drawn into the bulb and squeezed out again as the nozzle is creatively maneuvered over the surface of the leather-hard clay. The clay used for making the work should be the same clay that is slaked down to form the slip. The consistency of this slip should be monitored carefully. If allowed to become too watery it will shrink disproportionately and pull away. A modified version of this technique uses underglaze or glaze in place of the clay slip. Only instead of using the standard slip trailing bulbs and bottles or an enema bottle with the nozzle cut short, use an infant's ear syringe or hair color applicator bottle, with a finer nozzle tip, for applying the glaze.

Sgraffito

The technique of scratching through a layer of slip or glaze to reveal the clay beneath it is referred to as *sgraffito*. The decorative quality of the this line work is directly related to the wetness or dryness of the clay and to the type of instrument used. Sharp pointed tools are most frequently chosen for incising but knives, wood modeling tools and fine wire loop trimming tools can also be used to produce results that are highly detailed and as richly decorative. The tooling can be spontaneous and playful or precise and technical. The imagery can be figurative and symbolic or abstract and repetitious. It's up to you. And, if a large area of the original surface coating is removed, a second coating of a material of a different color can be applied and drawn or carved through to create a more complicated and visually interesting surface design. If the engraving is done through a terra sigillata or a once-fire glaze the pot can be fired when dry; if not, it will need to be bisque-fired and glazed.

Kurt Weiser, Porcelain Teapot, slip cast and single-fired to cone 04 in an electric kiln, 12″ × 11″ × 4″. A black slip (100 grams colemanite + 25 grams black stain) was brushed on the bone dry clay and the design scratched through with a needle.

Resists

A resist is any material that is used to mask out selected areas of a clay surface to prevent the adherence of glazes or colored slips. Resists can be applied to unfired clay, bisque fired clay or an unfired but glazed surface. Applied to greenware, and covered with a slip, the wax burns away in the bisque kiln, leaving areas of both bare and slip covered clay to be glazed. Wax applied over a glaze on a bisque pot will resist the second application of a different glaze resulting in two distinct but planned areas of glaze after firing. Wax, either in the form of hot melted paraffin or a cold liquid emulsion, is the most commonly used resist in the clay studio. The bottoms of pots are often dipped in wax to prevent glaze build-up and fusion to the kiln shelf, but for decorative use the wax resist is usually applied with a brush. To avoid disarranging the glaze paint the wax on between 5 and 15 minutes after glazing the surface. If done sooner the glaze will be too wet; if done much later it is too powdery and vulnerable to movement.

Masking tape, liquid latex, contact paper and dampened paper shapes applied to the leather-hard clay surface are also very useful approaches to decorating and creating designs by using resist techniques. Stencils in the form of cut-outs, screens and any number of found objects can be placed in front of clay surfaces while they are sprayed with slips or underglazes to create visual textures of contrast and interest.

Nancy Selvin removing a latex resist after spraying the piece with glaze.

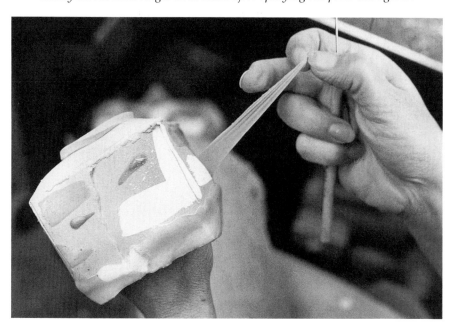

Clay resists, in the form of a medium-to-thick application of clay slip applied to a bisque surface, produce dramatic surface patterns when raku fired. When the clay slip dries it shrinks. In shrinking it forms a series of crackle patterns over the already shrunken clay form. Carefully taken to and from the raku kiln, to prevent the dried pieces from readily flaking off, the ware is heavily smoked. While still hot and in the post-firing reduction container, the surface exposed to the smoke from the cracks in the slip turns black. When cool, the clay resist is scraped away to reveal a gray and black harmonious design over the entire surface of the piece.

Heidi Ciofani using crumpled newspaper as a partial resist to a second glaze being sprayed over a previously glazed surface. The visual contrasts between these relatively accidental color patterns, created from the organic overlapping of different colored glazes, can be pleasingly dramatic.

Sandblasting

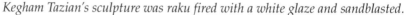

Many ceramic surfaces, both glazed and unglazed, often project a feeling of being far from complete and finished. One suitable way out of such an outlook, especially if the work in question has already been glaze fired, is to try sandblasting to bring new texture and expressive depth to the skin of the piece. The overall results of this powerfully abrasive technique can be extreme, but if used thoughtfully they can be more than complementary. An overly glossy glaze, for example, can be softened and made to appear almost warm and contemplatively satisfying. On certain forms entire sections can be taped over and the surrounding areas sandblasted to initiate a successful play between rough and smooth relationships. As a technique for enhancing the appearance of surfaces, and rendering them with more visual stimulation, sandblasting offers many attractive possibilities.

Kegham Tazian's sculpture was raku fired with a white glaze and sandblasted.

THE GLAZE JOURNAL

A glaze journal or glazing notebook is a personal diary of your glazing experiences. It is a place for keeping a running record of each pot and how it was glazed. It should contain a rough, but identifiable, sketch of the pot with numbered arrows showing where and in what order various decorative slips, glazes, etc. were applied. It should include dates, recipes, firing techniques and observations on the final results.

Your name, address and phone number should be clearly visible near the front or on the cover. This journal is a valuable source of both technical and aesthetic information. As time goes by, it will become even more valuable and you'll not want to lose it. In time it will be a document of how specific glazes look, not only by themselves but in combination with many other glazes. Normally this would be useful information that would go unremembered and be forgotten, but with the journal you can quickly refer back to your notes for advisement.

GLAZE RECIPES

Cone 9-10 Reduction Glazes

Piepenburg Matt Cone 9-10
35% Potash Feldspar
25% EPK Kaolin
15% Dolomite
10% Flint
10% Spodumene
 5% Whiting

Cornwall Clear Cone 9-10
70% Cornwall Stone
15% Whiting
15% Flint

Ivory Matt Cone 10
40% Potash Feldspar
20% EPK Kaolin
10% Spodumene
10% Flint
10% Dolomite
 5% Whiting
 5% Bone Ash

Laura's Turquoise Cone 10
35.3% Whiting
26.5% Kaolin
22.1% Custer Feldspar
 8.8% Flint
 2.9% Copper Carbonate
 2.6% Rutile
 1.8% Bentonite

Frosty Matt Cone 10
30% Nepheline Syenite
30% Flint
20% Whiting
10% Kaolin
10% Magnesium Carbonate

Doug's Rock Moss Cone 10
 35% Custer Feldspar
 25% Whiting
 20% Hawthorn Fire Clay
 20% Ball Clay
  5% Titanium Dioxide
0.25% Cobalt Oxide
0.25% Nickel Oxide

Turner's Cinnamon Cone 10
35% Custer Feldspar
25% EPK Kaolin
15% Kona F4 Feldspar
15% Dolomite
10% Whiting
 8% Bone Ash
 5% Tin Oxide
 5% Red Iron Oxide
 1% Bentonite

Hill's Blue Ash Cone 10
48.6% Albany or Alberta Slip
30.4% Whiting
18.2% Kentucky Ball Clay
 1.5% Cobalt Carbonate
 1.3% Red Iron Oxide

Weiser Moon Glow Cone 10
20.5% Custer Feldspar
20.5% Nepheline Syenite
20.5% EPK Kaolin
18.4% Dolomite
 8.7% Flint
 7.0% Superpax
 3.8% Whiting
 0.6% Bentonite

SNGN Stony Blue Cone 10
33.3% Kona F4 Feldspar
24.8% Kaolin
16.9% Dolomite
10.5% Talc
 6.9% Spodumene
 4.4% Whiting
 2.0% Bentonite
 0.9% Cobalt Carbonate
 0.3% Red Iron Oxide

Sargent's Matt Cone 10
25% Potash Feldspar
25% Dolomite
15% Nepheline Syenite
15% EPK Kaolin
10% Flint
10% Whiting

Sam's Matt Cone 10
50% Custar Feldspar
25% Dolomite
20% Ball Clay
 5% Kaolin

Tropical Clear Cone 9-10
30% Potash Feldspar
30% Flint
15% EPK Kaolin
15% Whiting
 5% Spodumene
 5% Dolomite

Rob Cone 10
29.9% Custer Feldspar
19.1% Whiting
18.6% Flint
15.4% Kaolin
10.4% Talc
 4.7% Rutile
 1.9% Bentonite

Piepenburg White Cone 10
50% Custar Feldspar
20% EPK Kaolin
20% Dolomite
 5% Flint
 5% Whiting
     Fawn
     4% Rutile
     4% Titanium Dioxide
     Temple Jade
     5% Titanium Dioxide
     2% Copper Carbonate
     Frog Belly
     3% Red Iron Oxide
     3% Tin Oxide
     Caramel Dynasty
     104% Red Iron Oxide
       4% Rutile
     Harvest
     4% Rutile
     3% Tin oxide

Gatsby Gloss Cone 9–10
50% Custer Feldspar
25% Flint
15% Whiting
 5% EPK Kaolin
 5% Dolomite

Lou Rainer #6 Cone 8-10
40% Nepheline Syenite
20% Flint
15% Talc
10% Gerstley Borate
 9% Dolomite
 6% Kaolin
     Snow White
     10% Opax

Ohata Iron Cone 10
43.0% Kona F4 Feldspar
19.0% Flint
 9.0% Bone Ash
 6.0% Whiting
 5.5% EPK Kaolin
 5.5% Talc
 2.0% Bentonite
10.0% Red Iron Oxide

Marine Blue Cone 10
45% Potash Feldspar
15% Cornwall Stone
15% Whiting
10% EPK Kaolin
 5% Gerstley Borate
 2% Red Iron Oxide
0.5% Cobalt Oxide

Abner Celadon Cone 10
66% Kona F-4 Feldspar
13% Flint
 6% Whiting
 6% Gerstley Borate
 5% Bone Ash
 4% Zinc Oxide

Bronze Cone 10
45% Cedar Heights Redart
33% Manganese Dioxide
 7% Copper Carbonate
 7% Cobalt Carbonate
 4% Ball Clay
 4% Flint

Tomato Cone 10
44.2% Kona F-4 Feldspar
23.7% Flint
10.7% Bone Ash
 6.6% EPK Kaolin
 6.6% Magnesium Carbonate
 6.6% Red Iron Oxide
 1.6% Bentonite

Cone 6 Reduction Glazes

Priscilla's Clear Cone 6-10
38% Nepheline Syenite
24% Kentucky Ball Clay
20% Whiting
13% Flint
 5% Gerstley Borate
   Mutant Ninja
   3% Copper Carbonate
   Jade East
   5% Titanium Dioxide
   3% Copper Carbonate
   Madonna White
   8% Titanium Dioxide

Spodumene Grey Cone 6
30% Spodumene
24% Dolomite
21% Custer Feldspar
12% Flint
 9% Kaolin
 4% Gerstley Borate

Stormy Matt Cone 6
37% Kona Feldspar
16% Gerstley Borate
15% EPK Kaolin
15% Dolomite
 6% Zinc Oxide
 6% Tin Oxide
 3% Whiting
 2% Bentonite
   Boa Skin
   8% Titanium Dioxide
   2% Nickel Oxide

Buttermilk Cone 6
30% Potash Feldspar
20% Gerstley Borate
17% Flint
 8% Whiting
 8% Dolomite
 7% Zircopax
 5% Kaolin
 5% Talc

P-5 Clear Cone 6
32% Potash Feldspar
22% Gerstley Borate
22% Flint
11% Kaolin
11% Dolomite
 2% Tin

Gloss Clear Cone 6
44% Kona Feldspar
20% Gerstley Borate
19% Flint
10% Kaolin
 7% Dolomite
   Creamora
   8% Titanium Dioxide
   3% Manganese
   Deep Sea Blue
   5% Rutile
   3% Manganese
   Ivory
   10% Zircopax

White Cream Cone 6
66% Kona Feldspar
 9% EPK Kaolin
 8% Dolomite
 7% Zircopax
 4% Zinc Oxide
 3% Gerstley Borate
 2% Whiting
 1% Bentonite
   Cream of Broccoli
   6% Rutile
   0.5% Cobalt Carbonate

D.B.S. Cone 6
33.8% Ferro Frit 3819
24.5% Kaolin
15.5% Flint
12.4% Wollastonite
 6.7% Lithium Carbonate
 4.7% Titanium Dioxide
 2.4% Dark Rutile

Cone 6 Oxidation Glazes

Matt White #536 Cone 6
41.7% Soda Feldspar
19.6% Kaolin
15.1% Whiting
12.6% Zinc Oxide
 6.2% Flint
 4.8% Tin Oxide

Gloss Base #537 Cone 6
35% Pyrotrol
33% Gerstley Borate
22% Custer Feldspar
10% Wollastonite
 Black
  8% Red Iron Oxide
  2% Manganese Dioxide
  1% Cobalt Carbonate
  1% Chrome Oxide

Base #540 Cone 6
28.1% Spodumene
26.3% Flint
21.9% Gerstley Borate
10.5% Nepheline Syenite
 8.8% Dolomite
 4.4% Zinc Oxide
 Grey
   7% Tin Oxide
  0.75% Mason Stain 6600

Base #547 Cone 6
28% Spodumene
26% Flint
18% Gerstley Borate
17% Wollastonite
11% Custer Feldspar
 Dusty Rose
  15% Mason Stain 6007
   5% Mason Stain 6006

Jackson's 41–A5 LClear Cone 5-6
60% Nepheline Syenite (Minex #7)
30% Wollastonite (NYCO 400 mesh)
10% Boroflux #1

Matt Base #548 Cone 6-10
34% Wollastonite
21% Ferro Frit 3269
18% Flint
17% No. 6 Tile Clay
10% Ferro Frit 3134
 White
 12% Superpax

Matt Base #533 Cone 6
30.5% D F Stone
21.8% Spodumene
21.8% Wollastonite
14.8% Georgia Kaolin Clay
 8.0% Red Iron Oxide
 Black
 12% Mason Stain 6600

Gloss Base #542 Cone 6
22.3% Gerstley Borate
19.1% Spodumene
18.2% Flint
14.5% D F Stone
11.3% Pyrotrol
 6.8% Wollastonite
 5.5% Custer Feldspar
 2.3% Zinc Oxide
 Deep Blue
   8% Cobalt carbonate
   5% Dolomite
   1% Red Iron Oxide
  0.25% Manganese Dioxide

Base #531 Cone 6
72.7% D F Stone
18.2% Gerstley Borate
 9.1% Whiting
 Pansy Purple
 10% Mason Stain 6385

Jeri's Turquoise Cone 04
70% Ferro Frit 3134
8% OM4 Ball Clay
22% Zircopax
4% Copper Carbonate

Yung's Satin Matt Cone 02
35% Flint
31% Gerstley Borate
16% Whiting
8% Lithium Carbonate
5% EPK Kaolin
4% Nepheline Syenite
Yellow Green
4% Copper Carbonate
4% Rutile

Arleo's Lithium Cone 04
41.3% Flint
20.2% EPK Kaolin
13.8% Lithium carbonate
11.0% Gerstley Borate
11.0% Ferro Frit 3110
2.7% Bentonite
Deep Blue
1.0% Mason Stain 6500
1.0% Copper Carbonate
0.4% Cobalt Carbonate

Nancy's Base Cone 04
54.7% Ferro Frit 3124
27.1% Flint
18.0% Kentucky Ball Clay
0.2% Bentonite
Black
11% Mason Stain 6600

J.S. Frozen Rain Cone 04-02
35% Nepheline Syenite
30% Ferro Frit 3124
12% EPK Kaolin
8% Wollastonite
5% Flint
5% Lithium Carbonate
5% Gerstley Borate

1-3 Base Cone 04
50% Ferro Frit 3134
24% EPK Kaolin
14% Flint
6% Lithium Carbonate
6% Wollastonite
Crimson
10% Mason Stain 6006

Yung's White Majolica Cone 02
64.7% Ferro Frit 3134
9.8% Flint
9.5% Zircopax
5.3% OM4 Ball Clay
3.3% Custer Feldspar
2.2% Calcined EPK Kaolin
1.9% Gerstley Borate
1.9% Bentonite
1.4% Tin Oxide

Shield's Smi-Matt Cone 05
65.5% Ferro Frit 3124
10.0% Whiting
9.5% Nepheline Syenite
9.5% EPK Kaolin
4.0% Lithium Carbonate
1.5% Bentonite

Arleo's Clear Gloss Cone 04
30% Ferro Frit 3124
26% Gerstley Borate
20% Nepheline Syenite
10% Flint
10% EPK Kaolin
4% Lithium Carbonate
Green Turquoise
3% Copper Carbonate

Pam's Smooth Matt Cone 05
30% Boroflux C-13
30% Nepheline Syenite
20% EPK Kaolin
20% Talc
Coffee
5% Manganese Dioxide

Jackson's 41-A Clear Cone 03-01
50% Nepheline Syenite (Minex #7)
30% Boroflux #1
20% Wollastonite (NYCO 400 mesh)

Midnight Blue Dry-Matt
49.06% Flint
27.55% Lithium Carbonate
15.31% #6 Tile Clay
 5.02% Boroflux C-13
 3.06% Bentonite
 5.00% Cobalt Carbonate

Jackson's 2C-C Low Gloss Sheen
Cone 03-01
47% Soda Feldspar (Minspar #7)
30% Wollastonite (NYCO 400 mesh)
23% Boroflux C-13

Suspension media for all of
   Jackson's glazes:
50-60% Hot Water
 0.20% Magnesium Hydroxide
 0.20% CMC-7M
 0.25% Bentonite 129

Raku Glazes

Piepenburg Crackle
70% Gerstley Borate
20% Nepheline Syenite
10% Flint

Wentworth Satin
45% Ferro Frit 3134
15% Wollastonite
14% Kaolin
11% Flint
 8% Lithium Carbonate
 5% Magnesium Carbonate

Bebe's Blue
67.6% Gerstley Borate
18.0% Nepheline Syenite
 9.0% Natural Bone Ash
 2.7% Copper Carbonate
 2.7% Cobalt Carbonate

Douglas Clear Cone 08-07
50% Gerstley Borate
20% Custer Feldspar
20% Strontium Carbonate
10% Flint

Bora-Bora
40% Bone Ash
40% Boroflux C-13
10% Nepheline Syenite
10% Copper Carbonate

Ingrid's Clear Crackle
80% Gerstley Borate
15% Custar Feldspar
 5% Whiting

Belanger Flat
45% Ferro Frit 3134
25% Flint
12% Whiting
10% Magnesium Carbonate
 7% Lithium Carbonate
 1% Bentonite

Hines Patina
7 parts Gerstley Borate
3 parts Bone Ash
2 parts Nepheline Syenite
1 part   Cornwall Stone
1 part   Copper Carbonate

Piepenburg Patina
4 parts Gerstley Borate
3 parts Bone Ash
2 parts Nepheline Syenite
1 part   Copper Carbonate

Copper Ridge Patina
4 parts Gerstley Borate
4 parts Bone Ash
2 parts Copper Carbonate
1 part   Nepheline Syenite

Terra Sigillata

White Body
70% Water
30% Kentucky Ball Clay
 2% Calgon

Red Body
 68% Water
 32% Redart Clay
 0.5% Calgon

Bonovitz Body
80% Water
20% Kentucky Ball Clay
 1% Calgon

Arleo's Body Colorants:
(Add to one cup of Terra Sigillata)
 Teal Blue
 8 tsp. Mason Stain 6305
 1/2 tsp. Mason Stain 6101
 Orange
 6 tsp. Mason Stain 6121
 Sage Grey
 6 tsp. Mason Stain 6500

Masuoka Body
 14 cups Water (warm)
 7.5 grams Tri Sodium Phosphate
 500 grams Ball Clay (OM4)
 1000 grams EPK

Slips

Seattle White Slip
(Wet to bisque ware) Cone 05-10
4 parts Ball Clay
2 parts Feldspar
2 parts Flint
1 part Kaolin
1/2 part Borax

Hall's White Slip
(Wet to bisque ware) Cone 05-10
4 parts Kentucky Ball Clay
3 parts Custer Feldspar
1 part EPK Kaolin
1 part Flint
1/2 part Borax (anhydrous)

Steven Hill's White Slip
(Wet to leather hard clay)
44.9% Kaolin
22.5% Kentucky Ball Clay
21.4% Flint
11.2% Custer Feldspar

W-W White Slip
(Leather hard clay) Cone 05-10
55% EPK Kaolin
35% Ball Clay
10% Ferro Frit 3134
 5% Zircopax

Stephenson White Slip
(Wet to leather hard clay) Cone 04
25.0% Ball Clay
20.0% Ferro Frit 3124
20.0% Flint
12.5% EPK Kaolin
12.5% Georgia Kaolin
 5.0% Talc
 5.0% Pyrophilite
 Chartreuse
 20% Mason Stain 5363
 20% Mason Stain 6483
 Turquoise
 24% Mason Stain 6390
 Pink
 30% Mason Stain 6020
 White
  5% Zircopax

Engobes

A1 Engobe
(Wet to dry clay) Cone 05-10
50% Ball Clay
20% Potash Feldspar
15% Flint
10% Boroflux
 5% Whiting

H - White Engobe
(Wet to bisque ware) Cone 04-10
4 parts   EPK Kaolin
2 parts   Flint
2 parts   Potash Feldspar
1 part   Ball Clay
1/2 part Borax
1/4 part Zircopax

English Engobe
(Leather hard clay) Cone 05-10
25% Potash Feldspar
25% Ball Clay
20% EPK Kaolin
20% Flint
 5% Whiting
 5% Zircopax

Stephenson Engobe VC3-1
(Leather hard clay) Cone 04
40% Ferro Frit 3124
25% Tennessee Ball Clay
15% Flint
10% Nepheline Syenite
    Yellow-Orange
    15% Mason Stain 6129
    Crimson
    30% Mason Stain 6006
    Rose Pink
    30% Mason Stain 6002

David Hines does not glaze his ceramic wall sculptures, he paints them. Bold washes of water color paints are brushed on after the bisque fired works are lightly smoked by burning small piles of twigs on their surface. In an attempt to avoid fading he will often add a water-base satin epoxy finish.

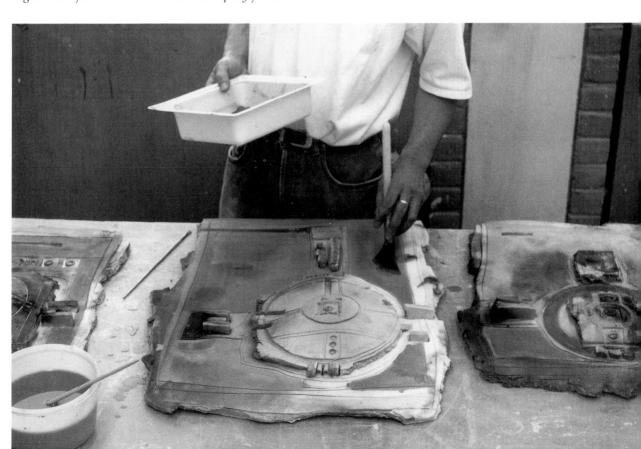

6

Kilns And Firing

Kilns are insulated receptacles designed to contain heat from one of many sources. The most efficient and common suppliers of heat are electricity, natural gas, propane and wood. While the designs of kilns are infinite, and can vary from simple box shapes or covered holes in the ground to Gothicized catenary arch structures and large hill climbing chambers, they are indispensable to the making of ceramics.

Kilns have the humblest of origins. They go back to the earliest uses of fire and the discovery of the hardened ground beneath those first warming and cooking fires. For many today, kilns remain every bit as mysterious, enigmatic and at times as frightening as fire must have appeared to our early human ancestors on the plains of Central Europe when a larger part of the world was still under ice.

Over the years, I've worked with college administrators and security personnel who viewed kilns as little more than big bombs waiting to explode or as apparatuses of excessive expense and pollution. Unfortunately, a great deal of misunderstanding and lack of technical knowledge concerning kilns exists within the clay community as well. I've known instructors of ceramics who fire kilns blindly. I remember my early days, could even call them years, of ignorance when it came to firing reduction glaze kilns. John Glick and especially J.T. Abernathy probably remember them too, as I sought them out for their expert advice and help in putting together pieces of the puzzle. Yet what was embarrassing and complicated then seems so obvious and simple now. To assist you with your puzzle, the following pieces are presented in a brief and comprehensible format.

Michael Gwinup's gas-fired car kiln.

KILNS AND FIRING

SOME FUNDAMENTALS

When it comes to building or firing kilns, the difficulties ceramists grapple with are commonly familiar. But, as with many situations in life, we can reverse the resistance of our fears through understanding. To make for a more cohesive picture, it might help to first explain some basics.

Cones

Pyrometric cones or firing cones are small triangular pyramids made of ceramic materials that melt at a predetermined temperature inside the kiln. Cones measure the effect of both time and temperature. When the clay or glaze being fired has reached maturity the cone will begin to soften and bend indicating that not only has the desired temperature been reached but that enough time for heat saturation has lapsed.

Each cone has a number imprinted into one of its three sides. This number indicates the melting temperature of the cone. The major supplier of these imaginative devices is the Orton Foundation in Westerville, Ohio. It numbers cones from 022 (1074° F), the lowest temperature, up to cone 42 (3659° F), the highest. A zero, pronounced "oh" is placed in front of the low temperature cones: cones 01 to 022. The higher temperature cones have no zeros for a first digit. At times this can become confusing and the numbers can get mixed up. Remember, cone 01 melts 34° F lower than cone 1. Time wise, this could be anywhere from 10 to 60 minutes sooner.

Three bent cones in a handmade clay pad that were used to fire a kiln to cone 9.

Cone / Temperature Equivalents

CONE NO.	TEMPERATURE 108°F/hr	60°C/hr	RELATED EVENTS
022	1074°F	579°C	GLASS SLUMPING
021	1105°	596°	
020	1148°	620°	ALUMINUM MELTS
019	1240°	671°	MOTHER OF PEARL
018	1306°	708°	CHINA PAINTS
017	1348°	731°	LUSTERS
016	1407°	764°	SMOKE FIRING
015	1449°	787°	DECALS
014	1485°	807°	GLASS FUSING
013	1539°	837°	
012	1571°	855°	
011	1603°	873°	COMMON BRICK
010	1629°	887°	START OF BODY REDUCTION
09	1679°	915°	FLOWERPOTS
08	1733°	945°	SILVER MELTS
07	1783°	973°	RAKU FIRING
06	1816°	991°	DUNCAN HOBBY GLAZES
05 1/2	1852°	1011°	GOLD MELTS
05	1888°	1031°	BISQUE FIRING
04	1922°	1050°	
03	1987°	1086°	COPPER MELTS
02	2014°	1101°	START OF GLAZE REDUCTION
01	2043°	1117°	
1	2077°	1136°	
2	2088°	1142°	
3	2106°	1152°	
4	2134°	1168°	FACE BRICK
5	2151°	1177°	EARTHENWARE
6	2194°	1201°	STONEWARE (ELECTRIC)
7	2219°	1215°	
8	2257°	1236°	BONE CHINA
9	2300°	1260°	STONEWARE (GAS)
10	2345°	1285°	
11	2361°	1294°	PORCELAIN
12	2383°	1321°	COMMERCIAL CHINA

The temperature equivalents in the table are from the Edward Orton Jr. Ceramic Foundation. They are for the large regular cones (the regular self-standing cones will bend at slightly higher temperatures). In degrees Fahrenheit they are rated at an average rise in temperature of 108° F per hour and in degrees Centigrade at a temperature rise of 60° C per hour.

Temperature equivalents are not necessarily those at which cones will deform under firing conditions different from those of calibration determinations.

The Orton cones come in four different sizes. The small cone and the mini bar are for use with a *kiln sitter*: an automatic shut-off device found on most electric kilns. From the kiln-sitter, mounted on the outside of the kiln, a hollow ceramic tube extends through the wall and into the kiln's interior. At the end of this tube two kanthal metal bars support the cone. A pivoted metal sensing rod, running through the tube from the sitter, rest on the middle of the cone. When the cone, which is laying perpendicular to the sensing rod, melts, the rod moves downward, disengaging the weighted breaker bar on the sitter and causing it to drop and shut off the flow of electricity. Many of these sitters are also fitted with limit timers as back-up safety systems for shutting off the kiln at a specified time.

When used with a kiln sitter, the cone is a trigger: an activating mechanism for shutting off the kiln. Its proper placement is very important. The small tip of the cone should never extend more than 1/8 of an inch beyond its metal support, neither should any part of the cone be closer than 1/8 of an inch to the ceramic tube. If the bending of the cone cannot initiate a quick and responsive movement in the sensing rod, the kiln can easily over-fire and damage the contents. As an added safety precaution kilns should not be left unattended at the end of firings.

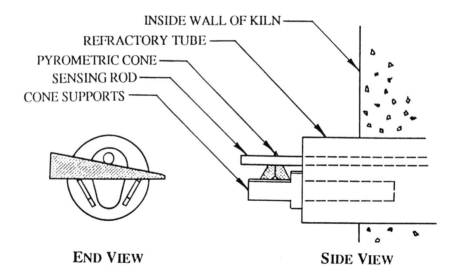

INSIDE WALL OF KILN
REFRACTORY TUBE
PYROMETRIC CONE
SENSING ROD
CONE SUPPORTS

END VIEW   SIDE VIEW

Kiln Sitter Cone Placement

The two other cones are much larger than the small cones and mini bars. They are also identical except for the extra clay at the base of the self-standing model. When compared to a smaller cone with the same number, the average temperature for a large cone is 50 degrees lower. Monitored visually, these cones are placed on the kiln shelf, in front of a viewing hole, at an angle of 8 degrees from the vertical. This angle is important in controlling the direction of bend, which should always be at a right angle to your line of sight for maximum readability. When the tip is bent over and almost touching the shelf its calibrated temperature has been reached.

Cones are usually used in consecutively numbered sets of three. If they are not free-standing they are placed, all facing the same direction, in a commercially made ceramic cone plaque or in a self-made cone pad formed from a small wad or coil of clay. Incidentally, cone pads should be given plenty of time to dry out so they don't blow up in the kiln and destroy any chances for an accurate firing. The middle member of this cone pack is always the firing cone. The first one to melt is the one with the lowest number. Called a warning or guide cone, it signals the approach, in 10 to 15 minutes, of the end of the firing and the downing of the center cone. Should the third one go over it would indicate that the kiln was over fired.

Victor Spinski, Breaking Into An Apple Box, slip cast, cone 04, 14" × 16" × 10".

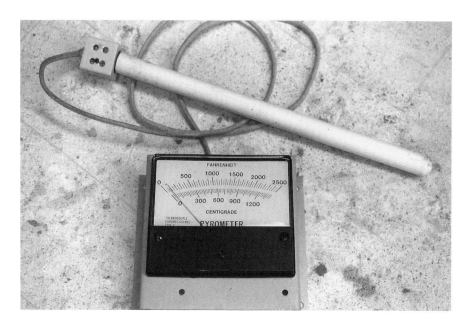

Pyrometer with a K-thermocouple inside a protective ceramic tube. This analog pyrometer is not nearly as accurate as the more expensive digital models.

Pyrometers

A pyrometer is a mechanical instrument for measuring the interior temperature of a kiln during firing. It consists of a needle-reading meter, located outside the kiln, connected by several feet of doubled wire to a chrome/alumel thermocouple. This thermocouple is housed inside a protective ceramic tube, projecting through the wall and several inches into the kiln. Unlike a cone, which indicates a single maturing temperature only, pyrometers give a continuous reading of the kiln's temperature at all times. Nevertheless, both are necessary for the successful firing of kilns. While the pyrometer measures the rate of temperature climb it doesn't necessarily inform you when the contents of the kiln have matured—a cone does. If, for example, a kiln is brought to temperature slowly, the cone may have already fallen, when the temperature registered on the pyrometer (even when properly calibrated) may still be 60 to 100 degrees lower.

Controllers are electronic devices with continuous digital temperature read-out pyrometers that act as automatic shut-offs. They can be preset to either shut the kiln off at a certain temperature or to maintain, on a soaking mode, a certain temperature in the kiln until it is turned off manually. The more sophisticated programmable controllers are capable of automatically firing a kiln by advancing the temperature at pre-determined intervals. They can also be set to maintain consistent soaking and precise cool-down cycles.

Oxidation And Reduction

Oxidation and reduction are two terms you'll hear a lot of whenever glazes, kilns and firing enter into a conversation. What they refer to is a type of atmosphere inside the kiln during a firing.

Oxidation describes an atmosphere where the normal amount of air—oxygen—in the kiln is not disturbed or reduced. In an oxidizing atmosphere the oxides that make up the clay and the glaze are allowed to chemically maintain their full complement of oxygen atoms throughout the firing.

Reduction describes an atmosphere where some of the air or oxygen inside the kiln has been removed or reduced. This act of withdrawing or denying oxygen to the kiln is called reduction. In a reducing atmosphere, which is easily obtained in a fuel burning kiln, there are not enough oxygen atoms available for complete combustion . The result is a drop in the rate of temperature climb and a chemical pilfering of oxygen atoms, from the clay and glazes, that promote dramatic changes in color. The effects of oxygen theft or starvation are most noticeable on copper glazed raku where glazes can become a vibrant copper and the clay a dark black. The same piece fired in oxidation would be totally different in color: the glaze would be green and the clay white.

Paul Kotula, 3 piece place setting, the highly refined forms and visually rich stoneware glazes were reduction fired, the large plate measures 2" × 10 1/2" × 14".

ELECTRIC KILNS

Electrically heated kilns are generally used for firing bisque and low temperature glaze ware. They can be used for cone 9 glaze firings, and are becoming increasing popular, due to temperature uniformity, as mainstream raku kilns. Electric kilns are a no-nonsense, if not consummate, means for firing ceramics. They are, in fact, authentic all-around kilns and might well be the only kind you'll ever need.

Electric kilns are made from soft, and extremely light weight, insulating fire bricks wrapped in a thin sheet of stainless steel. The interior face of the lining contains a series of recessed grooves that form circular rings, spaced apart every 2 to 3 inches, for holding a number of tightly wound electric coils. Made from 8 gauge Kanthal A-1 wire, these coils (elements) radiate heat generated from electrical resistance.

Electric kilns come from the manufacturer ready to use, that is if there is a 220 volt wall outlet with a 30 to 40 amp circuit breaker available to plug into. The larger kilns may require a 240 volt outlet, a 50 to 60 amp breaker and #6 copper wiring instead of the standard #8 or #10 wire. Most electric stoves and clothes dryers are on 220 power lines. Standard stoves or ranges use a #6 wire and 50 amp fuses or breakers; dryers use a #10 wire and 30 amp breakers. If the proper electrical requirements are not present a licensed electrician is needed.

Most models are top loading and have hinged lids. Extension rings can be stacked beneath these lids to increase the size and the height of the kiln. If the ring contains coiled elements no loss in temperature will be experienced. If the ring segment is blank, without coiled elements, the overall peak temperature of the firing will be less. Besides being economical, efficient, and reliable, electrical kilns do not require chimneys and can therefore be placed indoors and located with a great deal of flexibility. My wife, Gail, has two 7 cubic foot electric kilns on wheels that she conveniently rolls into a corner to obtain more studio space when they are not being used. During a bisque firing, as a fire-safety precaution, they are moved out into the room and away from the walls. For rakuing, they are unplugged and moved to another part of the studio—near an outside door. Like high-fire glazing, rakuing in an electric kiln shortens the life of the elements and lengthens the time of the firing, which may or may not be a relative concern based upon the uniqueness of each individual situation.

A common practice of firing new kilns, while still empty, is done to lengthen the working life of the elements. By turning all dials directly to "high" and firing straight to cone 05, the elements are oxidized and provided initial protection from organic and other destructive fumes.

Environmentally electric kilns are relatively merciful and benevolent yet they should never go unvented. For breathable, healthy and more comfortable surroundings, the heat and gaseous fumes produced during firings must be vented. Venting can take many forms from open doors and windows to mechanical hoods and fans. For me, and for this purpose, an air flow-through system does it all. The process is exceedingly simple. A self-cooling blower motor, mounted—out of the way—under the kiln, draws clean air from the room down through the kiln, from 3 to 4 small holes drilled into the lid, and out 3 other small holes drilled through the floor, just above the motor. Noxious fumes do not get a chance to enter the room, because they are immediately whisked away inside the flexible ducting attached to the motor. As these hot fumes become collected at the base of the kiln they are quickly diluted with additional air drawn from the room by the blower motor and cooled as they exit through the ducting to the outside of a building. Normally the ducting is externally vented much in the same way a clothes dryer is vented. The interesting aspect of this concept, although not originally foreseen, is that it promotes more even heat distribution and temperature consistency inside the kiln. And, it makes for brighter glaze colors by introducing a generous supply of oxygen for a more complete and proper oxidizing atmosphere. Color distortions in reds, a frequent problem when fired with other glazes or with insufficient oxygen, are eliminated. It would be an understatement to say that without this air flowing through, electric kilns are less than ideal for oxidation firings, because their interior atmosphere is neutral and somewhat lacking in free oxygen, but with it they become first-rate oxidation kilns, and even more worthy of respect.

An electric kiln flow-through fume venting system mounted under the kiln.

GAS KILNS

Gas fired kilns are generally used for firing high temperature glazes. Primarily because kilns fueled by natural gas and propane gas are the most efficient ways to high-fire glaze in a highly valued reduction atmosphere. Reduction kilns require combustion, or more accurately incomplete combustion, to alter the chemical composition and color of clays and glazes and, as such, can be fired with solid fuels such as wood or with liquid fuels such as oil. Today, gas happens to be the most plentiful and economical fuel available.

Gas can also be used as a heat source for oxidation firings, just as easily as it can be used for firing bisque kilns or raku kilns. Unlike electric kilns, which are commercially made, most gas kilns are self-made, custom designed and built by the artist to meet his or her own needs. Large, commercially manufactured kilns are too expensive for most individuals and are, more often than not, purchased by educational institutions with extensive clay curriculums.

The shapes and sizes of gas kilns vary dramatically, but fall into one of two categories known either as updraft or downdraft kilns. The concept of each is based upon a different principle of heat transfer. While the overall design for any one type may differ, the procedure for moving heat through the kiln will remain the same. For example, a kiln can have a flat, compression-type top, a sprung arch top, or even be a form that is one continuous catenary arch, and still be classified as a downdraft kiln.

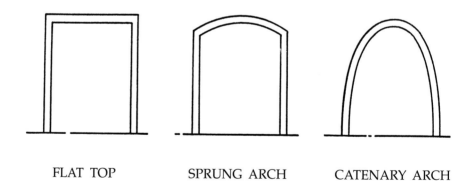

FLAT TOP   SPRUNG ARCH   CATENARY ARCH

Kiln Shapes

A small catenary arch kiln with 2 burners on each of the opposite side walls.

If a kiln is built from the hard, high-temperature, firebricks (which are the most affordable, but also the least efficient in terms of firing time and heat loss) it will have to be made with mortar. Because hard bricks are press-molded, and no two are the exact same size, the joints need to be filled with a 50/50 fire clay and sand mortar mixed with water. Soft, insulating firebricks, on the other hand, are accurately cut and sized from fired blanks of cast refractories and can easily be stacked, like building blocks, in place without creating any gaps or the need for any joint filler. Although more fragile and more than twice the price of the hard bricks, insulating bricks absorb or conduct very little heat and are therefore extremely cost and heat effective. These firebricks are numerically rated according to temperature: a number 20 brick will function at 2000° F, a number 23 at 2300° F and so on. The higher the temperature rating the denser, and consequently, the more durable, the brick. As this rating goes up so do the costs but, ironically enough, they become less efficient insulators. The number is a temperature service rating and not a service limit rating: a number 23 brick will not melt at cone 10.

Kilns built with soft insulating firebrick are built without the use of mortar.

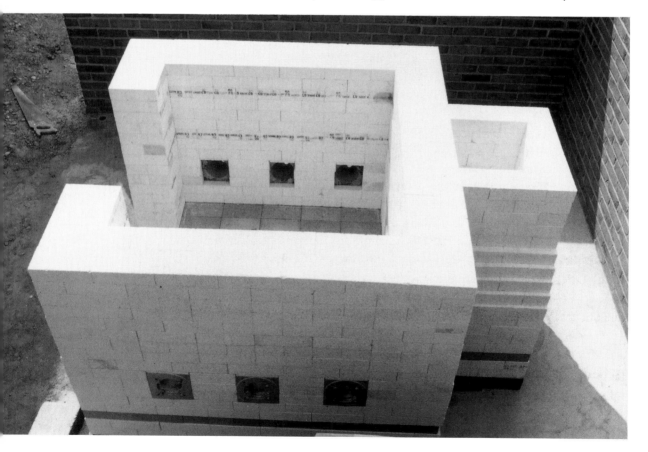

An opening is built into the chimney for a movable damper plate (kiln shelf).

The insulating bricks, which are several times lighter than the dense hard bricks, are still not as lightweight as the ceramic fiber or blanket products now being used to insulate the interior chambers of some kilns. With a melting temperature greater than 3000° F, dense ceramic fiber blankets, known by such trade names as Kaowool, Cerwool and Fiberfax, can be purchased in 25 foot rolls, in either 2 or 4 foot widths, and in several thicknesses up to 2 inches. As amazing as these alumina-silica blankets are, they are not without drawbacks and many ceramists see no real advantage to using them in place of the soft bricks. Unlike bricks, the blanket material reflects rather than absorbs heat, which is why it cools off rapidly. Also the stuff is costly, but more than financial disadvantages it's delicate and must be handled with extreme care. After being fired, especially to high temperatures, it loses resiliency and undergoes linear shrinkage, which make for joint problems. With the exception that fiber blankets don't weather well out of doors, their ability to withstand sudden and extreme changes in temperature make them a great insulator for raku kilns. Beyond these technical concerns, those of us who have worked with ceramic fibers know that they irritate the skin . . . and although the official word is still out as to what they do to the lungs, many of us view it as a very hazardous material to inhale and have chosen to play it safe and to play with bricks.

A wooden support form is used to support the brick arch during construction.

Angle iron and steel rods hold the arch of the kiln roof in place.

Upddraft Kilns

Kilns which have the inlets for the heat either in or near the floor and an exit flue at the top are called updraft kilns. The draft and heat movement passes up and through the chamber of the kiln. With the chamber itself functioning as the chimney there is no real need for an external structure to be built above the kiln to induce air movement. The draft, or the amount of air drawn through the kiln, as well as the inside temperature and atmosphere, is controlled by the movement of a damper plate over the flue opening in the roof. In theory and design these kilns are quite simple and became the earliest types to be made in the Middle East and Africa once it was discovered that pottery could be fired hotter if it were covered or enclosed than if it were fired in an open pit.

Downdraft Kilns

Kilns with both the heat inlets and the exit flue in or near the floor are called downdraft kilns. The heat, which is directed upwards either by a *bagwall* or target bricks, circulates inside the kiln chamber and is drawn back down to the flue outlet where it exits up the chimney built adjacent to the kiln. Because the flue opening is so close to the floor, a chimney 2 to 3 times taller than the inside height of the kiln is needed to provide a draft strong enough to pull the heat upward and then back downward through the ware. Once the chimney heats up this draft improves, becoming more effective, and an adjustable *damper* plate, placed either in the chimney or between it and the kiln, is used to control the temperature and the atmosphere of the kiln. Developed in Germany over two hundred years ago, the downdraft kiln fires more evenly and efficiently than an updraft kiln.

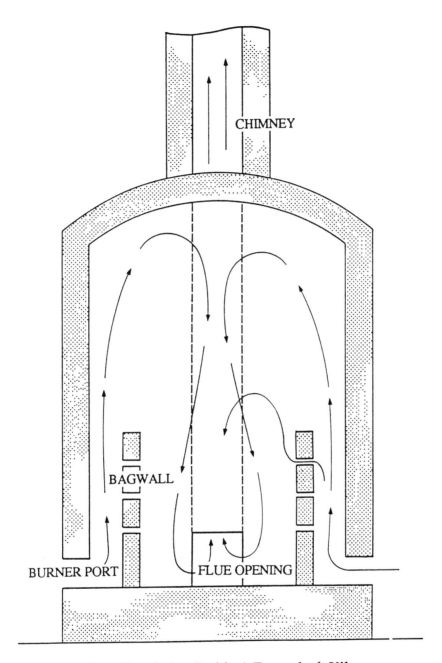

CHIMNEY

BAGWALL

BURNER PORT

FLUE OPENING

Heat Circulation Inside A Downdraft Kiln

Crossdraft Kilns

Kilns that have the heat inlets in one side of a kiln and the exit flue on the opposite side are called crossdraft kilns. Similar to downdraft kilns, the heat is directed upward and passes through or across the kiln chamber before being drawn out and up the chimney. Unlike a downdraft kiln, which has heat directed up two opposite side walls and the chimney flue on the back wall, the heat source for a crossdraft kiln comes from one side only. Many oriental kilns, known as climbing or chamber kilns, built up the sides of hills, banks of earth or other natural inclines, function on the crossdraft principle.

A hard brick catenary arch crossdraft kiln under construction. The 3 burner ports are located in the base of the wall opposite the chimney.

John Glick, Ewers, thrown stoneware with extruded parts and slip decorations. Reduction fired to cone 11, post-firing surface alterations, 4 1/2" high.

Burners

Gas fired kilns operate with a fuel burner system that uses either natural gas or propane as their fuel source. These two extremely clean burning fuels are mixed with air in a device called a burner to produce heat through a process of combustion.

Simple burners are made of an 8 to 10 inch long flame tube for mixing the air with the gas, an orifice for supplying the gas and an adjustable air inlet. This air inlet is the source for what is known as the *primary air* and is normally located just behind the orifice where it supplies the burner with half the air needed for combustion. The other half of the air mixes with the flame as it leaves the burner and is referred to as the *secondary air*. The opening around the burner, known as the *burner port*, is the source for the secondary air.

The orifice itself is located just inside one end of the flame or combustion tube which is usually 1 1/2 to 2 inches in diameter. Orifice sizes vary from burner to burner depending upon a number of local conditions, available gas pressure being one important variable. Propane burners have orifices that are much smaller than those found on natural gas burners owing to the fact that propane is supplied at a much higher pressure. Natural gas burners, for an average size kiln of 30 to 40 cubic feet, require less than 6 inches of water column pressure (equal to 1/4 pound per square inch) which is the regulated pressure available for most residential usage.

Burners are often classified, according to their primary air source, as being either atmospheric or forced-air. When the gas pressure is relatively low, which it is at 6 inches, an electric blower motor is often required to force an additional amount of air into the combustion barrel of the burner. If, as with atmospheric burners, the pressure is high, a half a pound or more, the gas draws enough air through the primary air inlet to produce an efficient flame without the use of a blower motor.

A forceful blue flame coming from the tip of the burner is an oxidation flame and an indication of a fairly good gas to air ratio. A lazy yellow flame is a reduction flame and indicates that there is a shortage of air. The hottest and most efficient flame is called a neutral flame which is blue at the burner tip and yellow 8 to 10 inches into the kiln. The size, condition and stability of this flame is controlled by adjustments made to both the air and the gas supply. Such adjustment, however, must be made slowly so that the results can be observed. If, for example, too great an increase in the primary air is made too quickly, relative to the gas pressure, it may blow the flame out. If it is too little it may cause *blow-back*, a condition that has the burning flame being sucked back into the burner. Blow-back often results in a sudden and dangerous back-fire, also known as flashback, at the primary air inlet as the flame seeks oxygen.

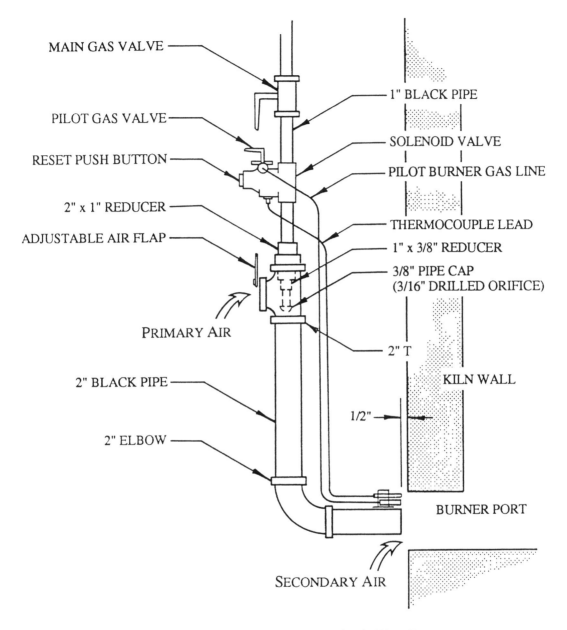

MAIN GAS VALVE

PILOT GAS VALVE

RESET PUSH BUTTON

2" x 1" REDUCER

ADJUSTABLE AIR FLAP

PRIMARY AIR

2" BLACK PIPE

2" ELBOW

SECONDARY AIR

1" BLACK PIPE

SOLENOID VALVE

PILOT BURNER GAS LINE

THERMOCOUPLE LEAD

1" x 3/8" REDUCER

3/8" PIPE CAP
(3/16" DRILLED ORIFICE)

2" T

KILN WALL

1/2"

BURNER PORT

Homemade (Natural Gas) Atmospheric Pipe Burner

The in-line gas solenoid safety valve is designed to shut down the main gas supply whenever there is pilot flame failure or whenever the flame from the pilot light (fixed to the tip of the main burner) fails to surround the tip of the thermocouple.

One of two forced-air natural gas burners on John Glick's downdraft kiln.

The small piece of sheet metal clamped to the burner aids in directing a greater portion of the flame from the pilot up to the heat sensitive thermocouple.

The pilot light clamped to this burner is also used to pre-heat (candle) the kiln.

Two natural gas forced-air burners with state-of the-art safety features including automatic electronic ignition, ultraviolet scanners and a digital limit controller for either soaking the kiln (maintaining a constant temperature) or shutting off the burners at a pre-determined temperature.

KILN FURNITURE

The shelves used inside the kiln for holding ceramic ware, and the posts that support them, are often referred to as kiln furniture. The kiln shelves used in most electric kilns are made with cordierite. This material is highly resistant to thermo-shock and seldom cracks during sudden changes in kiln temperature. The shelves that are 5/8 inch thick hold up exceptionally well at cone 6 temperatures. Shelves used in high temperature gas kilns range in thickness from 3/4 to 1 1/4 inches and are generally made from either a high alumina fireclay or from silicon carbide. These shelves can easily withstand cone 11 temperatures. The silicon carbide variety are held in higher esteem, especially among those who do reduction firing, and are often considered to be the stronger of the two. I've worked with both, and find the less expensive high alumina shelves to be of comparable strength and quality. In fact, I'm currently reduction firing to cone 10 with 3/4 inch thick high alumina shelves (hydraulically ram-pressed in England) measuring 12 by 24 inches that have not warped under the same conditions that have, in the past, caused 3/4 inch thick carbide shelves of the same size to warp. The slightly more expensive nitride bonded silicon carbide shelves are much stronger than regular high alumina and carbide shelves. The strength of a 1/2" nitride bonded shelf is equivalent to that of a standard 3/4" silicon carbide shelf.

Commercially extruded shelf supports can be purchased but many ceramists use hard firebricks (2 1/2" x 4 1/2" x 9") or *soaps*: hard firebricks cut lengthwise and then again into vertical modules. Such a system offers adequate stacking flexibility when it comes to adjusting the heights between shelves. For example, a half soap (2 1/2" x 2 1/4" x 4 1/2") could be used to provide a height of 2 1/2 or 4 1/2 inches between two shelves. When placed on top of a full soap the total distance could equal 13 1/2 inches: the recommended maximum height for stacking soaps. Beyond this height measurement full bricks and not soaps should be used for stability. If a little extra height is needed, a small piece of broken kiln shelf is often added to the top of each support to obtain 3/4 or 1 inch worth of additional clearance.

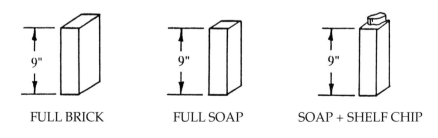

| FULL BRICK | FULL SOAP | SOAP + SHELF CHIP |

Shelf Supports

The placement of the shelf supports is important, especially with regards to shelf warpage and stability. A three post system is used to support kiln shelves. Like the three-legged milking stool, three points of support provide immediate stability. If a four point setup were used the shelves would not be as steady. Besides being wobbly, shelves are also placed under more stress with this arrangement and have a greater tendency to crack.

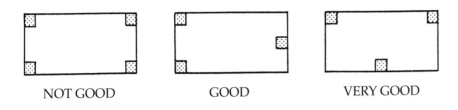

NOT GOOD   GOOD   VERY GOOD

Post Placement

For increased stability and maximum shelf area two shelves can share the same support post.

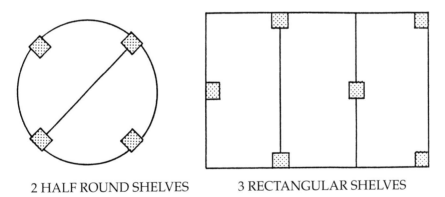

2 HALF ROUND SHELVES   3 RECTANGULAR SHELVES

Shared Posting

The warpage of kiln shelves can be minimized if they are turned over on a regular basis and if large, heavy pieces are not placed directly on the unsupported center. Still, the most practical way to avoid shelf warpage is to use in-line posting when stacking the shelves. By continuously placing each post directly above the one supporting the shelf it sits on, the weight is uniformly distributed and directly transferred down to the kiln floor.

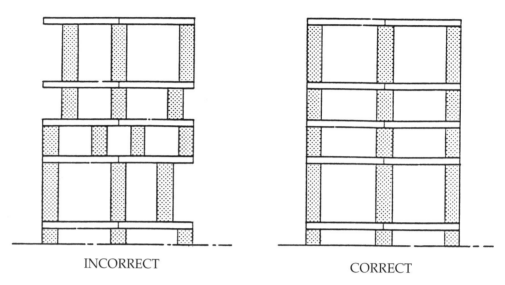

INCORRECT   CORRECT

Shelf Posting

Shelf heights are staggered for more efficient heat distribution.

Joe Zajack, Recycler, vessel made from masonry mortar and recycled refractory brick taken from a bag wall, a salt kiln, and a raku kiln, 52" × 22" in diameter.

Kiln Wash

Many ceramists coat the top surface of their kiln shelves with a layer of *kiln wash*. The standard wash is a 50/50 mixture of kaolin and flint. Sometimes a very small amount of ball clay or bentonite is added to aid adhesion. Enough water is added to allow the mixture to be easily applied with a wide brush or paint roller. Two flowing coats are usually applied, in opposing directions, with care being taken to leave an inch wide band around the sides of the shelf unpainted. If the wash is brought to the very edge, chips of it can easily fall off during the handling that occurs when the shelf is being loaded and land on the glaze ware already in the kiln.

Applying deflocculated kiln wash to a shelf with a sponge.

Kiln wash is used to protect the shelf from glaze accidents. Should a kiln overfire or a piece be too heavily glazed, a running of the glaze could fuse the ware to the shelf. If the shelf were protected by a layer of kiln wash any such piece could be released more easily and the excess glaze remaining on the shelf chiseled off. One disadvantage to applying kiln wash to shelves is that they can no longer be turned over periodically to reduce warping. There are other drawbacks. Shelves have to be recoated every so often; eventually coatings build up into an uneven surface which can induce shelf warpage and cause uneven pot bottoms.

Some potters have taken to not using kiln wash and, like my students and I, take special care in seeing that applied glazes are not at risk of running or in any way capable of presenting a threat to either the shelf or the pot. My studio assistant, Sandy, is very good at placing any piece on a glaze reject shelf, for future student clean-up, that looks potentially hazardous. If there is uncertainty she will fire the piece on top of a dusting of powdered *alumina hydrate* or a small, broken section of kiln shelf placed between the pot and the regular shelf for protection.

If a kiln shelf is in need of cleaning it should be laid flat on a thin but dense pad of foam and the glaze drips removed by gentle, glancing blows from a hammer onto the handle of a chisel held at a 30 degree angle, or less, to the shelf. If the chisel were held at a greater angle it could easily break the shelf. Portable electric grinders also work and can be used in place of a chisel and hammer. Be sure to always wear a dust respirator and eye protection when operating a grinder.

In the context of shelf restoration and the comparisons between alumina and carbide shelves take note that the carbide shelves clean-up easier and with reduced surface damage. Also, it appears that the high alumina shelves fire hotter and shorten the adhesive life-span of homemade shelf coatings Cleaning shelves, no matter how it is approached, is dangerous and should be done carefully and safely: eye goggles are an absolute must!

FIRING: AN INTRODUCTION

When it comes to firing kilns, especially glaze kilns, we can't expect text-book-type explanations for everything that may occur, but with greater understanding we can come to more consistent and rewarding results.

Firings are often treated as technical triumphs of temperature attainments, as though the firing of a kiln was simply a series of systematic mechanical operations practiced in a context of basic scientific theory. In fact, nothing could be farther from reality. The firing of a kiln is every bit an art, an expression of intuitive wisdom and creative vitality, as it is an elaboration of scientific principles. Kilns, like clay, are conduits for the metamorphosis of individual perceptions. There is useful wisdom in seeing firing as a generative process filled with the same formative spirit that accompanied the shaping of our clay. The possibilities of both call forth the potential of our own visions.

The kiln is an object, and firing is an activity. While it's true that a kiln is an environment for containing heat, artistically it's important to work with it as an atmosphere with powers of transformation, because what happens or doesn't happen, atmospherically, is every bit as important as temperature. Firing is an act of bringing clay and glaze to a determined temperature and, most profoundly, to an assumed condition over a controlled period of time. In this process there is no one right way, no absolute procedures, no rigid guide of operations on how to proceed.

Firing is about temperature, atmosphere and time. The challenge of bringing these three variables together, in coordinated union, is to live through the final story of conversion and, with creative impact, the spirit of clays completeness. Experience becomes the best way to meet this challenge. Until one has some of this priceless stuff one has to go carefully, gathering knowledge which seems, and in fact is, limitless. Learning from mistakes, dialogs, readings and surprises are a natural part of this script.

If reaching temperature is a problem the kiln or burners may be at fault by being inadequately constructed. It's not uncommon, for example, to find chimneys that are too short or their sectional area to small. Burner insufficiencies may exist, ports could be undersize, gas pressure too low or insulation inadequate. Kilns made of hard brick, remember, take much longer to fire than those made of soft insulating firebrick and more fuel. These and many other such physical realities of basic kiln design alter the firing temperature as well as the patience and frustrations of many ceramists. Where problems are revealed to be physical in origin they require their own brand of physical-centered solutions and are best approached in a direct, rather than in a roundabout, manner of resolution before they overpower the situation and hound the spirit.

Clayton Bailey, Hyperthermic Teapot, made from a blue shale terra cotta brick clay and covered with a porcelain slip. The clay contains enough carbon to cause it to bloat when over-fired. The firing is monitored through a "spy hole" and the kiln shut off when the desired results are obtained, 12" × 24" × 12".

Failures at reaching temperature may not always be attributed to kiln design, they may on occasion be incorporated in, or identified with how the firing is managed.

Atmospheric conditions inside the gas kiln may undergo many variations. Compared to the extreme atmospheric stability of an electric kiln, primordially characteristic of a toaster or an incubator, gas kilns are radical hallmarks of atmospheric instability, and all related to the chemistry of oxygen. The atmosphere, in the same firing, can be oxidizing (as it continuously is in electric kilns), neutral or saturated with carbon monoxide and is often manipulated back-and-forth to serve different needs. Knowing when, how and why to make these robust changes is at the heart of firing a fuel burning glaze kiln.

A reduction atmosphere is the key to successful surface color with stoneware glazes. It is the result of insufficient oxygen or an excess of fuel and is obtained by reducing the draft with the damper or by decreasing the supply of primary air to the burner. When a shortage of oxygen creates carbon monoxide, it becomes very unstable and seeks to become carbon dioxide by chemically taking oxygen atoms from the metallic oxides found in the glaze and clay body. When clay and glaze give up oxygen atoms they have undergone reduction. As an interesting side note relating to the modification powers of a reducing atmosphere, it can literally lower the maturing temperature of iron bearing glazes by several cones.

The temperature window for clay reduction is very narrow: between cone 012 (1571° F) and cone 04 (1922° F). At higher temperatures the clay begins to shrink and is no longer porous; becoming too vitreous for body reduction. Following this phase, either a neutral or a partial glaze reduction atmosphere is maintained until cone 7 (2219° F). At this temperature the kiln is put into full glaze reduction until cone 9 or 10 bends. Afterwards the kiln is often reoxidized for a few minutes and completely shut down or it is allowed to soak, at a slightly lower temperature, for half an hour to burn away excess surface carbon.

This quick and rather buoyant account of the reduction aspect of a stoneware firing belongs directly under the heading of "General Procedures." Exceptions and preferences meet frequently, however, when it comes to the intimacies of reduction firing. One of the things that should be recognized here is that different types of glazes require different treatments; copper reds need light reductions celadons and shinos heavier ones. Another construct that should be recognized is that carbon monoxide is virtually transparent and if the kiln interior is full of a hazy smoke that obscures a view of the cones, or if a dark smoke appears at a spy hole, there is an overabundance of free carbon. If allowed to continue these sooty particles weaken the reduction process and muddy the glaze.

When it comes to expressing a natural preference for certain glaze colors within the full range of colors available to the ceramist, it's important to understand and appreciate the qualities identified with oxidation and reduction firing. Many of the livelier stoneware colors, the yellows, aquas and purples, are only available when fired in oxidation on white clay bodies. The copper reds, celadons and rich irons, on the other hand, are only obtainable in reduction. Your attachment to one or the other of these firing processes will articulate many hidden emotions and unconscious feelings that you might want to identify and apply to your clay work with regards to form, design and content. While this may be a seemingly strange or back-door approach to creating with clay it is, never-the-less, appropriate; the noble origins of many clay pieces, as can be seen with some raku forms and brightly colored low-temperature ware, are the valid results of working with a specific surface treatment in mind beforehand.

"Time is man's most precious asset", Voltaire said. When it comes to firing kilns, time is not only precious but an honored necessity. It contains and nurtures the blossoms of transformation. In the beginnings of the bisque firing clay is brought to a time-centered crisis. If the temperature is increased in a short period of time the ware can explode. For the first hour or two the temperature should barely be allowed to advance beyond the lowest setting. If an electric kiln is being used the lid is often propped open to prevent the temperature from rising higher and to vent excess moisture. During the early stages, especially the first 500 degrees, water and organic compounds are being chemically released from the clay. If this release is accelerated too quickly they cannot escape to the surface fast enough and moisture will expand into steam while still trapped inside the clay walls where, if enough pressure is built-up, it blows the wall apart. After reaching 1000° F the temperature of the bisque ware can safely be increased at a rate of 300 degrees an hour.

Glaze firings also ask us to carefully manage time, but differently from that of the bisque firing. Start-up temperatures are still kept initially low to allow for moisture dehydration only now in the emergence of a glaze context. If glazes, and their binders, aren't heated slowly the intensity of the steam build-up can loosen glazes and cause them to crawl or, in extreme cases, to flake off. Sudden or fast temperature climbs at this time are also provocative with regards to refired ware often causing fractures and cracking. After 1000° F the stoneware glaze kiln can be advanced at a rate of 400 to 500 degrees an hour, although 200 to 300 degrees is more responsible.

The time/temperature union is given special attention at the end of the firing, during the soaking period, and again during cooling. A slow, even, cooling cycle reduces tensions between the glaze and clay body and prevents stress cracks. The real hidden danger in the cool-down process presents itself at 1060° F and is known as *quartz inversion*. On cooling, flint reverts back to its original state by undergoing a structural chemical contraction. If this crystalline inversion is not allowed to take place slowly the ware can crack severely. Because the shrinkage is greater than 10% the temperature drop between 1100 and 900 degrees should last almost two hours.

BISQUE FIRING

Most, but not all, greenware is bisque fired before being glazed and then glaze fired. With single-fire or onece-fire glazing the glaze is applied to leather-hard clay and the ware, when dry, is fired directly to maturity. While single-fired ware requires less handling, it is not without its problems. By bisque firing, the work is strengthened and is no longer in danger of being broken through the decorating and/or glazing process. Naturally, there is more work and expense in firing work twice but, at least in the initial stages of one's ceramic career, it favors the work and essentially pays off.

Loading The Bisque Kiln

Once the clay work is dry—bone dry—it can be loaded into the bisque kiln for its first firing. Assuming that the work will be fired in an electric kiln, start by placing the first level of shelf supports, three posts per shelf, in the kiln. Set one post aside for checking the height of the work being loaded. It should show a visible clearance. Also, these initial posts should only be tall enough to accommodate the height of the smallest pieces which are generally loaded first at the bottom of the kiln. The tallest forms are saved for the last shelf at the top of the kiln. Incidentally, the floor of electric kilns often takes the place of a shelf by serving as the supporting surface for both pots and posts.

Greenware pots to be bisque fired, because they are not coated with glaze, can be stacked inside of larger pots in an orderly manner to more efficiently fill the kiln.

Loading a bisque kiln is a challenge, almost in the same way locating and placing the pieces of a picture puzzle is a challenge. Unlike the loading of a glaze kiln, greenware pieces are allowed to touch each other, which has many practical implications when it comes to handling the ware. By addressing each pot as a piece of a puzzle, to be fitted in its proper place either in or around other pots, the loading process becomes a series of small creative choices that can make a labor intensive task pleasurable. Lighter and smaller pieces are stacked on top of larger and heavier ones. Open bowl shapes can be stacked inside of one another as long as an area of clearance is maintained between the rim and the wall of the piece in which it is nested to allow for any stress inducing shrinkage or warpage. By observing and considering the dynamics of such physical relationships stacking is easier.

GOOD   NOT GOOD

Bisque Stacking

Rules of common sense are always useful when stacking ware. Weight distribution, for example, needs to be considered whenever one form is placed inside of another form. If the inside form seems excessively heavy for its size or in comparison to the weight of the piece in which it sits, replace it with a different form whose weight is not threatening. By progressively and efficiently stacking pieces—always with some degree of sensible restraint that ultimately results in a placement of the delicate and more fragile works on top of rather than under other forms—it is not unreasonable for a bisque kiln to hold enough pieces, volume wise, for two glaze kilns.

When the floor area is full carefully place the first shelf on the posts. Next place the support posts for the second shelf directly above and in line with the ones below. Proceed to load this shelf without wasting any space. Choose pieces that are fairly uniform in height and nearly as tall as the posts. If you run out of such work nest 2 or 3 shorter pieces to form the needed height by stacking. Place the wider forms on the shelf first and follow-up by filling in the open areas with the thinner pieces. If there is room inside the wider forms fill them with smaller pieces. Do all of this maneuvering with a great deal of care. And, without forgetting that greenware is very, very fragile, handle the forms with both hands; never picking up a piece by the rim or by a handle.

If the kiln is not being fired with a programmable temperature controller, set your kiln sitter with a small cone or pyro-bar while it is still accessible and before any shelves are placed above it. I fire a cone 05 (1922° F) bisque. Most fire to cone 06 (1816° F) and some only fire to cone 010 (1629° F). Even at this low temperature the clay is strong enough to handle during glazing. As you proceed to load the upper half of the kiln it may become advantageous to place some pieces on end—supported by the wall of the kiln. While clay should never touch the electric coils of the kiln, or even be placed close to them for fear of cracking them, standing several flat pieces on end, as close to vertical as possible, is often the best way to bisque them. Large plates, on the other hand, are fired flat on a thin layer of sand. Any heavy or wide based forms should also be placed on sand to allow for movement during shrinkage. Soon, after all of your work and effort, you'll have gained something important: experience. As your confidence grows, you'll be placing pots on their side or in any number of contorted positions to make sure they get into the firing, realizing more and more that there are as many solutions to loading as there are pots and that some are more efficient than others.

Firing The Electric Bisque Kiln

With the kiln loaded, the kiln sitter set, its limit timer ready for use, and with all switches turned to the "off" position, the lid can be closed and power brought into the kiln by pressing in the plunger on the kiln sitter until it catches. The kiln can now be turned on by dialing the bottom switch to "low".

Electric kilns come with many types of control switches varying from the simple on-off switch to the rotary dial switch with three or more positions. The theoretical kiln referred to here has three rotary switches with "low", "medium" and "high" settings. Also, it is to be assumed that it is vented with a motorized down-draft vent system located at the base of the kiln. Kilns vented with this system, and only with these systems, are fired with the lid closed and the spy holes plugged during the entire firing. If the kiln you're doing a bisque firing in is not vented in this manner you must fire the first hour or two with the lid propped open an inch or two to allow for the evaporation and removal of the physical water. This water, which was added to the clay body and is also known as mechanical water or as the water of plasticity, is removed by the time the kiln reaches 250° F, which can easily take one to two hours; longer if the ware is thick. The top spy hole must also be left open during the entire length of the firing. This small opening provides a vent for the release of chemical water, most of which should be gone before the kiln reaches 900° F, after which the speed of the firing can be safely increased. Still, the opening must be left unplugged to allow for the escape of the various fumes and gases that develop throughout the firing. If this opening were covered these gases would exit through the tube of the kiln sitter and eventually cause the pivot mechanism to corrode.

	BOTTOM SWITCH	MIDDLE SWITCH	TOP SWITCH	LID	TOP PEEPHOLE
1st Hour	Low	Off	Off	Open 2″	Open
2nd Hour	Low	Low	Off	Open 2″	Open
3rd Hour	Low	Low	Low	Closed	Open
4th Hour	Medium	Medium	Medium	Closed	Open
6th Hour	High	High	High	Closed	Open

Bisque Firing Schedule For A Typical (unvented) Electric Kiln
(The firing schedule may be altered by varying the time between switch adjustments.)

After approximately one hour turn the middle switch to "low". In another hour the top switch is also placed on "low". At this point things become more subjective. In the forth hour some may want to proceed more cautiously, turning the switches to "medium" at different time intervals while others may feel comfortable with turning all the switches to "medium".

After the kiln has been on "medium" for a couple of hours all the switches can be turned to "high". In some instances, the kiln may fire-off before it is turned to "high". Firing times can vary according to load density and turn-up schedules. Also, as elements age, the kiln will take progressively longer to heat. Even though the kiln is set to fire-off on its own with the bending of the cone, and even though it may have a safety back-up system in the form of a limit timer to shut it down, one should always check its progress and manually turn it off if a peek into its interior reveals an orange color that intuitively seems brighter than it should be. Again, experience is a valuable asset, but if it looks hot, really hot, it could be turned off—especially in light of knowing that the temperature range for bisque ware can vary greatly.

The kiln should be allowed to cool slowly, generally overnight and well into the next day. Near the end of the cooling cycle the lid may be propped opened an inch or two to hurry things along, but only if necessary. Ware shouldn't be removed from the kiln until it is cool enough to be comfortably handled with bare hands. Otherwise the pots and kiln furniture are subjected to thermal stress. Once fired the clay has undergone a physical change that is permanent and irreversible. Not only is it a new color but it is now a new material . . . and immediately ready for your next activity— glazing.

Yoshiro Ikeda, coil built tea pot fired in an electric kiln to cone 02 and cone 07, 16″ × 11″ × 7″.

GLAZE FIRING

The real mysteries of glaze firing are the results, not the process. Firing the glaze kiln, as an activity of creating, involves all kinds of concentrated effort and preparation, but somewhere along the line something else takes over that mysteriously directs a course of events that can produce magical results that give delight beyond expectation—beyond mastery. If it were otherwise, if every aspect were predictable and controllable, we would soon become bored and quickly lose interest. As it is, the opening of a glaze kiln is never boring. At best it's an event, one of many in ceramics, that can be claimed as your own, to give depth and value to the life you've shaped for yourself.

No two kilns fire the same, nor are any two firings in the same kiln identical. Because of this, the act of firing a glaze kiln is also a sensory act of felt experience. As such, the senses of sight, sound, smell and touch become as valuable to the firing as the technical and theoretical information.

Loading The Glaze Kiln

Glazed pieces must be handled sparingly and delicately to avoid harming the powdery skin of glaze. Water and a small sponge should be at hand to wipe the bottoms of pots clean of any unwanted glaze. As with loading a bisque kiln, to which many of the same practices apply, flat and small

Like these plates by Ken Baskin, some pieces need to be loaded unconventually.

pieces are generally placed near the bottom of the kiln while the tallest pieces are reserved for the top. Only now, the pieces must not touch each other. In fact, there should be almost an inch of space separating the pieces to prevent glaze bubbles, which can be quite large and active during firing, from making contact with other pots and to allow for uninterrupted heat flow through the kiln.

If the shelves being used have kiln wash on one side they should be examined underneath and around the edges for any material which might loosen and fall onto the ware. Open forms, especially plates and bowls, should always be sheltered from any falling shelf wash or brick ceiling debris by being placed under a stacked shelf. To avoid chipping the kiln wash and knocking it onto other ware always set, rather than slide, the pots in place. Sometimes sheets of newspaper are placed over open forms until the loading is completed. Each paper shield is then carefully removed before the door is closed.

Assuming that the glaze kiln being loaded is gas fired, care should be taken to not let any ware overhang a shelf where it might be touched by flame from a burner. Larger forms should be located on the shelf first followed by the smaller, fill-in, pieces. Wide bottom pieces are still placed on a sprinkling of granular material to allow for movement during shrinkage, only now it should be a medium or coarse grog instead of fine sand to keep it from being blown around the kiln. Matching sets of forms should be fired on the same shelf when possible. Lids not fired in place should be fired on the shelf next to the container it belongs to. Again, all support posts must be stacked, in line, directly on top of those supporting the shelf underneath.

Glaze firings done inside gas kilns require more space between the pieces for heat circulation than those done in electric kilns. If an area is too densely stacked heat passage is restricted, if not choked off, and those pieces may be underfired. Likewise, if a specific part of your kiln continually fires hotter, pots and shelves could be stacked closer together to increase the density of the area and slow the convectional passage of heat.

The kiln should also be stacked for volumetric balance. If there are several large shapes to be fired, it is wise to place them evenly throughout the kiln to achieve uniform heat saturation. Avoid extremes. Do not have one section empty or skimpy with work and another section over-packed. Shelf placement also influences heat movement. By analyzing the heat paths inside the kiln you're using, you may see the importance of staggering the heights of each shelf to further stimulate temperature circulation.

If you have not positioned your cone packs in front of the spy holes when the kiln was being loaded, you'll want to do it before the door is closed and secured. And, if the myth of the firing spirits are stirring inside, you may want to fashion an icon in the likeness of a kiln god to place on top of the kiln door for metaphoric weight. Not all spiritual realities are explainable, or human.

Firing The Reduction Glaze Kiln

Just as each kiln fires differently, owing to its own uniqueness and individual character traits, each potter has their own personal agenda when it comes to firing a kiln. The firing sequence covered here is to be viewed as a guide and pertains to the firing of a medium size (30 to 40 cubic feet) downdraft gas kiln to cone 9 with a light-to-medium clay and glaze reduction.

With the kiln loaded, remove all spy hole plugs and, with the damper fully open to prevent a sudden build-up of heat, light the pilot burners. Leave the pilots on overnight to preheat the kiln. Sometimes referred to as candling, this gradual build-up of heat safely removes excess moisture from the ware.

The next morning, light the burners, cover the spy holes and adjust the damper plate to maintain a fuel efficient atmosphere inside the kiln. If you're working with forced air burners make certain that the blower motors are turned on before the burner gas valves are opened. If the blower has a variable speed control put it on a low setting. If not, close the air flap on the blower so that all but a small portion of the air grill is covered. To avoid *pre-ignition*, the burning of a flame inside the burner, open the burner gas valve with a quick, generous motion. Once the gas is ignited outside of the burner the gas valve can be backed down to a lower setting. The lighting of the burner should also be done at a full arms length distance from the body—with the face well away from the burner port—to protect against any *blow-back*. Blow-back, again, is a sudden backfire of flame at the burner port, usually the result of low gas pressure or wind gusts.

Around 1650° F the kiln is put into its first of two reduction cycles by closing the damper until enough back pressure is created to force a 6 inch yellow, but not smoky, flame to appear outside the highest spy hole. The atmosphere inside the kiln is now short of oxygen and a little long on free carbon monoxide hungry for oxygen. A look inside should reveal a slightly hazy interior with some yellow flames moving lazily about. Similar results can occur by increasing the supply of gas or decreasing the amount of primary air to the burner.

Some potters prefer to end the reduction after 30 or 40 minutes or when 1800° to 1850° Fahrenheit is reached. They call this phase of the firing *body reduction*. Then continue to fire the kiln with a *neutral* atmosphere (one without an excess of unused oxygen or carbon) until 2000° F, when the interior atmosphere is adjusted again for reduction. This second phase is known as *glaze reduction*.

Leave the kiln in glaze reduction and let it climb 100° to 200° F an hour. When the guard cone starts to bend, many potters slow the kiln down by adjusting the gas supply so that the final bending of the firing cone is drawn out and the ware is given a moderate-to-long beneficial soaking.

As soon as the firing cone goes down, open the damper and fire the kiln for three or four minutes with a neutral atmosphere to clean it out and burn away any carbon that may remain on the surface of the glazes.

Immediately turn off all burners, close the damper completely and seal the burner ports. The firing is now finished. If the kiln is well insulated and sealed it can be left on its own to cool down.

Ben Pearlman, drape molded bowl multi-glazed with 4 separate glazes thickly applied and reduction fired in a gas kiln to cone 10, 4‴ × 19″.

The Firing Cycle

The average length of time it takes to complete a glaze firing cycle can vary anywhere from eight to fourteen hours; some potters even prefer to take more time to reach cone 10. If there is no overnight preheat, the temperature should be brought up very slowly for the first hour or two, afterwhich it can be increased 150° to 200° F an hour. At the end of the cycle it becomes important to once again slow down the temperature's rate of climb to under 100° F an hour to allow the glazes to fully mature and take on the depth and richness that reduction glazes are noted for.

TEMPERATURE °F

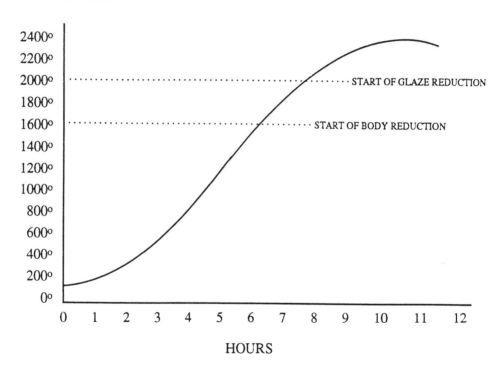

Reduction Glaze Firing Cycle—Cone 9
(with no overnight preheat)

Body Reduction

Altering the color of the clay body through reduction can only be effective within a very narrow temperature range of less than 200° F. The clay begins to be responsive to the needs of free carbon at 1650° F and is willing to give up oxygen atoms until 1800° to 1850° F. Afterwards the clay begins to vitrify and to lose its porosity. Any reduction before or after these temperatures is virtually ineffective and a great waste of fuel. Also, the emissions of carbon monoxide pollute our air.

Glaze Reduction

At around 1900° F glazes begin to give up oxygen and to react to the instability of carbon monoxide in a reduction atmosphere. Carbon monoxide, created by a deficiency of oxygen and an excess of gas in the form of hydrogen and carbon, seeks to become carbon *dioxide* by attracting an additional atom of oxygen. When glazes and glaze colorants undergo this chemical change of releasing oxygen atoms they are said to have been reduced.

Most potters wait until the firing cycle reaches 2000° F to begin the glaze reduction. By cutting off the draft with the closing of the damper or by cutting off the primary air supply to the burner, flames and black smoke are made to appear at the chimney, the spy holes and, in some cases, at the burner ports. While such strong, smoky reductions are thought to maximize results the opposite is often true and many glazes end up appearing lifeless.

Reductions do not have to be excessive to be effective. Remember, carbon monoxide is invisible. A smoky, cloudy atmosphere inside the kiln, one that literally obscures a view of the ware and cones, is a sign of too much free carbon and is left to continue for too long could seriously dull the color of glazes and leave dark carbon deposits on the glaze surface. The proper air-to-gas ratio for reduction can best be judged by the color of the flame at the burner and at the spy holes and not by the opaqueness of the kilns interior.

Back pressure, witnessed by the length and strength of the flame at the spy holes, is also a good way to visually determine the quality of the reduction. The damper should be adjusted to retard the draft just enough so that a continuous and even pressure is maintained inside the kiln. A six to eight inch flame at the highest spy hole, the one farthest removed from the draw of the chimney flu on the kiln floor, should be visible during reduction whenever the plug is removed. Thick black smoke need not be anywhere in sight.

For a truly accurate indication of the combusion atmosphere inside the glaze kiln I highly recommend the purchase and the use of an *oxygen probe*.

The insertion of the probe into the kiln during firing provides continuous digital readings that allow for greater control of the firing's fuel-to-air ratio. With a clear sense of this ratio, you can also save fuel and control environmental pollution.

Glazes fired slowly to maturity under a moderate reduction atmosphere, are given more time to assimilate the process—to heal—and to avoid potential defects such as bubbling and pinholing that can result from an excessive amount of chemical activity in too short a time frame. Both time and temperature are important to glaze development. Temperature is the major force affecting the chemical reactions that influence glaze maturity but time is the variagble that controls the porocess.

Removing the brick from the spy hole reveals the amount of back pressure present inside the kiln. The color of the flame indicates the degree of the reduction.

Soaking

The slowing down or the stopping of an advance in temperature is known as soaking. Soaking gives glazes an opportunity to equalize and to come together chemically to obtain certain and valued results. Its effects are very influential. By holding a relatively constant temperature for a period of time, for example, a glaze can be made to mature 200° to 300° lower than normal. While some potters prefer to time-soak their glazes at the same temperature for thirty minutes to an hour at the end of the firing, others find it more advantageous to simply slow down the rise in temperature for the last hour of the firing cycle; beginning with the bending of the guide cone and ending with the downing of the firing cone.

Cooling

To avoid thermo-shock and cracking, a glaze kiln must be cooled slowly and carefully after being fired. If the kiln is well insulated, and can be efficiently sealed up when the damper is closed and the burner ports are covered, it can be left for a day or two to safely cool down on its own to a temperature of 100° F or less. If, for some reason, the kiln cannot be tightly sealed the pilot lights may be left on for several hours after the firing has ended to prevent a sudden a drop in temperature.

Normally, high-fire kilns are built well enough to go through the cooling process slowly enough to avoid any cracking problems that could occur from the extreme contraction that crystalline silica undergo during the brief but critical quartz inversion phase. Quartz inversion begins instantaneously at 1060° F. It should take an hour for the kiln to pass through this hazardous zone. If it becomes necessary to speed-up the cooling process, by progressively opening the damper at various time intervals, wait at least until 900° F has been reached before attempting to do so.

Record Keeping

When firing a glaze kiln it's important to keep a record of the proceedings in the form of a logbook, a journal or charts. Such a document of the temperature changes, burner and air adjustments, damper settings and other events of importance, including weather conditions, provide a written account of each firing that can be referenced for information. Each log or chart contains a history of a firing that can aid in the explanation of results, both good and bad, and in the management of a repeat performance.

Susan Beiner, Screw Tea Set, made from a multiple number of slip cast parts in the form of various size screws, leaves and wiring conduit joined together with an Epson salt and water slip. Oxidation fired to cone 6 with a manganese base glaze and again to cone 018 with a silver luster glaze. 18" × 11" × 18".

Jay Gogin, The Reef Seekers, a cone 10 ceramic wall mural installed on the exterior walls of the Student Activities Center at Florida Keys Community College. Jay and his students have created several murals for their campus on the Gulf of Mexico, including a large "Cone Ten Sunset" surrounding the double doors to the clay studio.

Kiln Safety

When working with gas kilns you should *always be on the lookout for gas leaks*. The specific gravity of propane is heavier than air and the gas will collect at the bottom of kilns, the kiln room floor and inside of underground drains where it can become dangerously explosive. Natural gas is just the opposite. Being lighter than air it quickly moves upwards where it can build-up under the ceiling or roofing and pose a threat to the building.

Gas kilns are safest when *located out-of-doors* or in a separate building or enclosure away from the classroom or studio. They need to be well vented and especially need a continuous supply of fresh air for gas combustion and burner efficiency. If the flame of a pilot burner or a main burner should become extinguished while the gas valve is still open, the valve must be closed and the kiln purged of any gas accumulation before the burner is lit again. A burner could easily go out during the early stages of a firing when the flame is small and vulnerable to external air movements. Once a kiln reaches red heat, and the burner is operating with a larger flame, the threat is past and the burner should stay lit or reignite itself. As a safeguard against simple flame failure, burners should be used in conjunction with thermocouple-actuated solenoid or gas shut-down safety valves. They cut-off the supply of gas to both the pilot and the main burner in the event that the pilot flame goes out. Safety valves with an Off-Pilot-On gas cock allow pilot lighting to be done with less risk. The burner safety system on my high-fire gas kiln makes use of Ultra Violet Scanning and automatic ignition. It is electronically operated and somewhat expensive but defensively protective and very user friendly.

When lighting burners manually always protect yourself by keeping your face and body as far away from the burner as possible. Sometimes a burner will backfire and a sudden burst of flame will shoot back out of the burner port or the adjustable air intake on the burner. This is usually caused by sporadic gusts of wind or an inadequate amount of gas pressure.

When viewing the progress of the firing through the spy holes or burner ports always protect your face and especially your eyes from the invisible heat that may come from these openings. Wear infrared radiation blocking glasses or protective goggles with a shade rating of 3.0 when looking into a glowing kiln.

Eye protection, either in the form of infrared glasses, safety glasses or a heat resistant face shield, should be worn whenever inspections through spy holes or adjustments to the burners and damper are made. If the damper plate is located up high, above head level, you'll especially want to *protect your face and eyes from any injury that might occur from small, hot particles of debris* that can fall when the plate is moved in or out.

Protective non-asbestos gloves should also be worn, along with the infrared glasses, when removing the plugs from the spy holes and again when returning them.

Finally, *never leave your kiln unattended during a firing*. And, even though your gas kiln may be equipped with automatic shut-off controls, *never rely on gas kilns to automatically shut off or fail to be present to shut the kiln down when the firing ends*.

Sandy Happel loading an all brick Bailey natural gas shuttle kiln.

BUILDING A CAR KILN

Is there an ideal kiln? Of course, any answer is relative to subjective qualification. As much as anything else, a kiln's design is linked to a potter's personality, type of clay work produced and to a preferred firing process. As it turns out, many potters prefer to fire their wares at stoneware temperatures (at cone 9 or 10) and, for this very simple reason, I have chosen to include some detailed instructions for the building of a high-fire gas kiln.

I have personally built and fired several types of high-temperature brick kilns. Currently, my students and I fire in a 54 cubic foot, single car, shuttle kiln at least once every week. It is an all brick kiln made by the Bailey Pottery Equipment Corporation and is fired by two forced air burners to cone 10. After all these years, this is my first commercially made kiln and, even on a bad day, I love it. Shuttle kilns, also commonly known as car kilns or drawer kilns, are unique in that the floor and front wall are attached to a metal wheeled cart that is easily shuttled into, or out of, the kiln chamber along two metal rails. When fully open, the kiln can quickly and easily be loaded from three sides by several people simultaneously. Better yet, the stacking of both the ware and the shelves can also proceed in a much safer manner, with a lot less strain on the back.

Over years of traveling, I have seen many gas kilns throughout this country, as well as in other countries from as far away as Australia, but I have been most impressed by potter Michael Gwinup's car kiln. Michael has built several kilns based upon the shuttle design. The first kiln that I saw of his was at his Blue Spruce Pottery in Bend, Oregon. The kiln itself was located under a roof structure just outside of the pottery, facing a garage door. Whenever necessary, this door was briefly opened so that the cart containing the kiln floor could be rolled into the studio, either for loading or unloading, and then conveniently returned to its outdoor location where the heat and fumes from the firings couldn't disturb the air inside the building. In addition to being a talented artist, Michael is a skilled kiln builder and the supportive material that follows is based upon the 50 cubic foot car kiln he recently built at his new studio.

*By opening the garage door built into the side of his studio Michael Gwinup can
shuttle the cart of his outdoor car kiln into the studio for loading or unloading.*

Metal Framework

The frame for the car kiln is made from 3" angle iron, 3" channel iron and steel plate. All of these elements are 1/4" thick. The 2 wall support frames, the chimney-flue frame and the cart-door frame are welded. The remaining framing and arch buttresses are bolted together. The holes for the bolts should be slightly larger than the bolts to allow for expansion and contraction during firing.

On a level concrete slab, 6" thick, lay out the welded wall and stack supports around the angle iron track containing the cart. Roll the cart in and out between the wall supports to check the fit before securing the tracks and the legs of the wall supports to the concrete with anchor bolts. To keep the tracks from drifting apart, cross supports should be welded at three foot intervals.

Welded frame supports for the side walls and chimney on the concrete kiln pad outside the studio.

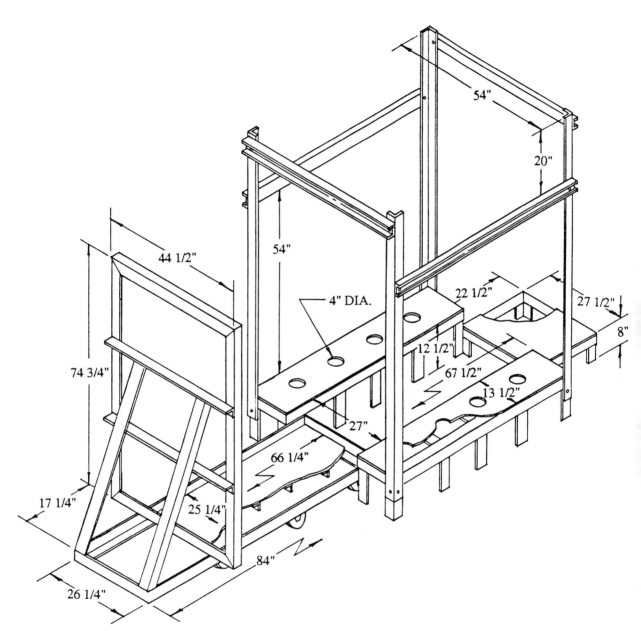

Steel Framework For Car Kiln

Securing the welded metal base frame to the concrete kiln pad.

Bricking

This kiln is constructed from 750 K-23 soft insulating firebricks and 425 high temperature hard bricks. Each brick measures 2 1/2" x 4 1/2" x 9".

Once the tracks and metal base frame are properly positioned and bolted to the concrete pad use a single row of hard bricks to form a mini wall (5 bricks high) as a foundational support for the back wall. This wall is stacked directly on top of the concrete slab, in front of the metal chimney frame, and marks the beginning of the flue opening. The flue opening forms a corbel arch. The area of this arched opening should at least be equal to the total number of square inches of the burner port openings. Whenever you're unsure of a flue size build it larger as it can always be dampered down later.

The brick foundation for the back wall and the first course on the chimney frame.

Next, lay the double brick floor for the side walls, cutting out the 4" diameter circles above each burner port with a hand held bone saw. Soft firebrick cuts easily.

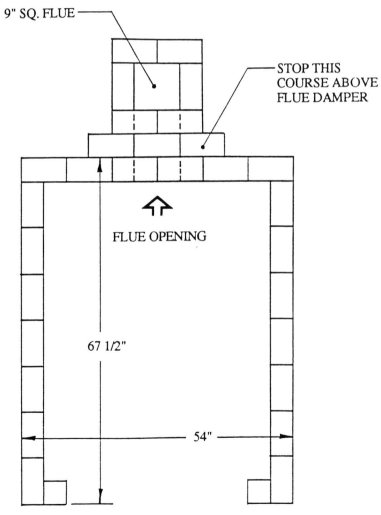

9" SQ. FLUE

STOP THIS
COURSE ABOVE
FLUE DAMPER

FLUE OPENING

67 1/2"

54"

Brick Stacking Diagram

After bricking the floor of the kiln, brick the floor of the cart and roll it in and out of the kiln to check or adjust the clearance.

The total wall thickness of the kiln is only 4 1/2" thick. The walls are made by stacking every other layer of soft brick, without mortar, in such a way that the center of each brick covers an underlying joint. The stacking is easy. Just take care to keep the door opening plumb and, along with the side walls, an equal distance apart. Use an old carpenters hand saw to cut the brick. For really straight cuts use a second brick as a saw guide.

After the last row of bricks are in place assemble the rest of the frame. Making certain that the channel iron, buttressing the arch supporting the skew bricks, is in the right position and tightly bolted in place.

Cutting a skew brick from a standard soft brick using a carpenter's hand saw.

Arch-supporting skew bricks on top of the kiln wall; buttressed by channel iron.

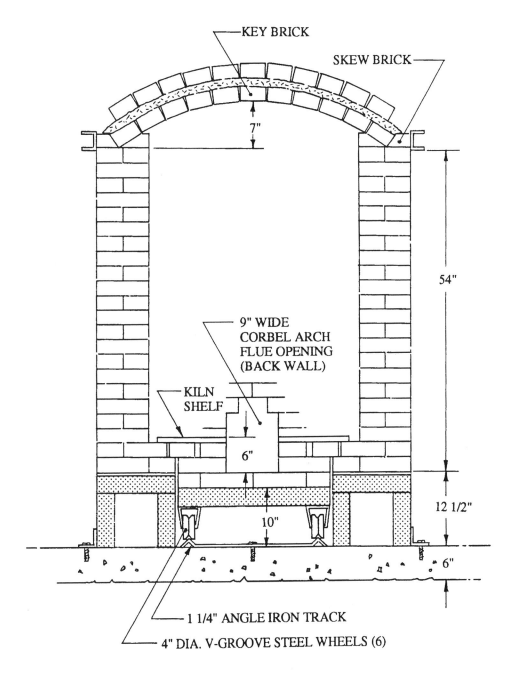

KEY BRICK

SKEW BRICK

7"

54"

9" WIDE
CORBEL ARCH
FLUE OPENING
(BACK WALL)

KILN
SHELF

6"

12 1/2"

10"

6"

1 1/4" ANGLE IRON TRACK

4" DIA. V-GROOVE STEEL WHEELS (6)

Section view — Looking Into Kiln

Arch

There are many ways to layout and build a sprung-arch roof for a kiln. The method Michael has chosen is fast and inexpensive.

On one edge of a 3/4" sheet of plywood mark out the distance between the 2 metal buttresses with a marker. Cut two skew bricks (or skewbacks as they are often called) and place them on these marks. With straight bricks, standing on end, begin to layout an arch that has at least a 7" rise. Start from both skew bricks and work towards the center. Keep an even number of bricks on each side of the key brick and try to form a smooth, even curve. Mark the curve of the arch with a marker and cut it out with a saber saw. Using it as a pattern, make two additional plywood forms. Attach the plywood shapes to 3 wooden 2 x 4's that are as long as the kiln and cover it with a flexible sheet of 1/8" masonite. Once the masonite is nailed in place the structure is complete and can be held in position with scrap 2 x 4's. Remember, this form is temporary and should be secured in such a manner that it can easily be removed when the arch bricks are all in place.

Arch bricks are stood on edge between two skew bricks to determine the exact curvature of the plywood support form.

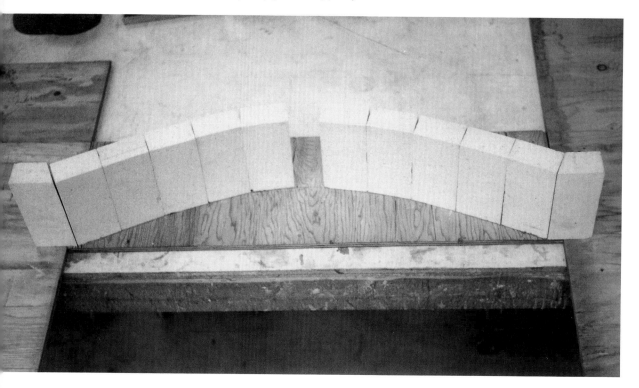

With the support form in place, lay the bricks flat on top of the masonite. Work from the skew bricks towards the middle of the arch. Stagger each course and keep the front of the arch flush with the wall of the kiln. Put the row of key bricks in last. The interfacing edges of these arch bricks could be cut for a tighter fit but Michael prefers to fill the spaces between each brick with a high temperature mortar and, when necessary, shims cut from broken bricks.

Once the arch bricks are securely in place carefully remove the support form. Seeing the arch, unsupported, for the first time is always a dramatic moment. Sometime prior to firing the kiln, a 1″ thick high temperature fiber blanket should be placed on top of the arch for added insulation and held in place by a second layer of mortarless bricks.

Adding the key brick which has been custom cut to fit snugly in place.

Cart

The brick floor of the cart is four layers thick. The upper two layers accommodate a 9″ wide flue channel that runs the entire length of the floor and are stacked in such a manner as to form a double heat seal with the side walls of the kiln. This part of the cart floor requires custom fitting, so don't hesitate to roll the cart in and out to check on the clearance.

The door is not added to the cart until the floor of the cart is bricked and the body of the kiln is completed. With the cart located all the way inside the kiln, position the door frame so that it is 3/4″ away from, and parallel to, the front wall. When in place, weld it and its supports to the cart.

Using a thin coat of mortar, brick up the door frame, leaving an opening for both an upper and a lower peep hole. When finished, use a marker to trace the contour of the door opening onto the inside face of the brick door. This needs to be done from inside the kiln with the cart pushed in all of the way. With the cart pulled out of the kiln carefully cut and grind away a portion of the brick surrounding this outline to make a more efficient heat seal.

One of four custom welded quick-release locking cams used to latch the kiln door.

Chimney

The stack is added after the brick work on the kiln is finished. It measures 18" square on the outside and has a 9" square flue opening inside. It is built 4 1/2" (the thickness of one brick) away from the back wall directly on top of the welded support platform. To close off the flue, a damper channel needs to be built into the wall of the chimney. A kiln shelf 9" x 24" can be used as the sliding damper. To allow for ease of movement, the channel should be made slightly larger than the thickness of the kiln shelf.

A kiln shelf is used as a horizontal damper to control the draw of the chimney.

Burners

There are several burner systems that could be made or purchased to fire this kiln to cone 10 in from eight to fifteen hours. Michael has chosen to use 4 eclipse venturi burners manifolded into 8 separate burner tips. Each burner has a 125,000 BTU rating, with a total BTU output of 500,000. He fires his kiln with propane, at a setting of 1 1/2 pounds of pressure, and rarely has the gas valves fully open.

For your own kiln and situation you may want fire with natural gas, use atmospheric burners or use two forced air burners, all of which could be done with Michael's kiln design. You may want to have your burners and safety shutoff controls professionally designed and manufactured for you just as you might hire a plumber to custom install the gas lines. The choices are yours to make. Where Michael's kiln ideas unfold yours should begin. By sharing his kiln with us, Michael has removed some obstacles and paved a welcoming way for our future actions in the engaging world of kiln building.

Michael assembling one of his kilns 4 manifold venturi burners.

Burners on one side of the kiln in their assembled position.

Flames from the burners, arising through the 8 burner ports, inside the kiln.

RAKU FIRING

The firing of raku pottery has become one of the most enlightening and enjoyable firing processes practiced in contemporary ceramics.

Its origins go back to 16th century Japan and the cultural aestheticism of the tea masters and their socially democratic order to drinking tea. Closely associated with the disciplines of Zen Buddhism, the drinking of tea soon developed into a highly civilized, yet gentle and amiable, ceremony that brought about contentment through contemplation and led to new perceptions of human consciousness. The tea ceremony, with the help of raku fired tea bowls, was used to bridge the distance between spirit and embodiment in Japan. It was, and still is, a way to view eternal virtues in ordinary things and events.

Part of the liveliness of making raku pottery today is attributed to the preservation of those same realities, and those truths, which are eternal in their nature and so important to the vitality of the senses and the humanness of the spirit.

Pots, especially raku pots, are not made simply for the sake of making something from clay. Nor are they necessarily made for culinary purposes. They may be formed to meet a utilitarian need or as an expression of self. More likely than not, they are formed for deeper reasons. At their best they are created to engage and to faithfully honor those human-felt aspects of our lives which are in harmony with nature, uniquely personal and fundamentally true to our being. Pottery, like any art object, lives from generation to generation when it speaks of eternal human truths. Raku pottery, because it doesn't live well in the kitchen . . . not being fired high enough to be water proof . . . has become artfully spirit-centered. It is profoundly important in the world of ceramic forms, without the normal rational of justifications, as a vehicle for gifting the individual. And, as a transforming force, where the one who shapes the pot is also shaped by it, raku has continued to reflect with subtle charity a significant heart-felt consciousness.

Clam shell raku kiln built by Ken Turner and co-designed by John Harris and Mike Blackwell. Made with angle iron, expanded metal, soft bricks and ceramic fiber, this movable kiln provides easy access to the fired ware, 34" × 24" × 24".

Technically, raku is low-temperature pottery that is placed into a cold or already hot kiln (with metal tongs) and fired to maturity in less than one hour. After reaching temperature the pots are immediately removed, while glowing hot, with long handle metal tongs and placed into a metal container (garbage-can) partly filled with a combustible such as dry hay or straw. Once the combustible is ignited by the hot pot, and the flames peak, the container is quickly covered with a lid and sealed to prevent air from entering and smoke from exiting. The flames inside the tightly sealed container now become desperate for oxygen, which is required for combustion, and chemically removes it from the clay and glaze before being snuffed out. This is known as the *post-firing reduction* phase. It's what turns the exposed clay surfaces a spirited black and the copper bearing glazes into voluptuous patinas. This alluring reduction phase is what captivates and engages contemporary raku potters. Its practice is a recent American adaptation to raku firing and was advanced a little over thirty years ago by Colorado artist Paul Soldner. Until this time the Japanese, and others, simply placed the hot pots on the ground to cool.

Glazes, applied to the bisque ware, can mature anywhere between 1700° and 1800° Fahrenheit. From experience, many rakuists develop a sense for judging the kiln's temperature by eyeing either the color of the pottery or the kilns interior. Others lay large ceramic firing cones (usually cone 07) on top of bricks with half of their length extending beyond the brick so that the cantilevered tips will bend down when the desired temperature is reached. Pyrometers, of course, are extremely useful for determining the kiln's temperature at any stage of the firing, and popular they are.

The major glaze ingredient and flux is Gerstley borate, although frits are becoming increasingly popular.

Gas fired kilns made from soft insulating brick or light weight insulating fiber blanket materials are the types used most often for raku firings. If an indoor electric kiln is situated near an outside door, in such a way that pots can safely be removed and taken outdoors for post-firing reduction, it too can be used to effectively fire raku pots. Old or retired electric kilns with lids still attached remain extremely valuable in that they can be easily converted into gas fired raku kilns.

For school situations, *counter-balanced* fiber kilns equipped with temperature indication pyrometers and gas burners activated with solenoid safety valves, thermocouples and electronic pilot ignition, forget the cullular phone, are modestly safer to use than other designs. They are decisively different in that students do not physically touch the kiln. Seattle Pottery makes a sensible counter-balanced kiln. Their kiln, aside from being classically simple, is remarkably portable and easily moved from place-to-place.

Used electric kilns are easily converted into top loading gas-fired raku kilns.

Raku venturi burner with pilot light and solenoid safety valve.

Indoor fiber-lined counter-balanced raku kilns, built by instructor Jay Gogian, are an important part of the exciting clay program at Florida Keys Community College. The kilns, and the reduction enclosure sunken into the built-up cinder block floor, are vented by a ten foot square over-head hood and two large window fans. Located in Key West, Florida these are the two southern most raku kilns in the United States.

Raku kilns manufactured by Seattle Pottery Supply being used in a workshop.

Patricia Cronin's front loading raku kiln with a ceramic fiber swing-hinge door, Manufactured by the Laguna Clay Company.

A P-240 Power burner with gas solenoid safety valve, manufactured by the Laguna Clay Company. Note the small piece of bent metal welded to the tip of the pilot light, it deflects and directs the flame onto the tip of the thermocouple.

Dry Matt Raku Glazes

Little by little, that captivating raku surface, the dry copper matt, is arousing, if not seducing, many raku potters. To be sure, they are alluring but they are also beguiling and difficult to obtain and to manage. Consider that these popular glaze surfaces are generally 70% to 90% copper carbonate with a little frit mixed in for control. Also consider that they have to be fired, at the very least, to cone 05 to become fortified. Otherwise they remain waywardly vulnerable due to oxidation over a short passage of time and to human handling.

Temperamental as these copper saturate glazes are, many potters have their own methodology for working with them. Some spray the glaze on the pot before it is bisque fired, and maybe spray on an additional application after it is bisque fired, and then raku fire it to temperatures well below cone 05 prior to removing it from the kiln for a post-firing reduction in an air-tight container. A few rakuists fire their ware to 1800° F, turn off the kiln and wait for the temperature to drop 400 to 600 degrees before removing it. Others use a procedure called *striking*. With this approach the gas kiln is fired to temperature, shut off, allowed to cool (to 1200°–1400°F: depending on the clay's wall thickness) and then relighted for a short stint of reduction to pre-activate the extensive copper portion of the glaze in advance of the reduction done outside the kiln.

Many rakuists are also highly scientific in how they manipulate the post-firing reduction. They take great pains to open the container after an exact interval of time, say two minutes, add a little more combustible and continue the reduction for an additional amount of time, say precisely seven, nine or ten minutes (depending on the size or wall thickness of the pot) before cooling it down with a quick application of water. Still, others obtain dry matt surfaces through the use of underglazes and/or commercial stains mixed into clay slip and applied to the pot while it is still wet or leather-hard. Such finishes cannot be over-reduced or reduced for too long a time after firing, otherwise they become dark, if not black. In some such cases potters completely remove the black carbon and restore the richness of the matt color by briefly torching the pot, while it is still warm, with the same gas burner they used to fire the kiln.

While there are many variables leading to the success of the miracle-like copper matt glazes, perhaps none of them are as important as clay thickness. Its an ever-reoccurring fact: the thinner the clay wall, the greater the possibility for surface color sovereignty. So! Don't postpone your birthing of thin raku clay pieces.

To minimize the effects of ultraviolet exposure and the chemical changes of oxidation, some individuals spray their dry matt surfaces with an invisible coating of silicone grout sealer. Protective silicone sealers, such as the one manufactured by the Jasco Chemical Corporation, can also be used as a water repellent barrier for unglazed ceramic surfaces and tiles.

Crackle Raku Glazes

If any one glaze surface is universally associated with raku it would be a shinny white glaze with a distinctive crackle pattern. These crackle glazes look their best when applied either to a white clay body or on a non-white clay body covered with a white clay slip.

The dramatics of this crackle pattern is easily obtained by waving the pot back-and-forth for a minute, after it has been removed from the kiln and while it is still being held inside the jaws of the tongs, to expose the hot glaze to the relatively cold air. The thermodynamics of this extended exposure intensifies a thermochemical phenomena that generates a myriad of invisible cracks. For these cracks to be made visible they must undergo post-firing reduction. For these cracks, and the patterns they form, to become more definitive, they must be *burped*. Not once, but two or three times. . . and at sixty second intervals. Burping is a process of momentarily opening the reduction container (to once again expose the glaze to cooler air), adding additional combustible, waiting until it ignites and then sealing-off the supply of oxygen by quickly closing the container. Each burping phase forces an additional chemical reduction of oxygen to occur and a darker display of the once invisible crackle pattern.

John Harris, Raku Basket with Oak Stand, white crackle glaze, 22" × 12".

Ana England, The Great Serpent: Awake!, low-fire white clay, burnished and pit fired. The clay slabs were fired in sections and glued to a plywood backing with PC-7 epoxy. 45" × 32" × 3".

SMOKE FIRING

Various primitive firing techniques have been used by the earliest potters in different cultures and regions of the world from Africa to Mexico. Many of these early forms of firing, with age-old names such as pit firing, open-pit firing, dung firing, sawdust firing, etc., are beginning to be used by more and more contemporary potters. Although not primarily for the production of utilitarian pottery as much as the aesthetic markings of the firing process. In America, especially in the southwestern states of Arizona and New Mexico, the ancient pottery making and firing methods of the native Anasazi are being resurrected in today's pueblos and receiving world wide recognition. Contemporary Native-American potters such as Julian and Maria Martinez, Lucy Lewis and Fannie Nampeyo have been credited with making some of North Americas finest pottery . . . and you'll get no argument there from me.

A low-tech variation on one of these so-called romantic firing techniques involves the use of a reclaimed steel oil drum, sawdust and scrap wood. My students and I have settled on this unique system for firing pottery in a campus setting because it is safe, dramatically effective and relatively consistent. We call it smoke firing.

For the fifty gallon oil drum (which functions as the kiln) to breath, and supply needed oxygen to the firing, it should contain either 21 half-inch diameter holes or 40 quarter-inch diameter holes. The holes are spaced uniformly and made with an electric drill. The top of this kiln, which is 24" in diameter, can be covered with an oversize metal lid, containing several air holes, or with a piece of corrugated sheet metal. Our choice for a cover, however, is slightly different. We find that a metal lid from an old garbage-can that is an inch or two smaller in diameter than the drum works very well. During the firing, the lid gradually settles downward as the wood burns. For safety purposes we keep a large piece of seventeen gage expanded metal mesh on top of the drum to catch and contain any flaming debris.

An equally effective firing chamber can easily be made from ordinary house brick. The kiln is formed by layering up rows of brick on top of a floor made from brick or by building up the brick walls directly on top of leveled ground. The bricks are quickly and loosely stacked without the use of mortar. Depending on the amount and the direction of the wind, a 1/8" to 1/4" gap is left between the ends of each brick to admit oxygen. The top of the kiln is covered with a non-combustible material such as a metal garbage-can lid or old kiln shelves.

It's not uncommon to load a primitive fired kiln by stacking the pieces to be fired on top of one another, beginning with the largest and heaviest forms on the bottom and ending with the smallest ones at the top. During the firing the pieces shift, as the combustibles separating the layers burn away, and eventually they end up in one big pile. Yet, because such firings are relatively slow to burn and are extremely gentle in their effect, few pots end up being broken. However, we have repeatedly found that reduction patterning is graphically more spectacular if only one tier of pottery is fired at a time. Likewise, we have come to recognize that the flashing and fuming that occurs favors certain forms. Tall flat forms, for example, often fair well, but it's the tumescent or spherical shapes that respond best—especially if a white clay body is involved. They are the ones that always seem to surprise and arouse excitement in the studio by the breathtaking richness of their impressively potent surface finishes. They are the ones that turn, sometimes in a matter of a smiling instant, so many onto smoke firing—making them feel that they have finally found something that up until now has eluded them. You know the feelings of such gifted discoveries.

Priscilla Marino, burnished white stoneware clay fired in an oil drum, 9" x 13".

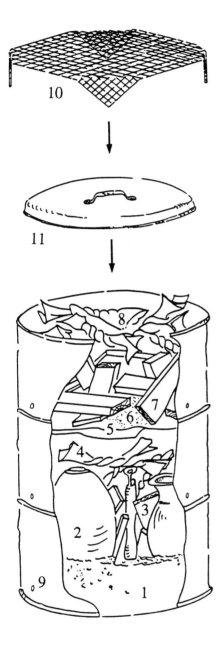

1. ADD 6" OF SAWDUST MIXED WITH 1/2 CUP COPPER CARBONATE TO THE BOTTOM OF THE CONTAINER.

2. ADD CERAMIC PIECES (PREFERABLY MADE FROM A WHITE CLAY BODY THAT HAS BEEN BURNISHED AND BISQUE FIRED).

3. PLACE SMALL BLOCKS OF WOOD (4" TO 8" LONG) AROUND EACH CERAMIC FORM.

4. FILL REMAINING SPACES WITH TWISTED SHEETS OF NEWSPAPER AND COVER WITH SAWDUST.

5. COVER WITH 3 SHEETS OF NEWSPAPER LAID FLAT.

6. SPRINKLE WITH A MIXTURE OF KOSHER SALT (1 PART) AND COPPER CARBONATE (2 PARTS).

7. ADD LARGER BLOCKS OF WOOD 10" TO 18" LONG, AVOID WOLMANIZED OR WOOD WITH BARK, TO 6" BELOW RIM AND SPRINKLE WITH MORE OF THE SALT AND COPPER MIXTURE.

8. TOP OFF CONTAINER WITH TWISTED SHEETS OF NEWSPAPER.

9. LIGHT KILN THROUGH THE 1/2" AIR HOLES WITH A BUTANE TORCH . . . START AT THE BOTTOM.

10. COVER WITH A SQUARE OF EXPANDED METAL MESH TO CONTAIN FLYING/FLAMING DEBRIS.

11. AFTER 15 MIN. PARTIALLY LIFT THE MESH AND INSERT A METAL LID THAT IS SMALLER IN DIAMETER THAN THE CONTAINER.

12. ALLOW TO BURN AND TO COOL-DOWN OVERNIGHT.

13. REMOVE FIRED WARE AND WASH CLEAN. FINISH WITH A POLISHED COAT OF SHOE PASTE OR LIQUID ACRYLIC FLOOR WAX.

Procedure For Smoke Firing In An Oil Drum

Still, that is not to imply that only classically round forms possess a distinctive secret or magical monopoly when it comes to successfully being smoke fired. It may help to know that an endless variety of forms are promising candidates. Forms made on or off the potter's wheel endure equally well. Bisque fired forms are stronger and ultimately run less of a risk but greenware forms, because they are not pre-fired, come closer in the quality and the intensity of their black coloring to the true spirit of primitive firing. Highly burnished pottery or those covered with terra sigillata can become exuberantly mirror-like, if not astonishingly ancient in appearance. Without question many forms beg, or in the very least envy, the engulfing fullness of nothing simpler than such a transformation process.

Begin the loading by adding 6″ of sawdust mixed with 1/2 cup of copper carbonate onto the bottom of the 36″ tall oil drum. The sawdust can be either softwood or hardwood but it should be dry. Wood shavings, because they burn too fast and admit too much air, are not recommended for this initial layer. As a single tier firing, this bed of sawdust is used to produce the strongest reduction and, subsequently, the richest black color. Pieces must be nested carefully, and in an advantageous way so that each form is favorably interfaced with the combustible to yield beneficial results. In some instances this may necessitate placing the pot into the sawdust upside-down; in others it may be desirable to lay the pot on its side. However you approach the task, *it is in your best interest to wear a dust mask and rubber gloves when reaching into the barrel and working with the finely powdered copper and wood dust.*

Unglazed bisque pots nested on a 6″ bed of sawdust inside a reclaimed oil drum.

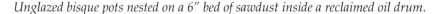

Priscilla Marino sprinkling a salt and copper carbonate mix inside the barrel.

After the pottery is loaded, with 2" of space left between the forms and the wall of the drum, small scraps of wood 4" to 6" in length are packed around them; followed by a layer of tightly twisted sheets of newspaper. Several flat sheets of newspaper are placed on top of the twisted paper and coated with a sprinkling of salt and copper. The mixture is made from 2 parts of Kosher salt and 1 part of copper carbonate. Larger scraps of wood, up to 18" long, are then added to the barrel until a height of 6" below the rim is reached. The remaining space is filled with more twists of newspaper and covered with the metal mesh.

Starting at the bottom, light the kiln through the air holes with a butane torch. The fire should burn and smolder evenly, so you may have to come back to some of the holes 2 or 3 times to relight until the fire establishes itself. Smoke will begin to appear and will continue to remain as a sure sign that the firing is progressing.

Heavy gauge metal mesh is placed over the drum to help contain burning debris.

Within fifteen to thirty minutes after lighting the kiln lift the metal mesh, *while wearing heat protective gloves*, and place the metal lid into the drum to cover the burning wood. After the cover is on and the mesh back in place the kiln sight may be periodically left unattended unless there is a site-specific fire hazard. After several hours the flames settle down and the kiln begins to smolder. At this point there is little danger of fire to the area and the kiln may be left to fire over night. The following day the pots should be cool enough to remove and clean-up. After cleaning, the surfaces can be brought to life by applying a thin coat of liquid acrylic floor wax or by buffing-out a coat of neutral shoe paste that has been rubbed into the clay.

Always remember—if the initial results are in any way disappointing the pieces can easily be refired.

Large pots can be smoked
fired inside an expansive
pit dug into the ground.

Small pots can be sawdust fired
inside a commercial trash burner.

7

Towards A Healthier Studio

The contemporary potter and student of ceramics is often in a more dangerous environment than they at first realize. Even today, the information associated with poisonous ceramic materials and detrimental studio procedures is incomplete. In general, the risks vary and are relative to the frequency and to the condition of your exposure to certain materials and circumstances. Exposure here refers to some form of body contact with a chemical substance or condition that is potentially harmful. Material toxicity, length of exposure time, condition and/or availability of protective safety equipment, personal work habits, cleanliness of facilities, ventilation, etc. are all threatening variables.

MATERIAL HAZARDS

Exposure

Damaging exposure to a hazardous material may result in one of the following ways:

> *Physical Contact:* Can cause burns, eruptive skin reactions, infections and blindness.
>
> *Inhalation:* Can cause damage to the throat, lungs and brain.
>
> *Ingestion:* Can cause injury to the mouth, throat, stomach, kidney, liver and lungs. Cancers, sterility and damage to the nervous system may also occur.

Acute health reactions to toxic chemical exposure are usually immediate and the symptoms severely apparent. Dizziness, nausea, headache, confusion and vomiting would be some examples of the short term effects. Not all hazards, however, are as immediately obvious. Chronic reactions, on the other hand, are usually hidden internally and do not manifest noticeable symptoms until much later. Often the results of low-level chemical exposure for an extended period of time can be serious. Lung cancer and emphysema are familiar examples of long term diseases with a latency period of years or even decades before symptoms develop.

Silica

Silicosis, a chronic and debilitating lung disease resulting from exposure to clay and silica dust, is a known threat in the ceramic studio.

In and of itself clay is not poisonous, at least not in the purely toxic way that lead and barium carbonate are, but in the form of dry airborne particles clay (which on the average is made up of 50% silica) can cause permanent damage to the lungs. External symptoms of pulmonary damage might include chronic coughing, shortness of breath, chest pain and lassitude, which might be characterized as an overall state of lethargic dullness and physical sluggishness.

Important ceramic materials that contain free silica and that are especially dangerous while in the dry powdered state include: clays, feldspars, silica (flint), talc and wollastonite.

Other chemicals such as bentonite, cobalt, copper, Gerstley borate, manganese, nepheline syenite, tin oxide, zinc oxide and zirconium products are respiratory irritants that may also contribute directly to pulmonary disorders when inhaled.

Toxic Materials To Avoid

Even if handled with the greatest of care, materials that are highly toxic or are potential carcinogens should be avoided. Not only are they a danger in the studio during mixing, handling and firing, they are a danger when used with food. In varying amounts, glaze materials tend to leach, or yield soluble matter overtime, depending upon their chemical reaction with other ingredients in the glaze recipe and the temperature of the firing.

The following glaze chemicals and all of their insoluble and soluble compounds are some, but not necessarily all, of the toxic materials that should be avoided: barium, cadmium, chrome, lead, lithium, manganese, nickel, potassium bichromate, uranium and vanadium.

Material Substitutes

Many compounds, such as cadmium and nickel, have no substitutes while others can often be replaced with suitable alternatives.

Spodumene, a feldspar, contains lithium yet, because of its integration within the compound, reduces the dangers of inhalation and is preferable to lithium carbonate.

Gerstley borate, borax, soda ash and unleaded frits are major fluxing agents and should be used in place of lead and leaded frits.

Barium carbonate is a *highly dangerous material* for potter and consumer alike. Fortunately, however, magnesium carbonate, dolomite, zinc, titanium dioxide, whiting and strontium carbonate can achieve the satiny soft surfaces associated with barium glazes when used in the 10% to 15% range.

Black iron oxide along with a pinch of cobalt can be a healthier colorant than the richly looking and forever tempting manganese dioxide. Manganese is the bad boy of colorants. Really!

The materials in ceramic glazes can be dangerous to your health! When working with glazes use every precaution available to protect yourself and to avoid the risks of being physically exposed, either by inhalation, ingestion or contact absorption, to any chemical hazards.

VENTILATION

More than any other single factor, *the health and well being of the ceramist is directly dependent upon the quality of air in the studio.* Breathing clean air must be a priority!

The upper respiratory system and mucus inside the nose can, to a certain extent, trap some of the larger dust particles but are no defense for the abundance of fine dust particles and fumes airborne in the ceramic studio. The 200 mesh particle size of many dry clays and chemicals can, in a relatively short period of exposure, lead to a permanent impairment of respiratory function. The avoidance of kiln fumes and dust from ceramic materials is best achieved by having separate and well ventilated areas for kilns, clay mixing, glaze making and art fabrication.

With electric kilns a negative pressure ventilation system, operated by a blower motor, is more effective at removing hazardous kiln fumes than overhead hood systems. Fumes do not enter the room with this arrangement. They are drawn down through the kiln, along with fresh air from small holes in the top lid, and vented outdoors through an exhaust duct at the base.

It is best to place gas kilns outdoors in an open area where polluted fumes cannot be trapped on windless days or, if indoors, in a separate room with a well engineered commercial ventilation system. Gas kilns, especially those that are heavily reduced, produce deadly carbon monoxide gases and other poisonous fumes from sulfuric clays, wax-resist, lusters, toxic glaze chemicals or, as is the situation with salt kilns, hydrogen-chloride acid: chlorine gas.

For clay mixing a separate air cleaning collector should be engineered and located as close to the clay mixing source as possible. If a dough-type mixer is used, for example, a hood vent with a long slot-like opening and a capture depth of at least 30 inches could be designed and positioned just above the area where the hopper and lid meet to exhaust the fine clay dust and free silica outdoors or indoors to a large, multiple filter, dust collecting unit.

Glaze making and mixing areas pose a highly hazardous health and ventilation problem. Since these chemicals can be toxic the air directly around the mixing and holding containers can become contaminated and must be vented away immediately. Here, a moveable or flexible air extraction system might be the appropriate solution. Such a local exhaust unit is often referred to as an elephant trunk. It consists of a of a small inlet hood connected to a counterbalanced arm assembly made up of both rigid and flexible ducting. The hood opening can be quickly and easily repositioned to any number of alternative positions. For flexible trunk ducts to be effective, they must be maneuvered as close, I'm talking inches, to the source of the contamination as possible. Consequently, the suction hood must be employed in such a manner as to always remain between the face and the perilous material and not above the head.

A small flexible trunk exhaust duct mounted on the ceiling of a glaze room.

Ventilation of the working centers of a clay studio or classroom can be maintained by open-air systems such as windows and doors or by a closed-air system of fans and recirculation. Because these spaces are generally large, and with differing requirements, you may want to consult a professionally qualified ventilation specialist. For the most part, however, dust contaminants can often be contained by initiating healthier work habits and hygienic housekeeping procedures that can help eliminate many problems before they become airborne.

Unfortunately, no one all-encompassing system of air cleaning or ventilation can provide complete protection from sub-micron particles but there have been substantial breakthroughs recently in air filtration. High efficiency air cleaning units with HEPA (High Efficiency Particulate Air) filters, rated as being 99.97% efficient at .3 microns, are easily available and easy to install. These air cleaning machines plug into standard 115V outlets, have variable speed controls and can easily operate for one year without requiring a replacement of the main fiberglass filter. However, the thick prefilter will have to be replaced or washed more often. For proper protection it is generally recommended that every hour ten to twelve complete exchanges of the studios air pass through such a unit, or units as the need of the room size may dictate. It should be noted, however, that there are many air cleaning devices designed and marketed to electrostatically remove smoke but these are completely unsuitable for studio dust control.

Activity Confinement

Frequently a ceramists choice of a workplace is strictly limited. Its location and layout are often determined by finances. If, however, there is a choice, the five major ceramic material handling stages (clay mixing, clay fabricating, glaze making, glazing and firing) should be physically separated from one another and should not be mixed with living, eating or children's play areas. It is in these five stages that the greatest risks to health exist. Ideally, each of these areas should have its own air transfer system.

A separate facility for mixing clay (removed from the main studio area and properly vented) is more than a protective health perk—it's an absolute necessity.

STUDIO SAFETY RECOMMENDATIONS

Clay And Glaze Making Safety Precautions

The safest procedures available for mixing these materials should be employed. Extreme care must be exercised to both contain and remove airborne particles during the mixing stages. Because the effects of exposure are long-term, where problems may not show up for twenty years, these areas should be especially well ventilated and maintained to prevent clay dust from accumulating. Frequent wet mopping and sponging is also a must. Otherwise clay dust is continuously kicked into the air as it is tracked through the studio. In addition, one should wear an appropriate respirator with an approved filter cartridge. Special work clothes or garments might be worn for these areas and removed after the mixing is completed; wash them frequently. Although it's more expensive, some schools and artists purchase commercially prepared clays and glazes. This is done not to save time as much as it is to eliminate the menacing risks involved with mixing and the need for air handling equipment. In many respects the safety concerns associated with the bulk mixing of hazardous materials justify the added expense.

Glazing Safety Precautions

When glazing it is important to work as neatly as possible. Spilled materials, wet or dry, should be cleaned up immediately. Formica or stainless steel table tops, because they are easily cleaned with a sponge, are good surfaces to work from when applying glaze.

Wear rubber gloves when glazing. The high quality, 5 mil thick, latex ones made for occupational safety rather than medical use are great and can be worn in the studio all day without tearing. I like the disposable soft rubber ones (No.W1005) from Best Manufacturing. Never stir or mix a glaze with bare hands. It is scary, for example, to know that a single gram of barium carbonate, if physically absorbed, can be fatal. Besides, a large cooking whisk or a paint mixer attached to an electric drill does a much better job.

Hands should be thoroughly washed after the glazing is complete. There is no justification, health wise, to subject yourself to inherent harm, *so make every effort to refrain from eating and drinking in the glazing or glaze mixing areas*. Don't hesitate to renounce using recipes that contain highly toxic materials. To *not* reject the use of harmful chemicals in the glazes you use would be unmistakably self destructive. Finally, if you're spraying glaze, do so only in a booth or manner that effectively removes airborne particles . . . and wear an approved respirator.

Safety Precautions During Firing

When fired, all kilns produce intense heat and give off fumes; some highly toxic. As various organic impurities in the clay break-down during firing, carbon monoxide and gases, such as sulfur dioxide, are formed. Exposure to these and other vapors, depending on the chemical make-up of the glazes involved, can cause harmful lung or respiratory tract reactions.

To reduce such irritating substances kilns should be located away from main work areas and be well ventilated with canopy hoods or by whatever means that best carries off the fumes and heat for a particular kiln's design and location. Outdoors kilns do not require mechanical ventilation. Indoor kilns, however, need to have an exhaust collection system and need to be located away from potentially flammable wall surfaces in case of overfiring or mechanical malfunction. Never fire a kiln in an enclosed and unvented area.

When firing kilns you should wear clothing, such as an apron, and use gloves that are heat resistant. For eye protection, safety glasses, a heat resistant face shield or infrared goggles or glasses with shade ratings between 1.7 and 3.0 should be worn.

PERSONAL SAFETY RECOMMENDATIONS

Dust Respirators

Your respirator is your most important piece of safety equipment. Whenever it becomes necessary, wear a respirator to avoid breathing in excessive dust and fumes. Breathing, after all, is one of the things you do. All of the time. It is ultimately your responsibility to know when to use a respirator and how to care fore it. True, you may not look as attractive with it as you might without it, but such thoughts make no sense to your lungs. For your protection, you'll need to do some research to determine which type is best for you and your situation. The mask should be approved by MSHA (Mine Safety and Health Administration) or NIOSH (National Institute for Occupational Safety and Health) and be issued an approval number such as TC-21C-287.

Generally you have a choice between the disposable mask and the reusable half-face mask. There are many designs and size variations; you will have to choose one that properly fits your face. If you choose the half-face cartridge mask you'll need to find out which filter to select and when to replace them with new ones. You will also need to learn how to perform a negative fit test on yourself. This simple test should be done *each time* you use the respirator.

A negative seal test is performed by cupping both hands over the disposable mask and inhaling deeply for several seconds. A negative (suction-like) pressure should be felt inside the mask. If you detect any air leakage around the edge, reposition it or its straps. To perform the same test on a reusable half-face mask cover the cartridge with your palm. A positive fit test can also be made by covering the exhalation valve while exhaling into the face piece and checking the pressure build-up inside the mask. Last, but not least, you'll need to know how to clean and properly store your mask. All too often I've seen masks left out on students' shelves face-side up and uncovered. Ceramics is a wonderful activity; a properly selected and cared for respirator makes it a safer one.

Lifting

Working in a ceramic studio inevitably involves the lifting and/or movement of many weighty items from large clay pieces to bulky ceramic materials. Where I teach we have hand trucks, Rubbermaid 4-wheel restaurant carts—regarded with much adoration—and even a hydraulic-fork pallet lift for transporting hefty or unwieldy loads. Still, a considerable amount lifting is done by hand. If the item lifted is too heavy or cumbersome and/or if it is lifted improperly, back problems can develop. With hindsight, as I look at my many years of studio work, I attribute poor lifting techniques as being a major cause of my low-back discomfort. If, irregardless of your age, you don't want to end up being a little slower on the draw because of a bad back heed the following:

1. *Lift only objects that are light enough for your own strength.* If a 100 or even a 50 pound bag of clay is too heavy to pick up have someone help you with it or open the bag and transfer it's contents in smaller and lighter portions.
2. *Lift with your leg muscles by keeping your back straight and bending at your knees.* Prior to lifting, stand close to the object with feet a shoulders width apart. During the lift keep the muscles of the stomach tight and be sure to bend at the knees and <u>not</u> at the waist.
3. *Lift and carry objects close to your body; near it's center.* To avoid twisting the body, first turn your feet towards any new change of direction.

Stretching

Often, especially while giving workshops, I am asked questions related to *potter's back* and how to avoid the common aches, pains and spasms that are frequently experienced in the back, shoulders and necks of people who spend long periods of time standing at work tables, sitting hunched over potter's wheels, loading kilns, mixing clay and so on. By way of confession, I am one of those people. One of many millions I'm sure, who's human anatomy gets out of whack from time-to-time and encounters lower-back pain. Like many of those people I, too, make my visits to the chiropractor and the massage therapist. I can vouch for their contributions. I can also vouch for the merits of staying as physically fit as possible through disciplined exercise. As a ceramist, I'm not alone when it comes to equating fitness with physical health. Among the ceramists featured on the pages of this book several are dancers, two are yoga instructors and one teaches aerobics.

I am not trained in the medical profession. I do know, however, that if a particular condition such as a back pain were to cause loss of body coordination or be accompanied by feelings of pain or numbness radiating through the arm or leg, or in any way appear to be potentially dangerous I would see a doctor immediately.

I am not attempting to identify or describe treatment for blown disks or any other form of physical exertion problem here. I am, however, talking *prevention*. Addressing what many potter's experience as, for the most part, not serious medical problems but rather as simple aliments that some pre-work stretching might eliminate and that in the past have been remedied with aspirin, ibuprofen, ice packs or Epsom salts baths.

At different times during the week I'll swim, do some running and lift weights, but daily I rebound (bounce) on a 38" diameter trampoline and do light stretching on a carpeted living room floor as body warm-up exercises to loosen muscles and prepare the neck, back, shoulders and legs for the physical demands of the day. My exercise routines vary, but each morning I usually include the following stretches beginning with a "Hip Roll".

Hip Roll Stretch

Laying flat on my back with both knees drawn upwards and feet off the floor I unceremoniously roll my hips from one side of the body to the other, gradually stretching the back and shoulder muscles and flexing the joints of the spine. Without lifting my shoulders off the floor I give my muscles to the pull of the stretch and continue moving back and forth until feeling fully extended.

Knee Tuck Stretch

While lying flat on my back with arms extended on the floor behind my head I lift and tuck one knee tightly to my chest while stretching the arm and leg on the opposite side of the body as far apart as possible. The tuck position is held for two or three deep breaths and the stretch repeated with the other knee. This extension always gets a "feels-good" sound out of me and helps me go through the day a little longer and stronger. I'll do several repetitions of this stretch or for variation bring both knees up together or use my hands to hold the knees in a tucked position.

Leg Crossover Stretch

With my back flat on the floor, legs straight and arms outstretched I cross my right leg over my left one and, twisting at the waist, touch the floor with my right foot as far from my left foot as possible. After holding the position for 20 seconds I release the stretch by slowly returning to the starting posture and then switch to stretching my lower back and buttocks with the other leg. Another leg crossover exercise that works the spine supporting muscles is done while sitting up-right. In this one both legs are extended forward and held, with knees slightly bent, just above the floor. One leg is then crossed over the other for a couple of seconds before reversing the leg crossover.

Leg Extension Stretch

While sitting on the floor with my left leg extended straight in front of me and the bottom of my right foot tucked high up against it's thigh I stretch my left arm towards my toes. With my left hand touching my left foot I then bring my right arm over my head and touch my left hand. After holding this position for several breaths I change leg positions and repeat the stretch on the other side of the body. As a dancer this stretch, and variations of it, were one of my favorite warm-ups for the lower back and hamstrings.

Toe Touch Stretch

To target those tight muscles running up the backs of my legs and across the width of my lower back I sit on the floor with my legs fully extended and my feet placed flat against the wall. Keeping my trunk straight I slowly extend my arms forward until a gentle tension is felt or till my fingers touch the wall. Initially, it's important not to over stretch yourself with this one, especially if you have lower-back problems. In time, however, you should be able to grab and hold your toes for several long breaths to gain the muscle elasticity and flexibility benefits of this stretch.

Back Bend Stretch

This hypertension back stretch strengthens back muscles while aiding flexibility, but one should be careful and not bend too far backward. Lying on my stomach, with feet together and toes extended, I assume a pushup position with both hands and slowly, while breathing in, raise my head, then my neck and gradually my chest and stomach, all with help from the arms, off the floor. With buttocks held tight, I'll hold the position for a few seconds then slowly return to the floor while exhaling. This stretch I seldom repeat more than twice and usually follow it up with a fetal-like curl formed by placing forearms, knees and forehead on the floor and maintaining a closely tucked position for a moments worth of restful stretching.

A person may start the day with a series of "feel-good" morning exercises that get the blood moving and warm up stiff, cold muscles; yet, by mid-afternoon, after long periods of standing or sitting—especially with bad posture—may experience muscle fatigue. For relief of mid-day muscle aches and back discomfort the following first-aid stretches can help to ease the tightness and keep you looser. Each is done from a sitting position. That's because sitting, jackknifed, at the potter's wheel is where a variety of those strange twinges, cricks and pangs of abuse first appear. To treat them you don't have to leave the wheel, just take a break from your throwing, push your stool back and, without rising, s-t-r-e-t-c-h . . . .

Rearward Reach

Seated, with arms straight at the sides, move both arms—thumbs pointing downward—behind your back until you feel the tension. Hold for several long breaths and do a few repeat performances.

The "Rearward Reach." By pointing the thumbs down resistance is focused on the muscles of the upper back and shoulders.

The "Overhead Reach." With the wrists crossed and the palms touching this stretch will relieve tension in back muscles running from the waist to the shoulders.

Overhead Reach

While seated, place both arms over your head. With your right palm facing right and the left one facing left, cross the arms at the wrists till the palms face one another and reach upwards. Hold for 10 seconds, take a rest and repeat once or twice.

Shoulder Lift

Sitting, with arms hanging at your sides, lift both shoulders up, hold and release. Repeat several times and then, with a continuous motion, raise them up again, only this time slowly roll them down and backwards. Repeat this circular rotation several times over.

Side Twist

Seated, with thighs parallel to the floor and knees spread wide, place a hand on each knee, lean forward and slowly twist from side to side until a healthy stretch is felt in the muscles of the back.

The "Side Twist." With the upper body supported by the hands on the knees, a band of muscle groups around the lower back can be loosened with slow body twists.

Arm Extension

Sit upright, with your hands on your knees and your thighs extended far apart. Move one hand down your leg and firmly grip your ankle. Raise the other hand and extend it straight upwards while slowly following it with your eyes and the careful turning of your head. Hold for a couple of breaths, return to your starting position, relax a moment and then stretch the other side of your body.

Neck Tilt

Sitting erect, slowly tilt your head towards your left shoulder until tension on the right side of the neck is felt. Hold for a couple of breaths, return the head to an upright position and repeat the slow tilting movement towards the right shoulder. When the cycle is complete tilt the head down, hold, return to the starting position and then tilt the head up and back. Do not make the mistake of just tilting your head from side to side without stopping to pause in the starting position.

Whether you participate in a therapeutic mid-day stretch break or not it's always beneficial to follow-up your work day with a short period of quiet rest and relaxation while lying supine (on the back) in a recumbent position. This can be an extremely rejuvenating experience. It takes the weight off of the spine, releases tensions and psychologically improves your mental state.

The mechanics are easy. Simply lay on your back and do nothing. It helps if you keep your eyes closed. It also helps if your arms are at a distance from your side, palms facing upward, and your legs are straight. The feet should be 10 to 12 inches apart and pointing outward. If you like, place a folded towel under your head or a rolled towel under your knees. Sometimes, if my lower-back is really feeling stressed, I'll lay with the calves of my legs resting on a chair, sofa or the bed. My experience with this position is that it produces results that are immediately noticeable and liberating.

To relax deeply you need to stay warm, which is why I like to keep something handy to cover myself with should I become chilled. At times you may doze off, as I frequently do. I think my dozing is associated with a yoga instructor I once had in Ann Arbor Michigan many years ago. At the end of each class she would have us lie on our backs for seven to ten minutes while she systematically talked our bodies—part-by-part—through a complete process of relaxation. Her transformations were complete enough to put me sleepily at rest. However, this session of quiet time need not be a nap period to be valuable. Ideally, the special delights of these empty yet divine moments will become favorable sources of health and strength in your everyday living.

Studio Housekeeping

A low cost way to eliminate studio safety hazards is to adopt a positive approach towards studio housekeeping. Work procedures can be reorganized, facilities rearranged, clean-up duties assigned and a new or revised studio code of conduct established to help reduce health and safety risks. The continuous wet cleaning of all flat surfaces, equipment and storage materials is necessary to keep dust from building up. To keep dust particles from flying about, table-top brooms need to be replaced with sponges. Floors should be wet mopped (or vacuumed using a HEPA filter) daily. If floors cannot be hosed or wet mopped every day they ought to at least be thoroughly swept daily with a soft bristle broom and sweeping compound, while wearing a respirator.

In addition to keeping a clean studio, serious consideration should be given to the proper storage and labeling of all supplies. Labels should be used to identify the contents of all chemical containers. Under OSHA (Occupational Safety and Health Administration) standards each label is required to provide hazard warnings and the name and the address of the manufacturer. By contacting the manufacturer a Materials Safety Data Sheet (MSDS) on a particular chemical can be freely obtained. Part of the information on the MSDS will include the physical health hazards (including signs and symptoms), primary routes of entry to the body and emergency aid procedures. Copies of these data sheets need to be compiled for school studios and located where they can be readily accessible.

Large buckets, partially filled with water and covered with metal racks, for the reclamation of clay scraps. When located adjacent to pottery wheels and within easy access of work tables the studio is kept considerably cleaner.

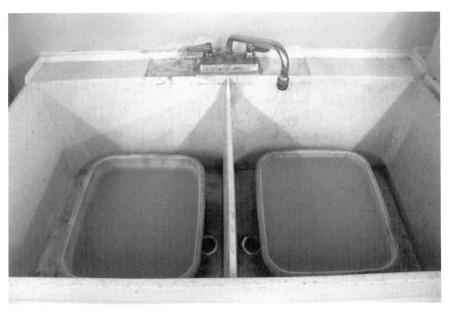

Removable plastic trays placed inside of studio sink basins prevent clogged drains by collecting clay scraps from the cleaning of tools and the washing of hands.

Personal Hygiene

Habits of personal hygiene, such as the frequent rubbing of the eyes, touching of the mouth or biting of finger nails must be altered to prevent dangerous materials from being absorbed by the body. The dangers to the body from eating, drinking and smoking in the studio work areas are clearly apparent and should be immediately recognizable. By frequently washing the hands, and studio clothing, exposure risks can be minimized further.

Open cuts on the skin, one of our body's largest defense perimeters, should be covered and protected with rubber gloves or clothing. Eye protection, either in the form of safety glasses or goggles, should also be used if circumstances require you to light or look into a kiln, chisel kiln shelves or to grind glaze from the bottom of a pot.

I hope that, by now, you are becoming more aware of the need to be personally involved in your own health and well being as an individual and as a ceramist.

And I hope that you take on the responsibility to genuinely care for yourself . . . and for others.

Adrian Arleo, Cairn #2, a low-fire clay and glazed sculpture with a rough, coral-like texture, 24" × 21" × 11". Cairns are generally stone piles used to mark a trail or place of spiritual significance but in this piece 3 figures in fetal positions form a cairn and make a primal reference to relationships with others and with one's self.

Why Clay . . .

This is clay, full and soft as I comfortably squeeze it between my fingers. Smooth and compact, it gently yields; responds to my touch as it curls up, like my cat "Boo", in the palms of my hands. It is simple; it is beautiful. Willing to take most any shape I might wish to give it. Life is like that isn't it—willing to take a shape of our own choosing?

Of course, many things affect and determine the shape of our life. Clay, I touch you, I look at your still shapeless form and, as always, you send my mind in quest, on a creative journey in search of answers. What shape can I give to my life today; to my clay work, that will give me peace with myself? I know the real answers have to come from within. But the outside forms give insight. Clay, there are many things we have no choice about. That is clear. Yet by working together in a world of freedom we can bring a miracle of form to each other.

Ultimately, one cannot answer the question, "why clay?" with the mind alone. One must also find answers through living life. Perhaps this simple, beautiful, yet important truth is why some of us live in relationship with clay. Like any living relationship we have the potential to evolve with it and grow to something else. Thoughts alone do not function here—best leave those for the observers. A personally nourishing relationship requires us to become interactive. To touch. To share intimate touch.

To the degree that we enter this relationship between a material: a medium, and the wholeness of ourselves, is the degree that we release our clay work and give it the freedom to visually resemble and carry forth the intimacy of our being. When the greeting between clay and person is complete and the heart is filled with joy and compassion there is little room for apprehension. Both are in harmony. At ease. Then and only then, does the resulting clay work nourish, invisibly, the human spirit.

How inexplicable this can become. Even in the best of circumstances there is no complete answer. How does one understand the spirit yet alone exercise the expression of this sensitivity in the midst of that which surrounds us. While it is true our own spiritual evolution need not be integrated with clay work, the contexts in which works of clay most naturally unfold and exist are ones with spiritual affirmations. Inevitably they constitute prophetic wholeness, and where insight is active and the senses awakened become a powerful witness to the inner life of self. Even the earliest of the sixteenth century raku tea bowls were not valued for their capacity to hold tea as much as they were valued for the self-realization and spiritual transformation that could not only be humanly felt but experienced.

Creativity, in its most unencumbered and universal form, is astonishingly spiritual when it is not economically driven and when it honors your own humanity. Being creative is being—and responding to—who you are. Living creatively means you're aware of the real you, and that your in touch with a natural essence of self called spirit: that knowing voice of personal truth held sacred deep within you. As a personal feeling of being, spirit is a perception as intimate as breath itself. Creativity, in the service of spirituality, is simply an affirmation of beingness. Working with clay is extra-fertile ground on which to greet, interact and to bond with the various aspects of spiritual wisdom. It is a place where the spirit is expressively anointed. Where, within a human context of emergent creativeness, important connections are made that help you to see how the truths of your authentic being have value and how they correspond with known realities, be they externally objective, culturally collective or internally subjective.

Clay work wears the freshness of an early dawn when it focuses on expanding the essence of physical presence through an inter-relatedness between object and perception. It will always move on to other levels of maturity whenever its genesis is engaged by our individual uniqueness. This self-enclosed process holds that the quality of our inward attentiveness not only determines the shape of our clay but the shape of our life. The experience of creating, how beautiful it is!

There is a natural pleasure that comes from creative work. The gratifying emotional enjoyment of the end product is mild by comparison to the ecstatic feelings during creation. Ecstatic, in fact, because our participation with this organic medium is not just physical. It is also infused with the spirit of our humanness, and the pleasures of making are further connected to a unique sense of contribution: an instinctive need to feel that we have given of ourselves purposefully. What we achieve as a result of our creating should enrich not only that which is around us but that which is inside us as well. Inevitably, the gentle simplicity of the relationship formulated by the question of "why clay?" . . . is that to create with clay is to create ourselves.

Richard DeVore, #723, 3 1/2″ × 15 1/2″. The strength and vitality of DeVore's finest forms is often found in the subtle dynamics of the undulating rims but the true strength of his aesthetic genius is revealed in the compositional cavities, often multi-level, carved within the floor's interior.

INSTRUCTIONAL VHS VIDEO CASSETTES

RAKU KILN BUILDING

The first video of a comprehensive set of three videos that visually outlines the process of contemporary raku ceramics. This video shows the fabrication of a top loading soft firebrick kiln. Details examined include: the foundation, layout of the floor, bricking of the walls, built-in shelf supports, the burner port, use of target bricks and construction of a liftable, compression brick top complete with flue openings. Seen also is a homemade natural gas burner with flexible fuel hose, snap-on fittings and a removable forced-air blower unit. Following instructions on the safe lighting of the burner, equally as precise fabrication details are shown for building a fiber blanket kiln with an expanded metal frame. And, for those with access to them, approaches to converting old or unused electric kilns to gas fired raku kilns are explained and displayed. VHS 43 minutes

RAKU FIRING AND REDUCTION

Raku artist and teacher Robert Piepenburg demonstrates his approach to firing raku ceramics and reveals the fascinating dynamics of the post firing reduction process. With a seasoned awareness he explains the theory and the technical aspects behind the sequence of events employed to achieve the glossy richness of a white crackle glaze and to effectively realize the full color spectrum of a "dry" copper surface patina. The intricacies of this ceramic phenomena are so subtle that only a film as fully illuminating as this could enhance the viewer's understanding of current raku practices. Equally rich in primary source material and visual detail it profiles the firing of two kiln loads of work, of significantly different shapes, to demonstrate how various forms might best be reduced after they leave the kiln. Contains coverage of the kiln loading and unloading, lighting the burner, reduction inside the kiln, preparation of combustible materials and the stimulating impact of the smoking applications on the finished pieces themselves. An invaluable supplement to any perspective on raku! VHS 30 minutes

RAKU CLAY GLAZES AND TONGS

A to-the-point demonstration and explanation of how various ingredients can be integrated to formulate handbuilding and wheelthrowing clay bodies capable of withstanding, continuously, the thermo shocks of the raku firing process. Equally as focused coverage is given to glazes. Formulas are shared, chemicals are mixed by volume and a straight forward application of glaze is applied to both traditional and sculptural forms. Through sequential steps of bending and shaping, with common tools, an inexpensive yet practical pair of long handled tongs are formed from flat iron. In total, this definitive film spotlights a number of highly technical and significant ceramic processes that, within a raku context, become an invaluable complement to an expanded overview of information. VHS 33 minutes

BEGINNING WHEELTHROWING

A step-by-step introductory reference guide to learning the potter's wheel. Visual close-ups of techniques, detailing precise hand and tool positions, balanced with an informal dialogue on expression and form analysis, Robert Piepenburg provides an invaluable supplement to "hands-on" learning. Filmed in a clear and lively style, the visual images and information effectively help viewers to understand and learn wedging, centering, opening, raising the wall, shaping from the cylindrical form, throwing open and closed shapes, trimming right side up, use of throwing ribs and a whole array of other significant fundamentals that enable them to advance their skills in one of the world's oldest yet most contemporary art forming processes. VHS 53 minutes

BEGINNING HANDBUILDING

A stimulating introduction to the basic and innovative ceramic handbuilding techniques including external support molds, internal support molds, stiff slab construction and sectional form fabrication. Following each demonstration, creative forms by various other individuals are shown. While emphasis is on the processes and procedures of construction, a great deal of discussion centers around design, application and sources of inspiration for personal expressions in clay. VHS 56 minutes

SMOKE FIRING

Presents the groundwork for beginning practitioners of simple, primitive fired clay by presenting the basic procedures and follow through of the wood firing of several works, of various shapes, in a reclaimed oil drum. Features clay body selection, clay form recommendations, burnishing, selection of combustibles, placement of pottery, use of salt and copper chemicals for fuming, possible experimental innovations, application of waxes on fired pieces and discusses health and safety issues. By using realistic examples and a non-technical approach for clarity, beginners are encouraged to proceed from practical tips, trial efforts and inner expectations. VHS 25 minutes

A VISIT WITH THE ARTIST

This videotape focuses on the human dimensions of Robert Piepenburg the artist and presents a personal perspective on ceramics, the creative process and self-empowerment. While working with clay he freely talks about his experiences, beliefs, insights and hopes in ways that engage personal reflection and motivate action. As he intimately shares his own thoughts and as we watch him trustingly explore the experience of his own humanness with the clay, we begin to understand what he means when he says ". . . clay requires resolution through individual uniqueness." VHS 28 minutes

ORDERING INFORMATION

If you would like to purchase any of Robert Piepenburg's videotapes, order autographed copies of his books *Raku Pottery*, *The Spirit Of Clay* and *Treasures of the Creative Spirit* or receive information about arranging for workshops please write to: Robert Piepenburg, c/o Pebble Press Inc., 24723 Westmoreland, Farmington Hills, MI 48336-1963

Payment And Mailing Information

Checks or money orders should be in US funds only. Purchase orders will be invoiced. Videotapes are $49.95 each. The price for *Raku Pottery* is $26.95 and *Treasures of the Creative Spirit* is $12.95. Shipping and handling charges in the continental US are $2.50 for the first book or cassette and $1.00 for each additional item. For non US and overseas orders, including Alaska and Hawaii, shipping and handling is 25% of the total order. These shipments are sent Parcel Post and may take 4 to 8 weeks.

Acknowledgments

This book is the result of many years of professional experiences as a practicing artist and art teacher. As a humane being it is also a personal statement, enmeshed with as much aesthetic, spiritual and human affirmation as is inherent in any work of art. Still, the supportive help of talented students, a nurturing family, inspiring friends and gifted colleagues is an important part of this book's success. I especially would like to acknowledge the highly respected technical expertise of **John Glick** and **J.T. Abernathy** and thank them for their assistance with the chapters on clay, glazes and kilns. I am deeply grateful to **Michael Gwinup** for sharing his valued kiln building skills and car kiln design. My warmest appreciation goes to **Wendy Piepenburg** for her intellectual and literary talents and for always being a perceptive critic and loving daughter during the many hours spent working with the manuscript. To Vivian Bradbury I extend my thanks, once again, for her professional contributions with layout and production assistance. To Morris Last, whose guiding support I cherish, and for his reading of the manuscript. Finally, I again thank all of those who expanded the scope of this book through their gracious cooperation by contributing information and photographs.

John Glick   *Michael Gwinup*   *Wendy Piepenburg*   *J.T. Abernathy*

Photo Credits

All photographs and illustrations by Gail and Robert Piepenburg except: John Buffington & Eve Vanderweit: front cover, pp. 9, 425; Bob Schatz: p. 3; Bill Pelletier: pp. 11, 291; Gene Ogam: p. 12; Joe Schopplein: p. 16; Judy Eliyas: p. 34; 6th Street Studios, San Francisco, California: p. 36; Tom Holt: pp. 37, 199, 251, 395; Lars Speyer: p. 38; David Browne: pp. 40, 422; Jesse L. Nusbaum, Courtesy Museum of New Mexico: p. 44; Courtesy The Museum of Modern Art, New York; p. 46; Jerry Nymshack: p. 48; Verne Funk: p. 54; Richard Olinger: p. 68; Jerry Anthony: p. 69; Kim Kauffman: p. 70; Bob Barrettp. 71; David G.Wright: pp. 71 (bottom), 297; Charles Frizzell: p. 74; Jane Selser: p. 86; Roger Schreiber: pp. 87, 121, 301; Montie Mayrend: p. 88; Jerry Kobylecky: p. 89; Suzanne Coles-Ketcham: pp. 299, 300; Wayne Fleming: p. 90; David Roberts: p. 95; Richard Sargent: pp. 96, 231; Rafael Duran: p.97; Joan Rosenberg-Dent: p. 99; Mark Masuoka: p. 98; D. James Dee, Courtesty Worth Gallery, Taos, New Mexico: p. 117; O'Gara: p. 122; Brian Oglesbee: pp. 123, 150, 166, 167; Patrick Young: p. 131; Bob Rush: p. 133; Caroline Court: p. 135; Steve Selvin: pp. 136, 265, 308; Kim Kauffman: p. 137; M. Lee Featherree, Courtesy Frumkin/Adams Gallery , New York: p. 139; Denis Deegan: p. 140; David Browne: p. 141; Paul Soldner: p. 142; Ana England: pp. 146, 396; Raymon Elozua: p. 152; Steve Wieneke: p. 153; Jeri S Hollister: p. 154; Tim Thayer: pp. 153, 327; John Addison: p.157; Sam Jornlin: pp. 160, 241; G. Carr: p. 162; Brian McGrath: p. 163; Al Surratt: pp. 205, 228, 246; Jim Ball: pp. 217, 302; Joe Schopplein: p. 230; Taylor Collins: p. 239; Dirk Bakker: pp. 242, 260; W. Mitch Yung: p. 280; Clark Peters: pp. 284, 359; James Evans: p. 295; Jerry Kobylecky: p. 296; Gary McKinnis: p. 305; Craig Smith: p. 307; Michael Gwinup: pp. 321, 373, 374, 376, 377, 378, 379, 380, 382, 383, 384, 385, 386, 387; Victor Spinski p. 325; John Glick: p. 339; Jeremy Bricker: p. 347; Clayton Bailey: p. 351; Tim Thayer: p. 368; Kevin Chancey: p. 369; Ken Turner: pp. 388, 389; Jim Copper: p. 393; Brad Iverson: pp. 396, 398.

Glossary

Aesthetics Philosophical theories of visual beauty.

Air drying The process of drying clay without the use of mechanical heat.

Albany slip A natural clay slip used as a reddish black stoneware glaze. Mined in New York state, this once popular slip glaze is no longer obtainable.

Alkaline glaze A glaze highly fluxed by any one of the alkaline earth minerals such as sodium, borax, calcium or lithium.

Alumina oxide An important stoneware clay and glaze strengthening component.

Applied decoration Adding additional clay to the surface of a form as a decorative design.

Arch brick A brick whose width has two tapered faces on opposite sides.

Art The universal language of humanity.

Ash glaze A stoneware glaze that uses a large percentage of wood ash for a flux.

Avant-garde art Non-traditional artwork that is experimental in content and use of materials.

Bag wall Bricks stacked inside a kiln to direct the flames and prevent them from touching the ware directly.

Balance The visual distribution of form through the use of design elements such as weight, scale, form, texture and color.

Ball clay A very fine-grained sedimentary clay added to clay bodies for plasticity and lightness of color. Mined in Kentucky and Tennessee, it is also added to glazes as a refractory and a source for alumina.

Banding wheel A turntable for manually rotating artwork during fabrication and decorating.

Bat A flat plate, usually circular in shape and often made from plaster, that is placed on top of the wheel head as a surface for throwing on. It is easily removable, enabling the work to be safely transferred from the wheel.

Bisque firing The firing of unglazed pottery to around cone 06 (1816° F) to remove moisture and harden the clay for handling during glazing.

Bisque ware Unglazed low-fired pottery.

Bone ash A calcium phosphate ash made of ground and calcined cattle bone.

Bone dry Unfired clay that is completely dry and ready for firing.

Burnishing Polishing leather-hard clay by rubbing with a smooth, hard tool.

Calcine The removal of chemical water from ceramic materials by heating them to red heat.

Celadon A pale gray-green high-temperature glaze.

Ceramics Fired clay, objects made of fired clay and/or the making of fired clay objects.

Ceramic fiber A high-temperature **refractory** blanket material for insulating kilns.

Ceramist A person who works with clay.

Chammy A soft piece of leather for smoothing the rims of thrown pottery.

China paint A low-temperature decorative glaze painted over a fired glaze surface.

Chuck An open clay form used to support inverted pots for trimming.

Clay A plastic medium made from fine-grained igneous rock and water.

Coiling Creating ceramic form by joining coils of clay.

CMC A cellulose gum used as a binder and suspension agent for pigments.

Combustibles Materials that will burn.

Commercial glaze A commercially manufactured glaze ready for use.

Composition The overall arrangement of the separate parts that make up the whole.

Conceptual art Artwork that emphasizes a concept or pivotal idea more than an object, material or technique.

Contour The linear outline or edge that defines the shape of a form.

Cone A clay/flux material in the shape of a small, elongated pyramid that bends at a pre-determined temperature. Known also as **pyrometric cones**, they are used as temperature guides inside the kiln during firing.

Corbel arch An arch formed by extending each course of brick further over the opening than the course underneath.

Crackle glaze A glaze with surface cracks as a result of **crazing**.

Crawling A shrinking separation of glaze resulting in bare spots of clay.

Crazing Glaze cracking resulting from a difference of expansion and contraction between the glaze and the clay body.

Crafts Disciplines of workmanship involved in the physical creation of handmade objects.

Crossdraft kiln A gas kiln with the flue/chimney exit in the wall opposite the burner ports.

Damper A movable plate inside the chimney of a gas kiln for controlling draft.

Deflocculant A material used to reduce shrinkage and obtain fluidity with less water than normally needed.

Design The arrangement of visual elements to satisfy a personal and/or functional need.

Dough mixer A large bakery mixer used for mixing clay.

Downdraft kiln A gas kiln with the flue/chimney exit at the floor of the kiln.

Drape mold A concave support form for holding and shaping clay slabs while they stiffen.

Dunting The cracking of pots during the glaze firing caused by rapid cooling.

Earthenware A red to brown low temperature clay that is soft and relatively porous.

Element A coil of high temperature wire used to heat an electric kiln.

Engobe A decorative slip made from clay and glaze materials.

Extruder A plunger activated device that presses soft clay through a die to form an infinite variety of solid or hollow shapes.

Feldspar A high-temperature clay and glaze flux obtained from granite.

Fettling knife A knife with a long tapered blade used for working clay.

Filler Any coarse mesh material added to a clay body for strength, texture and shrinkage reduction.

Fireclay A high temperature sedimentary clay that is highly refractory.

Firebrick A type of hard refractory brick made from fireclay.

Firing The process of bringing a kiln to maturity.

Firing temperature The peak temperature at which the ceramic ware reaches maturity.

Flint Ground **silica.**

Flocculation The massing together or aggregation of clay or glaze particles.

Flux A material that promotes melting.

Form A descriptive term for three-dimensional objects.

Foot The base of any form, or in the case of thrown pottery, the trimmed bottom.

Frit A glaze flux formed by rapidly cooling and shattering a melted glass-like material.

Functionalism A theory which values art in terms of its usefulness in daily life.

Glaze A glassy or matt decorative and/or waterproof surface applied and fired to ceramic forms.

Greenware Unfired bone-dry clay work.

Grog Fired clay that has been crushed and graded in particle size for use as a **filler** in stabilizing clay bodies.

Hard edged An exact boundary marking the separation between surfaces and/or forms.

Hump mold A raised form over which clay is placed for shaping until it stiffens.

Hydrometer Instrument for measuring the specific gravity of liquids or the ratio of water in glazes.

Insulating brick A type of soft refractory brick that is porous and light-weight.

Intaglio Designs carved beneath a form's surface.

Kaolin A nearly pure white high-temperature clay also known as **china clay.**

Kiln A refractory enclosure for firing clay.

Kiln furniture The refractory shelving and support posts used inside of kilns.

Kiln sitter A mechanical shut-off apparatus for electric kilns that is triggered by a pyrometric **cone** when the desired temperature is reached.

Kiln wash A refractory mixture of flint, kaolin and water applied to kiln shelves as a protective coating.

Key brick The center brick in an arch that holds the other bricks together.

Leather-hard Clay that is not yet bone-dry but stiff enough to support itself while remaining workable.

Line A directional marking.

Luster An iridescent metallic low-temperature finish applied to a previously glazed surface.

Majolica Centuries old Italian form of pottery where colorful decorations appear to float over an opaque glaze background.

Matt A dull, non-glossy surface.

Maquette A small scale model for a larger sculptural project.

Medium The material used to create artwork.

Mesh Calibrated and numbered size openings through which ceramic particles can pass.

Mishima Decorative cuts made into leather-hard clay and filled with colored slip.

Mold A plaster form used to give shape to clay.

Molochite A high-fired white clay that is ground and used as a porcelain grog.

Mullite A high-fired refractory clay that is ground and added to porcelain clay bodies to resist thermal cracking.

Negative space The empty space around objects.

Nepheline syenite A low temperature soda feldspar.

Nichrome A metal alloy used in the making of elements for electric kilns.

Non-objective art Artwork without recognizable subject matter.

Organic A non-angular form with biological associations.

Overglaze China paints and metallic lusters that are applied over a fired glaze.

Oxidation firing A kiln firing in which the atmosphere contains enough oxygen to allow for normal fuel combustion.

Pin tool A long handled awl-like tool with a needle at one end.

Pinching A method of shaping clay by pressing it between the thumb and fingers while holding it in the palm of the other hand.

Pinholes Small holes left in a glaze surface by escaping gases during firing.

Pit firing A wood/sawdust firing done inside a covered hole made in the ground.

Plasticity The workable qualities of a clay body.

Porcelain A high-fired white **vitreous** clay body.

Potter A person who makes functional ware.

Pottery Utilitarian clay ware and/or the making of functional ware.

Press molding The pressing of soft clay into or onto a **mold** for shaping.

Primary air Air that mixes with the gas inside the barrel of the burner.

Primary clay Clay taken from the site where it was formed.

Propane A liquefied gas widely used as a fuel for firing kilns.

Pug mill A mechanical clay mixer that extrudes the clay.

Pyrometer A calibrating instrument used to indicate the interior temperature of kilns during firings.

Raku A low-temperature type of ware and firing procedure that makes use of a reduction process outside of the kiln immediately after reaching temperature.

Rakuist A person who makes raku ware.

Reduction firing A firing in which the kiln's atmosphere contains an insufficient supply of oxygen for complete fuel combustion thereby causing oxygen to be chemically reduced from the clay and glaze.

Refractory A heat resistant material.

Rib A flat metal, wood or rubber tool used for shaping clay.

Relief Three-dimensional form that projects from a background surface.

Rhythm Movement created by a repetition of visual elements.

Saggar A protective clay container placed inside a kiln to isolate ware.

Salt glaze A clear textured high-temperature glaze formed by vaporizing salt inside the kiln immediately after reaching temperature.

Sandblasting The use of fine sand and compressed air to etch or alter a clay or glazed surface.

Sawdust firing A firing process that uses sawdust to turn unglazed ware black.

Scoring Making incised lines on the mating surfaces of clay to be joined.

Sculpture A constructed, carved, modeled or cast three-dimensional work of art.

Secondary air Air that enters the kiln through the burner port.

Secondary clay Clay geologically removed from the site where it was formed.

Sgraffito The process of creating a decorative design by scratching through a slip or glaze to expose the unfired clay body.

Shape A distinct two-dimensional outline of a flat area.

Shivering The flaking of glaze off the edges of ware due to excessive clay shrinkage.

Short Clay that lacks **plasticity**.

Shrinkage Clay contraction that occurs during drying and again during firing.

Single fire The glaze firing of ware that has not been bisque fired.

Skew brick The supporting bricks, also called skewbacks, on each end of a kiln arch.

Slab A flat broad sheet of thin clay.

Slab roller An adjustable device for rolling out slabs of clay to a uniform thickness.

Slaking The breaking down of clay or plaster through the absorption of water.

Slip Liquid clay.

Slip casting The pouring of **deflocculated** clay slip into a plaster mold for shaping.

Slip glaze A glaze containing a clay that becomes a flux during the firing.

Smoke firing A firing process that uses sawdust, pieces of wood and a copper/salt mixture to give unglazed ware a red to black finish.

Soak To hold a kiln at a constant temperature.

Space The volume that a form occupies, encloses or defines.

Spirit An intangible animating force.

Spray gun A device for spraying on glazes with commmpressed air.

Stain A metallic oxide or commercially prepared pigment added to clay bodies, slips, engobes and glaze for color.

Stoneware High-fired ware that becomes vitrified above cone 6 (2194° F).

Straight brick The standard brick size 9" x 4 1/2" x 2 1/2" used in kiln building.

Style Those qualities and means of artistic expression that are uniquely personal.

Subject The central focus or theme in a work of art.

Organic Having non-angular properties and/or characteristics related to living organisms.

Terra-cotta Low-fired reddish-brown clay or ware.

Terra sigillata A thin slip made up of very fine clay particles that is applied to leather-hard clay and burnished prior to being fired to a low temperature.

Texture The visual or tactile quality of a surface.

Thermal shock The physical stress placed on ware due to a sudden change in temperature.

Thermocouple The electrical probe placed inside the kiln to measure the temperature for the **pyrometer** located outside the kiln.

Throwing The centering, hallowing and shaping of clay on a potter's wheel.

Tongs A plier-like device with two long steel rods joined near one end by a pivot bolt for gripping and removing raku ware from a hot kiln.

Tooling Trimming leather-hard clay on a potter's wheel.

Traditional art Artwork that is continuously created around the same elements from time honored customs.

Underfire Clay or glaze fired below their maturing temperatures.

Underglaze Ceramic colorants applied to ware prior to it being covered with glaze.

Updraft kiln A gas kiln with the flue/chimney exit at the top of the kiln.

Viscosity A resistance to running or flowing.

Vitreous Hard, glassy and non-porous.

Ware A generic name for clay objects.

Warping The deformation of a clay form.

Waster A piece of disposible clay used in the kiln to support pottery.

Wax resist The application of liquid wax to a clay or glazed surface to repel glaze from the area.

Wedge brick A brick with two tapered faces running length-wise on opposite sides.

Wedging A manual technique of kneading clay to remove air pockets and render it homogeneous.

Wedging table A table with a plaster top on which clay is wedged.

Aleis Branzei makes porcelain wheel-thrown pots that are seldom larger than 3–4 inches. As personal affirmations they serve as powerful reminders that we too can embrace and realize our dreams as creators through the smallest of forms born in the magic of the human spirit rather than by the largest of forms fashioned by ego, aesthetic imitation or rational invention. Spirit, not scale, is the highest authority in ceramics. Can I say it one other way? . . . clay work always benefits when the spirit of clay succeeds the techniques of clay.

Index

Robert Piepenburg, altered wheel-thrown form, raku fired, 15″ high.

Robert Piepenburg is an instructor of ceramics, a best-selling author and an internationally known artist. He has been a recipient of a National Endowment for the Arts Fellowship and several Michigan Council for the Arts Creative Artist Grants. His works are in public and private collections from the Smithsonian in Washington, DC to the State Foundation on Culture and the Arts in Honolulu, Hawaii. He lives in Michigan with his wife Gail, who is also a well known artist and teacher, and their two youngest girls Leah and Jessica. Just as this book went to press Robert was selected by his college and colleagues as *Outstanding Teacher of the Year.*